The Europeanisation of National Administrations

Patterns of Institutional Change and Persistence

Christoph Knill's book analyses the impact of European policies on national administrations. Under which conditions can we expect domestic change, particularly the convergence of administrative styles and structures? How can we explain national patterns of administrative transformation in the context of Europeanisation?

Knill's study is a comparative assessment of the factors influencing administrative adjustment to European policy demands in the member states. It addresses the topic from an innovative theoretical perspective, combining institution-based and agency-based approaches, and includes a detailed account of the administrative impact of EU environmental policy in Britain and Germany. *The Europeanisation of National Administrations* will be of great interest to students, scholars and practitioners in the fields of European studies, public administration and public policy, environmental politics and European administrative law.

CHRISTOPH KNILL is Professor for European Studies at the University of Jena. His publications include *Ringing the Changes in Europe: Regulatory Competition and the Transformation of the State* (1996; with A. Héritier and S. Mingers) and *Implementing EU Environmental Policy: New Directions and Old Problems* (2000; with A. Lenschow).

Themes in European Governance

The evolving European systems of governance, in particular the European Union, challenge and transform the state, the most important locus of governance and political identity and loyalty over the last 200 years. The series *Themes in European Governance* aims to publish the best theoretical and analytical scholarship on the impact of European governance on the core institutions, policies and identities of nation-states. It focuses upon the implications on issues such as citizenship, welfare, political decision-making, and economic monetary and fiscal policies. An initiative of Cambridge University Press and the Programme on Advanced Research on the Europeanisation of the Nation-State (ARENA), Norway, the series includes contributions in the social sciences, humanities and law. The series aims to provide theoretically informed studies analysing key issues both at the European level and within European states. Volumes in the series will be of interest to scholars and students of Europe, within Europe and worldwide It will be of particular relevance to those interested in the development of sovereignty and governance of European states and in the issues raised by multi-level governance and multi-national integration throughout the world.

The Europeanisation of National Administrations

Patterns of Institutional Change and Persistence

Christoph Knill

CAMBRIDGE
UNIVERSITY PRESS

PUBLISHED BY THE PRESS SYNDICATE OF THE UNIVERSITY OF CAMBRIDGE
The Pitt Building, Trumpington Street, Cambridge, United Kingdom

CAMBRIDGE UNIVERSITY PRESS
The Edinburgh Building, Cambridge CB2 2RU, UK
40 West 20th Street, New York, NY 10011–4211, USA
10 Stamford Road, Oakleigh, VIC 3166, Australia
Ruiz de Alarcón 13, 28014 Madrid, Spain
Dock House, The Waterfront, Cape Town 8001, South Africa

http://www.cambridge.org

© Christoph Knill 2001

First published 2001

Printed in the United Kingdom at the University Press, Cambridge

Typeset in Plantin 10/12pt   System 3B2   [CE]

A catalogue record for this book is available from the British Library

ISBN 0 521 80632 1 hardback
ISBN 0 521 00092 0 paperback

Contents

List of tables	*page*	ix
Preface		xi
List of abbreviations		xiii

Introduction   1

**I   Theoretical frame of reference and analytical
approach**   7

1   The keywords: European integration, comparative
administration and implementation   9

2   An institutional approach to administrative change   20

3   The analytical framework   35

**II   Administrative traditions in Germany and Britain:
opposing patterns and dynamics**   59

4   The institutional foundation of German and British
administrative traditions   61

5   Administrative reform capacity in Germany and Britain:
autonomous versus instrumental administration   85

**III   Domestic change and persistence: the
implementation of EU environmental policy**   117

6   The administrative implications of EU environmental
policy   119

7   Germany: the constraints of a static core   135

8   Britain: the opportunities of a dynamic core   164

**IV The Europeanisation of national administrations:
     comparative assessment and general conclusions   199**

  9 Comparative assessment: the explanatory value of
     institutions   201

 10 Towards generalisation: different mechanisms of
     Europeanisation   213

References   228
Index   250

Tables

3.1 The dependent variable: dimensions of administrative
    change   *page* 41
3.2 The independent variable: dimensions and levels of
    adaptation pressure   47
3.3 Patterns of administrative change across member states   50
6.1 Administrative implications of the policies under study   134
9.1 The explanatory value of a 'simple' institutional
    perspective of sectoral fit and misfit   203
9.2 The explanatory value of a differentiated institutional
    perspective   206
9.3 Administrative convergence/divergence under the impact
    of European legislation   211

Preface

The underlying study was written in the context of a broader research project on 'European Integration and the Transformation of the State' which was funded under the Leibniz Programme of the German Science Foundation (*DFG*) and conducted by Adrienne Héritier. I am particularly grateful to Adrienne not only for her continuous support and encouragement, but also for providing me with the great opportunity to carry out my work at three of Europe's 'finest addresses' in political and social science: the University of Bielefeld; the Max-Planck Institute for the Study of Societies in Cologne; and the European University Institute in Florence.

I am also particularly indebted to Yves Mény. It was on the basis of his initiative that I was able to carry out a research project on 'The Impact of National Administrative Traditions on the Implementation of EU Environmental Policy' at the Robert-Schuman Centre of the European University Institute. This project, which was financed by the European Commission, is of major theoretical and empirical relevance for the underlying study. I am grateful to Yves for the provision of administrative and logistical support through the Robert-Schuman Centre as well as his scientific commitment to the project and his continuous advice. Furthermore, I want to express my particular thanks to Roland Czada, the director of the Institute of Political Science at the University of Hagen. Roland positively affected my scientific career in many ways, most notably in 'setting me on track' to Bielefeld some years ago and by his spontaneous preparedness to take this study through the habilitation procedure at the University of Hagen.

Invaluable and constitutive for this study was my collaboration with Andrea Lenschow. Many parts of this study draw heavily on ideas developed in close co-operation with her. She was always there when I had a problem and spent much of her time in reading, commenting and improving my draft pages. I also had the pleasure to share my office with Dirk Lehmkuhl. I find it hard to imagine that one could have a better mixture of constructive collaboration, fruitful conversation and fun.

In different, but equally important, ways, many other people have contributed to the production of this study. Besides my colleagues in the Leibniz project, Dieter Kerwer and Michael Teutsch, I am grateful for critical comments and suggestions by James Caporaso, Maria Green Cowles and Thomas Risse as well as the participants of their project on 'Europeanisation and Domestic Change'.

Abbreviations

BAT	Best Available Technology
BATNEEC	Best Available Technology Not Entailing Excessive Cost
BImschG	Bundesimmissionsschutzgesetz
BMU	Bundesministerium für Umwelt, Naturschutz und Reaktorsicherheit
BSI	British Standards Institution
CBI	Confederation of British Industry
DIHT	Deutscher Industrie- und Handelstag
DoE	Department of the Environment
DWI	Drinking Water Inspectorate
EIA	Environmental Impact Assessment
EMAS	Environmental Management and Audit Scheme
EPA	Environmental Protection Act
FOI	Campaign for the Freedom of Information
GFAVo	Großfeuerungsanlagenverordnung
HMIP	Her Majesty's Inspectorate of Pollution
LCP	Large Combustion Plants
NPM	New Public Management
NRA	National Rivers Authority
OFWAT	Office of Water Services
RCEP	Royal Commission on Environmental Pollution
RWA	Regional Water Authority
SRU	Sachverständigenrat für Umweltfragen
TÜV	Technischer Überwachungsverein
UBA	Umweltbundesamt
UIG	Umweltinformationsgesetz
UKAS	United Kingdom Accreditation Service
UVPG	Gesetz über die Umweltverträglichkeitsprüfung
WSA	Water Services Association
WVU	Wasserversorgungsunternehmen

Introduction

At first glance, a study of the administrative transformation in Europe seems to imply nothing new. There is an ever growing body of literature analysing the impact of global reform waves associated with what is known as New Public Management (NPM) on the structure and practice of public administration. There are a large number of country studies and a growing number of comparative studies on this subject (cf. Wright 1994; Pierre 1995; Flynn and Strehl 1996; Olsen and Peters 1996). However, this kind of public sector reform is not the central concern of this study. Here the analysis focuses on the *Europeanisation* of national administrations; i.e., the crucial question of how European integration affects domestic administrative practices and structures.

One could argue that the selection of this research focus does not necessarily make sense, as there is no European administrative policy *per se* which is explicitly concerned with the structure and practice of domestic administrations. Administrative policy, as a policy field in its own right, only exists in the national context, and it is still a very basic domain of the member states. This argument, however, overlooks one significant – although less spectacular – fact: the administrative impact of other European policies. Thus, for appropriate implementation, policy decisions to some extent always entail decisions on corresponding administrative arrangements. In other words, policy content and administrative implementation requirements are often closely related. While being aware of the fact that the degree to which policy contents and administrative implications are coupled may vary from policy to policy and from sector to sector, it cannot be ignored that the growing importance of European policies leaves its mark on domestic administrations. It is these subtle and less obvious forms of administrative change that this study is about.

The link between European policy content and domestic administrative implications indicates a basic tension. On the one hand, it is well documented that national administrative styles and structures reveal a considerable degree of divergence, which can mainly be traced to

1

differing institutional contexts and developments at the national level. On the other hand, the increasing Europeanisation of domestic policy-making implies converging policy contents. Based on the insight that there is often a correlation between policy content and necessary administrative provisions, the question arises concerning whether policy convergence leads to administrative convergence. This study is meant to analyse the concrete implications of European policies on national administrations. Under which conditions can we expect administrative change, and more specifically the convergence of national administrations?

Empirically this study focuses primarily on the implementation of EU environmental policy in Britain and Germany. The selection of environmental policy offers four analytical advantages. First, with respect to national administrative arrangements EU environmental policy can generally be expected to have far-reaching institutional effects. There is a tight coupling of European policy content and administrative requirements for domestic implementation. Second, the case of environmental policy seems to be quite illustrative, since it has been characterised by a rapidly expanding Europeanisation during the last fifteen years. Therefore, it can be expected that the implementation of European policies will lead to significant effects on national administrations. Third, given that EU environmental policy is an area where implementation gaps are particularly prevalent (CEC 1996), this policy area is a rather 'interesting' case with respect to patterns of domestic adaptation. Finally, because EU environmental policy is characterised by a high variety of regulatory strategies and instruments, it allows for the comparative assessment of the varying implications for domestic adaptation. To account for this variety, the empirical focus is on five pieces of European legislation with distinct administrative implications, namely: the Directives on Large Combustion Plants (LCP), Drinking Water, Access to Environmental Information, Environmental Impact Assessment (EIA), and the Environmental Management and Auditing Systems (EMAS) Regulation.

The selection of Britain and Germany allows us to assess the role of national administrative arrangements in a comparative fashion. As a result of far-reaching macro-institutional differences concerning the state tradition, the legal system and the political-administrative system, both countries have contrasting administrative traditions (Héritier, Knill and Mingers 1996).

Two dimensions of the administrative impact of EU policy are assessed: administrative structures and styles. On the one hand, EU policies put pressure on national administrations because of the structural requirements they tend to imply. These requirements may address concrete institutional structures related to the presence, design or integration of regulatory authorities in the overall system. For instance, a regulation may call for the creation of new structures (e.g., an environmental agency), the centralisation or decentralisation of regulatory processes (e.g., by introducing uniform reporting requirements to a central authority), or it may demand horizontal organisational change (e.g., by requiring the co-ordination of previously distinct administrative tasks). On the other hand, European adaptation requirements may refer to the dimension of administrative style, including the patterns of regulatory intervention and administrative interest mediation. Two contrasting types of regulatory intervention are often distinguished, namely, a hierarchical style of intervention imposing uniform, substantive standards, and a more flexible and discretionary style allowing for some level of self-regulation. Different forms of regulatory intervention tend to go hand-in-hand with particular patterns of interest intermediation, ranging from formal and legalistic styles of interaction between public authorities and the addressees of the regulation to more informal and pragmatic patterns with administrative actors playing a more mediating role between the different interest groups involved.

As revealed by the empirical evidence, the domestic impact of European policies is not characterised by a clear and consistent picture. The level of administrative adaptation cannot be directly deduced from the respective policy (where one regulation facilitates the national adaptation more than another) nor do systematic differences exist in the countries regarding their capability to adapt. In other words, domestic change and persistence follow no simple 'country-based' or 'policy-based' logic. As a consequence, we not only observe administrative convergence, but also (and to a similar extent) divergence – or persistence of administrative differences across member states.

Britain abolished its existing regulatory arrangements in favour of corresponding EU requirements in the cases of LCP and Access to Information, but resisted changing administrative styles and structures in the case of EIA. While changes to comply with the Drinking Water Directive took place only after a delay of several years, the EMAS Regulation was basically in line with already existing arrangements, hence there was no particular need for adjustment. In the implementation of the LCP Directive in Germany there was a similar compatibility between the European and domestic arrangements. In the remaining cases, Germany needed to adjust the existing administrative arrangements. These adjustments, however, took place only in the case of EMAS and, although delayed, also in the case of Drinking Water, while we observe a strong resistance to administrative change regarding the cases of Access to Information and EIA.

How can the diverse national responses to European policies be explained? Which factors affect whether there is administrative change or the persistence of earlier administrative styles and structures? In this book, three main arguments are advanced in order to account for the impact of Europe on national administrations. First, a perspective taking the institutional compatibility of European requirements and domestic arrangements into account provides a useful basis for an analytical framework. In this context, the historical institutionalist framework serves as the theoretical starting point. Based on the understanding that institutionally grown structures and routines prevent the easy adaptation to exogenous pressure, the level of pressure to adapt to the European policy demands (resulting from the 'fit' between European policy requirements and the existing national structures and procedures) is conceived of as the basic explanatory variable.

Second, the historical institutionalist framework has to be modified and qualified in order to address two major analytical weaknesses generally associated with institution-based explanations; namely, their deterministic and conservative bias. The problem of determinism emerges from the fact that, by conceiving of institutions as the sole explanatory factor, these models generally do not say much about the conditions under which and the degree to which factors other than institutions, such as the interests and strategies of the actors involved, play a role in explaining political outcomes. In other words, we need analytical criteria in order to determine when a mere institutional explanation is sufficient and when the institutional approach has to be supplemented by focusing on the underlying constellations of strategic interaction.

In this book, it is argued that in answering this question it makes a crucial difference whether European policies challenge core institutional patterns of national administrative traditions or only require adjustments within the institutional core. In this context, administrative traditions are defined as general patterns of administrative styles and structures which are strongly embedded in the macro-institutional context of the state tradition, the legal system as well as the political-administrative system of a country. If European policy demands stand in contradiction to core institutional elements, a merely institution-based perspective is sufficient to account for the expected outcome, i.e., the domestic resistance to change. A contradiction to the institutional core represents an institutional 'misfit' of such magnitude that the institutional perspective alone allows us to predict the pattern of domestic adaptation – or the absence of it, as the case may be. By contrast, if European requirements do not challenge the core of national administrative traditions, a mere institution-based focus is no longer sufficient to account for patterns of domestic adaptation. We find ourselves in the 'undetermined' realm of the historical institutionalist framework where non-institutional factors also have to be considered. National responses must also be explained in the light of the underlying constellations of interests and actors. In other words, agency-based approaches have to be considered as subsidiary in cases where a mere institution-based perspective provides no sufficient explanation.

The conservative view on institutional change constitutes a further weakness of the historical institutionalist framework. The 'normal life' of institutions is characterised by continuity and persistence; change is confined to minor adaptations, and fundamental reforms are restricted to highly exceptional cases of historical shocks or crises. The theoretical and empirical findings of the underlying study indicate the need for a more dynamic perspective on core institutional developments. Although a static core of national administrative traditions can be considered the 'normal case', we cannot preclude the possibility of core changes which, in turn, alter the scope for domestic adaptation to European requirements. To grasp the structural potential for such developments I shall introduce the concept of administrative reform capacity. As will be shown, the high level of administrative reform capacity in Britain implied changes in the level of adaptation pressure quite independent from European influences, and this partially facilitated the domestic adjustment to supranational policy demands.

Third, and implicit in the previous paragraphs, in taking the historical institutionalist perspective as the analytical starting point, I suggest that it is useful to structure the analysis according to the principle of 'decreasing levels of abstraction' (Lindenberg 1991), which supplements institution-based explanations by an agency-based perspective only in cases where the former provides no sufficient results. The alternative would have been to immediately follow an agency-based approach. Although a mere agency-based perspective should explain patterns of domestic change and persistence equally well, the chosen explanatory hierarchy benefits from the more abstract institution-based explanation which allows for the *ex ante* hypothesising on administrative adaptation.

The exploration offered here concerning how and why national administrations change or persist when implementing supranational policies is structured as follows. In Part I I explain my theoretical frame of reference, the analytical approach and the methodological procedure.

Several leading hypotheses are developed which guide the empirical analysis. Part II provides a comparative overview of the two administrative systems being compared. Based on these findings, it is possible to explain the observed patterns of administrative transformation in the environmental field. Part III aims to test empirically the theoretical and analytical considerations. In Part IV, the empirical and theoretical findings are interpreted from a general perspective, exploring the validity of these findings in the context of other European policies.

I

Theoretical frame of reference and analytical approach

To study the impact of European policies on domestic administrative systems one could think of many theoretical starting points, including not only research on European integration, but also on comparative public administration and policy implementation. I argue, however, that the research questions dominant in these fields differ from the focus taken by this study; and thus only provide limited analytical insights for our context. More promising starting points are offered by new institutionalist approaches. Since they reflect a broad variety of different theoretical conceptions, I shall develop and specify a more integrated perspective in the light of the underlying research question.

1 The keywords: European integration, comparative administration and implementation

This study is concerned with the impact of European policies on national administrations. In selecting this research topic, one could in principle focus on both the formulation and implementation of European policies. One could argue that explaining domestic administrative change in the light of European policy requirements is not merely a matter of analysing the process of implementation but also, and primarily, a matter of analysing why and how certain policy choices have been made at the supranational level. Several studies on the dynamics of the supranational policy-making process seem to underline this necessity. Both research carried out in the field of health and safety at work and environmental policy indicates that supranational policy-making in these areas is characterised by a process of 'regulatory competition' between member states (Héritier *et al*. 1994; Héritier, Knill and Mingers 1996; Eichener 1996). Individual states strive to avoid potential costs of administrative adjustment emerging from European policies that diverge from domestic provisions. The competition between the existing national administrative systems, which is inherent in regulatory competition, may therefore be taken as the basic starting point for studying the impact of European policies on national administrations.

Although many analytical insights can be gained by examining administrative changes in the context of the whole European policy cycle, this study takes another path. Its main focus is on the process of European policy *implementation* at the *national* level and the administrative changes following from this. Hence, the patterns of administrative transformation at the national level are the dependent variable to be explained. The explanation of the supranational policy formulation process which led to the selection of the policy to be implemented is not within the scope of this study.

This is not meant entirely to exclude supranational policy formulation from the analysis. Rather it has to be considered in order to get a full understanding of the concrete content and the administrative implications of the policy decided upon. While being aware of the complex

9

constellation in which national administrative systems are both influencing and being influenced by European policies, an exclusive focus on implementation allows for a transnational comparison of administrative systems which are confronted with an identical set of European requirements. In other words, treating the EU legislation as independent input into the national sphere allows for a focus on the distinctive impact of national factors in shaping domestic responses to European policy demands.

In view of the underlying research focus, there are at least three research areas related to this study: namely, research on European integration; public administration; and policy implementation. To what extent can we rely on results from related research areas and to what extent can the analysis make new contributions potentially relevant in these fields?

1.1   Europeanisation and domestic change

An important characteristic that distinguishes this study from earlier research on Europeanisation is its exclusive focus on domestic arrangements. They are conceived as the dependent variable which is affected by European policies. This contrasts with 'traditional' concepts of Europeanisation research, which are basically concerned with developments at the supranational level. Broadly speaking, these concepts examine the causal chain the other way round, by focusing on the extent to which domestic conditions affect the outcome of supranational institution-building and policy-making. Without neglecting this causal relationship, focusing on the Europeanisation of domestic arrangements examines the impact of already-established supranational arrangements at the national level.

With respect to 'traditional' research on European integration, two broad strands can be distinguished: intergovernmental relations and comparative politics. Whereas the discussion in intergovernmental relations is dominated by the two competing paradigms of intergovernmentalism and neofunctionalism, there are a growing number of European policy studies which bypass this long-standing debate by focusing on comparative politics and public administration literature (cf. Hix 1994; Héritier et al. 1994; Marks, Hooghe and Blank 1996; Héritier, Knill and Mingers 1996; Jachtenfuchs and Kohler-Koch 1996). The basic focus of both strands of research is on supranational institution-building and policy-making. Consequently, they provide only limited insights when it comes to the impact of European integration at the domestic level.

The two competing paradigms of neofunctionalism and intergovernmentalism were developed to explain the respective absence or occurrence of supranationality (Keohane and Hoffmann 1991; Moravcsik 1991, 1994; Burley and Mattli 1993).[1] With respect to institution-building, an important part of Europeanisation research focuses on the emergence and the development of European interest associations (Eising and Kohler-Koch 1994; Kohler-Koch 1994; Greenwood and Cram 1996; Knill and Lehmkuhl 1998).

Since the basic concern of these studies is related to developments at the supranational level, the impact of these developments on domestic structures and processes is hardly subject to consistent analysis. Domestic structures are not considered as dependent variables, but are analysed as factors which affect the interactions between the supranational and domestic levels. An important discussion in this context refers to the extent to which European integration might imply a redistribution of resources between national actors and institutions. Moravcsik (1994), for instance, argues that the political co-operation at the European level strengthens the autonomy of the executive actors in favour of other domestic actors, such as the parliament, interest groups, and regions.[2] This view is challenged by those claiming that the process of European integration provides subnational and societal actors at the domestic level with new resources that allow them to circumvent the national executives (Sandholtz 1996). A third position in this debate takes the view that the redistribution of resources among supranational, national, and subnational actors may neither strengthen nor weaken one level at the expense of the other, but that it implies a tendency towards shared and interlinked decision-making, and thus leads to new forms of co-operative governance (Kooiman 1993; Kohler-Koch 1998; Kohler-Koch and Eising 1999; Lenschow 1999).

For the purpose of this study, however, these findings seem to be of only limited relevance, since they contain no theoretical generalisations that allow for hypothesising on the scope and mode of domestic administrative change. First, traditional integration research is not directly concerned with domestic institutional change, but with potential power redistribution between domestic and European actors. Second, although the redistribution of power can be seen as a basic condition for

---

[1] Susanne K. Schmidt (1997a) demonstrates the explanatory deficits of each of these approaches, which she classifies as 'sterile debates' relying on 'dubious generalisations'.

[2] Moravcsik focused on this issue by arguing that national executives have powerful resources (they control and define policy initiatives, institutional procedures of domestic decision-making as well as the supply and access of information and ideas) that enable them to acquire some turf advantages by transferring policies from the national to the supranational arena. This argument of the 'paradox of weakness' is also inherent in other analyses (cf. Grande 1996; Kohler-Koch 1996).

subsequent institutional change, the above-mentioned concepts do not specify general conditions under which such changes actually take place. For instance, concepts like policy networks or multilevel governance, which are applied to integrate the national and subnational levels into the analysis, are basically metaphorical and allow only for limited generalisations about the extent to which European integration might result in changes of domestic institutions (Aspinwall and Schneider 1997). This deficit is further enhanced by the fact that there is obviously no agreement on the extent to which the European influence has affected the redistribution of domestic power or the direction of that redistribution. A third aspect which restricts the relevance that these concepts have to this study is their focus on political rather than administrative institutions and actors. Although political and administrative changes might be closely related, administrative changes are only indirectly integrated into the analysis.

It is only since the mid-1990s that research on Europeanisation has begun to focus more systematically on the domestic impact of EU policy. Andersen and Eliassen (1993) or Mény, Muller and Quermonne (1996), for instance, examined how activities in Brussels impacted upon the national policy-making processes. Héritier, Knill and Mingers (1996) analysed the impact of European environmental policies on domestic regulatory regimes from a cross-country perspective. Vivien Schmidt (1996) examined the Europeanisation process in reference to domestic governance structures in France. Kohler-Koch and others (1998) have documented this process at the subnational level by examining the influence of the EU on regional governments, policies and outcomes.

Notwithstanding a growing number of studies characterised by a systematic and exclusive focus on the domestic impact of Europe, however, we are still confronted with rather limited and inconsistent empirical and theoretical findings (Knill and Lehmkuhl 1999; Radaelli 2000). On the one hand, empirical evidence indicates rather contradictory patterns with respect to the scope and direction of national change. While some authors emphasise that European policy has led to a convergence of national styles and structures (Harcourt 2000; Schneider 2001), others stress the ways in which it has had a differential impact, with domestic responses to EU policies varying considerably across policies and countries. The same European policy might cause fundamental reforms in one country while having no impact at all in others. In the same country we might observe considerable regulatory adjustments to certain European policies, while nothing at all happens in other areas (Knill and Lenschow 1998, 2001; Héritier *et al.* 2001; Caporaso, Cowles and Risse 2001).

On the other hand, we are confronted with a rather unsystematic theoretical picture when we look at the varying explanations developed in order to account for the impact of Europe on domestic arrangements and structures. There are a number of studies which rely on the institutional compatibility of European and domestic arrangements; i.e., the level of European adaptation pressure, as the most important variable in order to account for the domestic impact of Europe (Olsen 1995; Héritier, Knill and Mingers 1996; Börzel 1999). Others completely discard this institutional argument, focusing instead on the extent to which European policies have affected domestic opportunity structures and interest constellations (Majone 1996; Lehmkuhl 1999; Haverland 2000; Schneider 2001). Still another group of scholars emphasises the impact of European policies on belief systems, ideas and the expectations of domestic actors (Lavenex 1999; Checkel 2001).

In the literature, there is currently a broad discussion of how to link the different approaches within a more comprehensive and systematic framework. In this context, several approaches can be distinguished. Cowles and Risse (2001) define the existence of European adaptation pressure as the necessary condition for domestic change. For these changes actually to take place, a second, sufficient condition has to be fulfilled (see also Knill 1998; Börzel and Risse 2000; Knill and Lenschow 2001a). There have to be some facilitating factors which provide the basis for corresponding responses to the adaptational pressures, such as changing beliefs and preferences of domestic actors, the emergence of 'change agents' or 'favourable' institutional opportunity structures.

Héritier and Knill (2001), by contrast, emphasise that the existence of European adaptation pressure does not constitute a necessary condition for domestic change. They base this on observed cases in which European policies led to national reforms, although European and domestic arrangements were fully compatible. They suggest a dynamic approach which conceives of European policies basically as input into the domestic political process that might be exploited by national actors in order to enhance their opportunities for achieving their objectives. In this context, the degree and direction of domestic change depends on the distinctive constellation of three interacting factors: namely, the stage of national regulation in relation to European policies (pre-reform, reform, post-reform), the level of sectoral reform capacity, as well as the prevailing belief systems of the domestic actors. The particular combination of these factors not only affects which domestic actors are strengthened or weakened by EU legislation, but also whether those actors benefiting from European influence are actually able to exploit effectively their new opportunities, putting through regulatory reforms consistent with their interests.

While the above approaches argue in favour of a comprehensive approach to the study of Europeanisation, Knill and Lehmkuhl (1999) suggest differentiating and qualifying different explanatory approaches depending on the particular mechanism by which European policies impact upon domestic arrangements. They argue that the more European policies positively prescribe or impose a concrete model for domestic compliance, the more relevance the level of adaptation pressure has for explanation (cf. Kohler-Koch 1999: 26). The perspective on the level of adaptation pressure is of limited use, however, when the impact of European policies basically operates through the mechanism of changing domestic opportunity structures and/or belief systems. In such cases, approaches focusing on the European impact on the strategic opportunities and constraints as well as on the preferences and beliefs of national actors provide a more promising analytical starting-point.

While this theoretical debate offers important analytical insights for this study, we are still confronted with a variety of different and partially opposing approaches. More specifically, there still seems to be a strong disagreement as to whether either institution-based perspectives (starting from the concept of adaptation pressure) or actor-based perspectives (focusing on belief systems, preferences and the strategic interaction of domestic actors) constitute the most fruitful approach to account for the domestic impact of EU policies.

In view of these inconsistencies, in this book I intend to contribute to this ongoing debate on the empirical and theoretical impact of Europeanisation. In focusing on national administrative systems, the study provides empirical knowledge on the domestic impact of Europe in a field which has thus far received comparatively little attention in Europeanisation research. Moreover, by taking a comparative focus (across different policies and member states) I aim to offer new theoretical insights to account for the different national responses to European policies; this will help to improve and qualify existing explanatory approaches. In this context, the main concern is to establish a complementary link between different theoretical perspectives on Europeanisation.

1.2   Comparative public administration

Given its focus on the comparative analysis of domestic administrative change, the underlying study is closely related to the field of comparative public administration. However, findings from this field provide only limited theoretical insights concerning the European impact on national administrative systems. Hardly any comparative studies exist which systematically investigate the conditions for administrative change from a cross-national perspective.

The generally limited theoretical development of public administration research is certainly one important factor in explaining this lack of systematic comparison (Peters 1988). On the one hand, there is a broad range of studies which focus on the micro-level of administrative organisations. This body of literature is generally descriptive and characterised by a normative and ameliorative bias; i.e., with an emphasis on improving administrative practice. In addition, most of these studies are based on single countries, and they do not seek to provide broader theoretical and conceptual perspectives (cf. Ridley 1979; Derlien 1995; Pierre 1995). On the other hand, to the extent to which students of public administration have been interested in theory, it has been theory (like Weber's) which stressed structural similarities of all public administrations (cf. Crozier 1964; Wilson 1989; Page 1992); for example, the political influence exerted by the bureaucracy on policy formulation and implementation has been examined. Hence, it was frequently assumed that very little variation did occur in public administration (Peters 1996: 15). In short, research in public administration lacks a systematic theoretical linkage between the descriptions of minute differences in structures and processes and the macro-perspective emphasising bureaucratic similarities across countries.

This general statement does not imply that no efforts have been made to bridge the gap between micro-level description and macro-level theorising. There are at least some studies which provide more conceptual and analytical insights into administrative differences across nations (cf. Aberbach, Putnam and Rockman 1981; Jann 1983; Page 1992; Peters 1995; Bekke, Perry and Toonen 1996). However, all of these studies are based on a static comparison; they do not systematically explain the dynamics of the administrative systems in question (Peters 1996: 16). While providing important analytical insights for the comparative analysis of public administration in general, they contain little information which would allow for hypothesising on the patterns of administrative adaptation to external (in our case European) requirements.

This deficit still applies, notwithstanding the fact that – in the context of the global wave of NPM concepts – there has been a growing interest in investigating administrative reforms across countries (cf. Wright 1994; Pierre 1995; Flynn and Strehl 1996; Olsen and Peters 1996;

Hood 1996). These studies start by examining differences in domestic administrative changes in the light of the convergent pressures emanating from the cluster of reform ideas that have been dominating the international discourse since the 1980s. These ideas provide a global diagnosis and a standard solution to the ills of the public sector; they recommended replacing the concept of administration based on due rules and process with NPM concepts emphasising goals and results and giving private firms an exemplary role in public-sector reform (Wright 1994; Olsen and Peters 1996: 13).

The analytical insights gained in these studies are nevertheless of limited value for the purpose of this study. First, this study is concerned with the impact of European policy requirements on domestic administrations rather than the diffusion effects of international reform waves and public sector management ideas. Given that there is a qualitative difference between the need to comply with European legislation and the opportunity to engage voluntarily in management reforms circulating on the international agenda, generalisations on administrative change have to be treated with caution. Second, many studies on public sector reforms are characterised by the deficits of the study of comparative public administration in general. In particular, they lack an analytical framework that allows for the comparative assessment of the scope and mode of administrative change across countries. Furthermore, they reveal important deficits with respect to comparatively operationalising the scope and mode of administrative changes in different countries.[3]

Besides administrative research with a purely national or cross-national focus, there is a growing body of literature which investigates the effects emerging from the interaction of national and supranational bureaucracies (Toonen 1992; Page and Wouters 1995; Wessels and Rometsch 1996). However, in taking a rather descriptive focus, these analyses contain no systematic information on the extent to which the interactions of European and domestic administrations yield domestic adjustment. Wessels and Rometsch (1996), for instance, provide quantitative evidence which underlines their hypothesis that there has been a 'fusion' of supranational and national bureaucracies. However, they are not specifying the ways in which increasing interactions and linkages between national and European administrations may lead to changes in domestic administrations. Toonen (1992) explicitly addresses this ques-

---

[3] For instance, in comparing the contributions of Derlien (1995, 1996a) and Hood (1995, 1996) in the same volumes (Pierre 1995; Olsen and Peters 1996), it becomes obvious that, although both authors use the language of 'reform'; the use of this term by Derlien seems to be highly exaggerated when contrasting the piecemeal German adjustments with the large-scale developments in Britain.

tion, but he confines his analysis to comparing the administrative conditions for the effective formal adoption of European legislation in the member states. Page and Wouters (1995), by contrast, hypothesise on the likelihood of domestic change, but their perspective concerns the extent to which the Brussels bureaucracy is seen as a model to be imitated at the national level,[4] rather than investigating the impact of European policy requirements, as is the purpose of this study.

In sum, given the lack of comparative theoretical and conceptual studies in the field of comparative public administration, it is difficult to develop general conclusions and assumptions on the scope and likelihood of administrative adjustments to external pressures emanating from EU legislation. This is not to say that past research in comparative public administration is not of importance for the purpose of this study. However, this requires that the findings from this field of research have to be linked to a comparative and conceptual framework. In this respect, this study addresses important research deficits in this field of inquiry.

1.3   Implementation research

A study which is concerned with domestic administrative changes emerging from the supranational policy requirements is closely related to questions of policy implementation. Assuming that European legislation contains administrative implications differing from domestic arrangements, implementation effectiveness can be expected to increase as domestic administrative arrangements are adapted to European policy requirements. From this perspective, effective implementation and domestic administrative change are congruent variables expressing similar research interests.

It must be emphasised that such a perspective necessarily implies a narrow definition of implementation. To be congruent with the conception of administrative change, effective implementation must be defined as the degree to which the formal transposition and the practical application of supranational measures at the national level correspond with the objectives defined in European legislation (Knill and Lenschow 2000). Hence, it is the *administrative compliance* with these objectives which is the concern of this study, rather than the evaluation of European policy outcomes and impacts.

---

[4] Page and Wouters (1995: 202) argue that despite the frequent interaction of national and supranational administrations, the 'isomorphy effects' (DiMaggio and Powell 1991) leading to a structural convergence of European and national bureaucracies will be limited. Given the 'adolescent' character of the Community bureaucracy (Peters 1992), it does not offer a coherent enough set of administrative principles, practices and rules to challenge the well-established administrative institutions of the member states.

In addition, its distinctive analytical focus implies two further restrictions in the way this study is linked to the huge body of implementation research. First, given the emphasis on administrative compliance with European requirements, the study necessarily analyses implementation 'from above'. Supranational legislation is taken as a starting-point and analysis concerns the extent to which European objectives have been complied with by corresponding domestic administrative adjustments. Hence, this study does not take the perspective of 'bottom-up' approaches which emphasise the importance of 'street-level bureaucrats' (Lipsky 1980) on the context-specific definitions of policy objectives and instruments (cf. Windhoff-Héritier 1987: 86–104; Peters 1993; Lane 1995). Second, by taking European policy programmes as an independent factor, I restrict my focus to a distinctive stage within the supranational policy cycle; namely, to the process of implementation. Although the benefits of analytically distinguishing different policy stages have been called into question (Sabatier 1993; Baier, March and Sætren 1990), for reasons outlined at the beginning of this chapter this study takes another path. European policies are 'taken for granted' (regardless of potential doubts on their quality), and the study concerns whether their institutional implications have been complied with or not.

Similar to the situation in the field of public administration, implementation research provides us only with limited theoretical concepts which can be usefully integrated in the context of this study. This can be explained by reference to two factors characterising implementation research in general. First, despite significant efforts during the 1980s, where implementation research was a 'flourishing industry', theory-building remained comparatively underdeveloped. With the increasing number of empirical case-studies it became more and more apparent that, given the high variety, singularity and contingency of implementation results, the ambitious plans for developing comprehensive and general theoretical models had to be abandoned (cf. Mayntz 1983: 8; Windhoff-Héritier 1987: 88). Hence, the number of generally applicable concepts remained low. They included, for instance, the assumption that implementation effectiveness decreases with the number of structural 'clearing points' which are involved during the implementation process (Pressman and Wildavsky 1973). Another argument refers to the fact that the success of implementation is not only dependent on policy characteristics and contents, but also on the preferences, capabilities and resources of subordinate administrative actors dealing with practical enforcement as well as societal actors addressed by the policy in question (Hanf and Downing 1982; Mayntz 1983). Without questioning the validity of these arguments, their limited degree of specification hardly allows for general statements on the scope and mode of domestic administrative change with respect to particular European policies.

Second, in contrast to this study, most of the literature on implementation concentrates on policy types and policy problems rather than institutions. Thus, even where more systematic and comprehensive concepts were developed, they were either focusing on the appropriateness of certain policy instruments in the light of distinctive policy problems or on the design of optimal implementation structures, given a certain policy to be implemented (Hanf and Scharpf 1978; Linder and Peters 1989; Ingram and Schneider 1990; Peters 1993).

Given the peculiar focus and problems characterising implementation research, even those implementation studies taking an explicit focus on European policies provide only limited systematic insights into the question of domestic administrative change. The focus of European implementation studies is either descriptive, and restricted to the formal mechanisms of policy adoption in the member states (Siedentopf and Ziller 1988; Schwarze, Becker and Pollak 1994), or directed towards the improvement of overall implementation effectiveness by focusing on statutory design and sanction mechanisms (Collins and Earnshaw 1992).

In view of the theoretical and conceptual weaknesses characterising implementation research, a systematic investigation of the conditions affecting the adjustment of national administrative arrangements to the requirements spelled out in EU legislation has considerable potential to offer new insights on the factors shaping the implementation effectiveness of EU policy.

2 An institutional approach to administrative change

The brief review of the broader research context in which this study is embedded has revealed the analytical problems present in the development of an analytical framework aimed at accounting for the impact of European policies on national administrations. On the one hand, this can be traced to the fact that the leading questions analysed in those related areas are only partially congruent with the analytical focus underlying this study. On the other hand, research deficits emerge from theoretical gaps prevalent in these fields. This does not imply, however, that in order to address these analytical deficits we have to start from point zero. Bearing in mind that explaining administrative transformation is mainly a matter of studying institutions and institutional change, there is a certain common sense in putting institutions at the heart of administrative analysis (Lowndes 1996: 181). In this context especially, the approaches linked to the concept of the new institutionalism have contributed to a renewed interest in the study of public administration. At the same time, the new institutionalist approaches play a prominent role in Europeanisation research, and, more recently, have also been applied to implementation research (Knill and Lenschow 2000).

New institutionalism does not constitute a single and coherent body of theory, but comprises many different streams of argument. Although sharing a basic common assumption, namely that institutions do matter, there are a variety of conceptions of *how, why and to what extent* institutions make a difference. The different theoretical variants are grouped into sociological institutionalists, focusing on normative and cultural institutions that establish a 'logic of appropriateness' for human behaviour, the rational-choice institutionalists, focusing on strategic, goal-oriented behaviour within institutional limits, and historical institutionalists, borrowing somewhat eclectically from the other two schools though with a special appreciation of the influence of history on present-day policy-making (Hall and Taylor 1996; Immergut 1997; Nørgaard 1996).

Notwithstanding the important theoretical and ontological differences existing between these views, I argue in this section that, from an explanatory perspective, they can be divided into *institution-based* and *agency-based* approaches. As both approaches have explanatory strengths as well as weaknesses, the crucial question is not to decide which approach is theoretically superior, but to link them in a complementary way. In so doing, I develop a framework that uses the historical institutionalist approach as a starting-point, specifies the conditions under which this model needs to be complemented with an agency-based perspective and introduces a new dynamic element to the analysis.[1]

2.1   Different concepts of institutional change: institution-based versus agency-based approaches

In distinguishing institution- and agency-based approaches I follow the argument made by Mayntz and Scharpf (1995: 52), emphasising that from a merely explanatory perspective the crucial question is not *how* institutions exert their influence, but *how much* they explain. To what extent can we conceive of institutions as independent or only intervening factors in accounting for administrative change?[2]

Institution-based approaches

Institution-based approaches emphasise the role of existing institutional configurations as *independent explanatory factors* in the analysis of political outcomes and institutional development. Existing institutions are considered the primary explanatory factor in shaping institutional change. The attribution of far-reaching structuring impacts to institutions favours conservative expectations. Institution-based approaches, regardless of their distinctive ontological conception of institutional impacts, emphasise the stability and continuity of institutions and policy legacies.

As a general rule, adaptation processes remain incremental or path-

---

[1] It ought to be emphasised in this context that my concern in this section is pragmatic rather than theoretical. The primary objective is to develop a sound explanatory framework to account for the impact of Europe on national administrations; it is neither my intention to join nor to resolve the discussion on how to integrate the theoretical and ontological differences underlying varying theoretical views of the new institutionalism (on this issue see, for instance, Finnemore and Sikkink 1998; Katzenstein, Keohane and Krasner 1998; Barnett 1999; Schoppa 1999).

[2] Mayntz and Scharpf (1995: 52) further legitimise their approach in view of empirical ambiguities. Thus in many instances it is difficult to tell whether empirically observed behaviour was consequential or appropriate. There might well be constellations where egoistic self-interested behaviour is exactly what is expected as institutionally appropriate from certain actors.

dependent, without challenging well-established core patterns of existing arrangements. This does not mean that external pressures have no impact on existing institutional structures. But they are not the single factor to be taken into account. Rather the process of institutional adaptation to exogenous factors is crucially influenced by endogenous institutional dynamics determined by the institutions' 'roots and routes' – the origins and the paths by which they have arrived where they are (Olsen 1995: 4).[3] Hence, institutions persist over time, although their environments may change. It is only in exceptional cases of fundamental performance crises or external shocks that the discrepancy between exogenous pressure and adaptive capacity becomes too big and old continuities are given up in order to create new continuities (Krasner 1988; Powell 1991; Thelen and Steinmo 1992). In this way, institution-based approaches provide us with rather clear expectations concerning the scope and mode of change.

However, by emphasising the structuring impact of institutions and claiming that institutions influence both the strategies and interests of actors, this relatively parsimonious model risks explanatory determinism, ignoring the possibly independent influences of actors and their strategic interaction on political outcomes (Mayntz and Scharpf 1995). Although we are assured – especially by historical institutionalists – that institutions constrain and refract politics but *never* solely cause certain outcomes (Thelen and Steinmo 1992: 3), we receive little guidance with regard to the extent to which institutions pre-structure the outcome, that is, *how much* institutions matter.

A further weakness emerges from the conservative bias inherent in institution-based explanations, ignoring the possibility that the dynamics of strategic interaction might break the boundaries of the institutional frame of reference or existing power structures. Considering that there are instances in which institutional change goes beyond routine adaptation,[4] this conception seems too narrow and needs to be complemented with concepts that allow for more than incremental change from the 'inside'.

The conception that institutions are independent variables cuts across the ontological boundaries between different institutionalist approaches.

---

[3] A similar interpretation is offered by DiMaggio and Powell who explain institutional change and persistence in reference to the striving of institutions to increase their social legitimacy by embracing forms and practices which are widely valued within the 'myths' of the broader institutional environment. Isomorphism, i.e., the demand for similarity of structure and functioning, rather than increased efficiency, drives institutional change (DiMaggio and Powell 1991: 63).

[4] The numerous moves towards the privatisation of public utilities taking place in many Western democracies serve as an example in this context.

To be sure, institution-based approaches are particularly dominant in the sociological institutionalist corner, with institutions not only enabling and constraining the specific strategies and choices of actors, but also influencing the way actors conceive of their ultimate interests in the first place. Institutions do not simply affect the strategic calculations of individuals, but also their most basic preferences and very identities. Institutions are frameworks that structure choices by providing appropriate routines and standard operating procedures (March and Olsen 1989; Jepperson 1991; Dobbin 1994; Scott 1995).

The conception of institutions as independent variables is also an important feature of historical institutionalism (Thelen and Steinmo 1992; Immergut 1992; Pierson 1996), which takes a rather eclectic view when explaining the independent structuring impact of institutions, relying on concepts which rely more on either rational choice or sociological institutionalist perspectives. In their rationalist variant, historical institutionalists emphasise the structuring impact of institutional 'lock-ins', where deviations from the initial path become increasingly costly or difficult as a result of the institutionally structured distribution of power between different actors (Arthur 1988; North 1990). In its sociological perspective, historical institutionalism conceives of institutions as affecting the actors' conception of their own interests by making some political outcomes seem more feasible than others and by propagating some worldviews more widely than others (Hall and Taylor 1996). Historical institutionalists point out that for explaining institutional change it is more important to recognise that 'history matters' than to figure out whether path-dependency is the result of lock-in effects, the distribution of bargaining power or the institutional reproduction of standard operating procedures (Hall 1986: 19; Thelen and Steinmo 1992: 9).

Agency-based approaches

Agency-based approaches attach a less determining explanatory role to institutional factors. In contrast to the analysis from institution-based approaches, change is analysed from the perspective of methodological individualism. Human action is the cornerstone of these social-science explanations. Institutions still matter, but they operate as *intervening rather than independent variables* between the interaction of actors and corresponding outcomes.

Agency-based approaches explain institutional developments (their continuity or change) by reference to the prevailing actor constellation in a given institutional context. Hence they do not face the problems of determinism and conservatism in the same way that institution-based approaches do. They are not biased in favour of institutional stability, thus they can equally well account for stability and change.

However, at the same time, their openness constitutes a major analytical weakness. A sound agency-based explanation would need to account for high empirical complexity. In practice, it is an enormous challenge to accurately attribute the resources, preferences and strategic orientations to the diverse set of actors involved, and hence to offer an accurate *ex ante* assessment of the conditions for institutional change. In this respect, the more abstract and parsimonious institution-based model is superior, and I shall argue below, can be fruitfully combined with the agency-based perspective, which also makes it possible to compensate for its implicit determinism.

The conception of institutions as an intervening variable is most prominent in rational-choice forms of the new institutionalism. Rational-choice institutionalist approaches emphasise that institutions matter because they structure the opportunities for strategic choice and interaction. Existing institutional structures – such as the definition of responsibilities and the decision rules or procedures, including 'veto points'[5] – restrict or provide opportunities for institutional change either by affecting the cost/benefit calculations of the actors involved or by defining a certain distribution of powers and resources between them. In this way, institutions influence the strategies of actors to achieve their interests, but institutions have no impact on the formation of these interests, which are conceived as exogenous to institutional analysis. According to this conception, rational choice institutionalists focus on interests as the primary, independent explanatory factor; institutions are considered to be a secondary, intervening factor for explaining political outcomes (Shepsle and Weingast 1987; Shepsle 1989).

Within the rational-choice branch of the new institutionalism, two perspectives on institutional development can be distinguished. In the field of new institutional economics, institutional development is interpreted purely from an efficiency perspective; i.e., the concept of institutions as an opportunity structure is interpreted in terms of the benefits they provide for the actors involved (Williamson 1985; North 1990: 24). Since efficiency is the rationale for institutionalisation, existing institutional arrangements will only persist as long as the costs of effecting changes outweigh prospective gains (Shepsle 1989). The second approach within rational-choice institutionalism emphasises the distributional effects and the struggle for power involved in creating,

---

[5] Immergut (1992: 27) refers to veto points as 'critical points of strategic uncertainty where decisions may be overturned'.

changing and maintaining institutions (Moe 1990; Dunleavy 1991; Knight 1992).

In conclusion, for the purpose of this study the consideration of the explanatory power of institution-based and agency-based approaches yields a dilemma, as both concepts are characterised by analytical strengths as well as weaknesses. Although providing sound explanations which are very close to empirical reality, agency-based approaches suffer from their low level of analytical abstraction. Hence, *ex ante* hypothesising on institutional change is difficult; explanations are only possible from an *ex post* perspective. This problem is avoided by sociological and historical institutionalism, given the conception of institutions as an independent variable. However, the independent explanatory value assigned to institutions at the same time implies the rather deterministic bias of these institution-based approaches; the role of actors and the dynamics emerging from strategic interaction are ignored. Both agency-based and institution-based approaches are therefore characterised by distinctive deficits, indicating the need to link both approaches in a way that partly compensates for their respective weaknesses.

2.2   Linking different perspectives on institutional change: a modified concept of historical institutionalism

In this section I argue that it is possible to link institution-based and agency-based approaches by using historical institutionalism as a starting-point. To address the specific explanatory weaknesses associated with this approach, its basic argument is modified in two ways. The deterministic bias is avoided by specifying the conditions under which the institution-based model is to be complemented with an agency-based perspective. In a second step, a new element is introduced into the analysis in order to reduce the static bias inherent in historical institutional explanations.

Before turning to these suggestions about how to modify the historical institutionalist model in order to deal with these analytical problems, let me justify why I adhere to historical institutionalism as an explanatory starting-point and do not turn to a rational-choice or a sociological institutionalist perspective. In my view this choice offers three analytical advantages. First, in contrast to agency-based rational-choice explanations, the historical institutionalism provides a more abstract and parsimonious basis which allows for the development of *ex ante* hypotheses on institutional change. In this respect, and not in its general explanatory value, historical institutionalism is superior and,

I shall argue below, can be fruitfully complemented with the agency-based perspective in order to deal with the weakness of its implicit determinism as well.

Second, historical institutionalism makes an important contribution by emphasising that the structuring effects of institutions may not only be the result of their normative and cognitive impact, but can also be interpreted in terms of lock-in effects and power distributions defined by distinctive institutional configurations. The more pragmatic, albeit to some extent eclectic, historical approach offers a more realistic view in the light of potential empirical ambiguities. To tell whether empirically observed behaviour was 'consequential' or 'appropriate' is difficult, if not impossible in many instances. There might well be constellations where egoistic self-interested behaviour is exactly what is expected as 'institutionally appropriate' from certain actors (Mayntz and Scharpf 1995: 52).

Third, historical institutionalists in general apply a more narrow conception of institutions, which is restricted to sets of formal and informal rules, norms and conventions that prescribe behavioural roles, shape expectations, and constrain and enable activities (North 1990; Thelen and Steinmo 1992). As it is only from such a less encompassing conception of institutions that problems of determinism can be effectively avoided (Mayntz and Scharpf 1995: 46), the comprehensive approach taken by sociological institutionalists, who conceive of institutions as symbolic and cognitive maps constituting individual beliefs and behaviour (Scott 1995: 31), constitutes a less promising analytical starting-point in this context.

Restricting determinism: linking institution-based and
agency-based approaches

In suggesting a link of institution-based and agency-based approaches, I follow Mayntz and Scharpf (1995: 43), who emphasise the pitfalls of a deterministic institutional explanatory framework and suggest that models focusing on the independent impact of institutions on political outcomes should be supplemented by explanations which take into account the independent role of interests and actors. Recognising the explanatory relevance of institutions as both independent and as intervening factors, they propose a pragmatic analytical solution to overcome the dilemma between an inappropriate determinism, on the one hand, and a general explanatory openness, on the other. Following the principle of 'decreasing levels of abstraction' (Lindenberg 1991), explanations should take the more abstract and parsimonious institution-based approach as a starting-point, considering strategic behaviour as an independent factor only if institutions provide no sufficient explanation. In other words, the more indeterminate interest-based approach plays a subsidiary role in explaining political outcomes.

However, without neglecting the benefits of this explanatory 'procedure', we are still left with the problem of defining the criteria indicating when we have to switch from one approach to the other. In other words, the development of *ex ante* hypotheses on administrative change requires analytical criteria which define the explanatory scope of institution-based or agency-based approaches. To what extent can we rely on the more abstract historical explanation, and in which cases do we have to step down the ladder of abstraction, applying a more open, rational-choice explanation? I argue that these questions can be addressed by explicitly acknowledging that different institutional approaches analyse and evaluate the same empirical phenomena from different levels of abstraction; they hence arrive at different conclusions concerning the impact of institutions on political outcomes. This aspect, which is often overlooked when assessing the strengths and weaknesses of varying approaches, might serve as an important starting-point for linking institution-based and agency-based approaches.

Different institutional approaches and their level of abstraction
While there is a long-standing scientific debate on the different ways institutions affect individual behaviour and political outcomes (i.e., by providing cognitive frames of reference or merely opportunity structures for strategic interaction), little attention has been given to the fact that different institutional approaches explain the same cases not only on the basis of distinctive ontological perspectives, but also from varying *levels of abstraction* (Knill and Lenschow 2001b). The distinctive levels of abstraction chosen in different institutional approaches are closely related to their conception of institutions as independent or intervening variables in explaining individual action and political outcomes, the former taking a bird's-eye view and the latter remaining on the spot.

A remote level of abstraction, i.e., taking a bird's-eye view in evaluating institutional change, is typical for institution-based approaches. The levels of empirical development and analytical evaluation are not identical. Thus historical institutionalists (regardless of whether operating on the basis of a more rationalist or a more constructivist framework) typically prefer to analyse sectoral developments against the background of the general macro-institutional context. Immergut (1992), for instance, analyses developments in health policies in the light of varying political structures that confront reformers with different institutional veto points. Steinmo (1993) explains the succession of different tax policies by reference to distinctive national political structures. Dobbin (1994) explains cross-national variation in nineteenth-century railway policies in reference to the impact of the varying conceptions of the state and the market in different countries. This is not to say that approaches that emphasise the importance of institutions as independent explanatory factors automatically focus on state structures. There are many sociological studies that are explicitly concerned with organisational life (March and Olsen 1989). But these studies also evaluate developments on lower, for instance, departmental levels in the light of the more abstract, in this case, organisational perspective.

By contrast, agency-based approaches, which conceive of institutions merely as an intervening variable structuring strategic interaction, tend to assess institutional changes on the spot, i.e., they view the levels of empirical observation and analytical evaluation as identical. The analyst follows the affected actors through the institutional jungle, viewing change through his or her eyes. Changes in the structure of regulatory agencies, for instance, are not evaluated in the light of a macro-institutional context (such as the conception of state and market relations), but by reference to the distribution of power between different actors situated in the respective regulatory environment (Moe 1990).

The distinctive level of abstraction, as inherent in institution-based and agency-based approaches, has important consequences for the interpretation of political developments. With increasing remoteness, the scale of change is diminishing. For instance, the privatisation of the state-owned utilities is dramatic from an individual or organisational perspective; it might even constitute a sectoral revolution. But at the same time the mode of the reform may remain in line with the legal and administrative traditions of the country in question and, on this basis, be judged as incremental. Given the adoption of a more remote level of abstraction by institution-based approaches, their emphasis on persistence and continuity is hardly surprising. On the other hand, the proximate perspective taken by agency-based approaches explains their more open expectations towards change or persistence.

Let me illustrate this point by way of an example and consider the recent global reform wave in the telecommunications sector and the different interpretations offered by historical and rational-choice institutionalist explanations. Whereas the telecommunications industry was considered as a classical case for a public monopoly for a long time, most industrialised countries (including the US, Japan, Britain, France, Germany and Italy) have broken up the former public utilities and transformed them into competitive markets, implying the privatisation of state enterprises and the establishment of regulatory regimes for market control (Schneider 2001; Vogel 1997).

When considering the distinctive explanations for these changes, as they are offered by rational-choice and historical institutionalists, it becomes evident that both approaches focus on the same phenomena from different analytical levels. Rational-choice institutionalists interpret the changes basically from a sector-based perspective. Given this view, it comes as no surprise that rational-choice scholars characterise the institutional transformations as path-breaking reforms which cannot be explained by emphasising piecemeal institutional routine adaptations. They argue that rapid technological innovation combined with the globalisation of markets has significantly altered the powers, resources, as well as the costs and benefits of the sectoral actors, thereby challenging the existing institutional equilibrium, and in fact favouring new arrangements. Given the overwhelming effects of innovation and globalisation, some authors point out that national institutions only affected the process of change, but had no impact on the outcome of the reforms, which show a converging tendency across countries (Schneider 2001).

Scholars applying a historical institutionalist perspective to assess the changes in the telecommunications sector, however, come to rather different conclusions. This can be traced to the fact that they evaluate change not from a sectoral but from a macro-institutional perspective. Taking this more remote analytical focus, sectoral changes are characterised as 'appropriate adaptations' in the light of the particular macro-institutional background of the state and administrative traditions. Rather than emphasising institutional convergence, these scholars point to the path-dependency of sectoral changes. Following this line of argument, Vogel (1997) points out that the arrangements to regulate the privatised telecommunications sector look quite different in Britain and Japan. Whereas in Britain privatisation is accompanied by a pattern of 'competitive deregulation', the Japanese arrangements reveal a more protectionist approach based on 'competitive reregulation'. According to Vogel, these sectoral differences can only be understood against the distinctive macro-institutional background given in both countries, namely the differing bureaucratic traditions and state–society relations.[6]

Given the general preference that different institutional approaches have of evaluating change from different analytical levels, there is a risk that the varying approaches ignore each other's contributions and analytical insights. This problem becomes particularly prominent when

---

[6] Vogel (1997) develops a similar argument with respect to the financial services sector.

different institutional explanations are compared without acknowledging that they operate from distinctive analytical reference levels. On the other hand, as will be shown in the following, the use of different levels of abstraction – when explicitly acknowledged – might serve as important starting-point for linking deterministic and indeterminate approaches in a complementary way.

Complementary perspectives on institutional change: combining varying levels of analysis

We have seen that institution-based and agency-based approaches not only operate from distinctive levels of abstraction; they are also characterised by particular explanatory strengths and weaknesses. While the conservative bias of institution-based approaches provides us with clear expectations on the scope of institutional change, the inherent deterministic bias is at the same time a major weakness. Agency-based approaches, by contrast, avoid the problem of determinism, but suffer from their openness, which makes *ex ante* hypothesising very difficult. I argue that the acknowledgement of different levels of abstraction, and hence the distinctive explanatory value associated with institutions, opens up an interesting space for linking the institution- and agency-based approaches in a complementary manner (Knill and Lenschow 2001b).

On the one hand, the deterministic bias of institution-based explanations was rooted in the presumption that everything could be explained by reference to institutional factors. Once we explicitly account for different levels of abstraction, such institutionalist determinism may be limited to the more remote level. This implies that from the macro-level of governing institutions we might only be able to delineate the range of options for sectoral adjustment, and claim that sectoral developments are constrained by the broader institutional context. In the case of Japanese telecommunications policy, for instance, these options reach from telecommunications as a public monopoly to privatisation combined with competitive reregulation of the sector (Vogel 1997). However, while restricting the range of options for sectoral change, the institution-based perspective provides no sufficient basis for explaining whether sectoral change takes place at all and which concrete option is selected. To answer this question, we have to step down on the ladder of abstraction, and rely on the agency-based perspective of rational-choice institutionalism. On the other hand, because macro-institutional rules do impose certain constraints on sectoral choices, they partly contribute to reducing the problem of openness that underlies agency-based approaches. Referring to the example of Japanese telecommunications policy, the macro-institutional background, in contrast to that of Britain, excluded the emergence of competitive deregulation. Hence, both approaches are characterised by a distinctive, albeit complementary, explanatory scope.

On the basis of the previous discussion, we are able to narrow down the set of cases for which institution-based approaches have to be complemented by an agency-based perspective in order to account for institutional change. Assuming that institutional adaptation is path-dependent or follows the 'logic of appropriateness', the institution-based perspective underlying historical institutionalism suggests that sectoral institutional change can only be expected when adjustment requirements remain within the scope of macro-institutional rules and standard operating procedures. In this way, the institution-based perspective allows for the preclusion of those sectoral options which exceed the constraints defined by the macro-institutional context.

We only need to descend the ladder of abstraction to agency-based approaches in those cases where the adaptational requirements emerging from European policies remain within the range of options defined by the macro-institutional context. Here, the institution-based perspective provides us with few insights about the actual occurrence and mode of sectoral changes. To answer these questions, we have to rely on the less abstract, agency-based perspective. It is necessary to consider whether the European policies have sufficiently altered domestic opportunity structures so that national actors are able to successfully challenge the existing institutional arrangements. To what extent are domestic actors able to exploit the new opportunities emerging from European policies so as to successfully challenge the existing institutional equilibrium? While actors move within the constraints of an institutional opportunity structure, their behaviour cannot be predicted beforehand and needs to be investigated in detail *ex post*.

While I cannot pretend to have a theory for the domestic adaptation under the impact of Europeanisation that has full predictive capacities, this pragmatic but no longer entirely contingent explanatory model helps to sharpen our view of the nature of the institutional limits to change and the degree of those limits. In the following section I will add one more modification to the historical institutionalist framework that deals with its conservative bias.

Avoiding conservatism: a dynamic perspective on institutional change

In linking the institution-based and agency-based perspectives I have so far assumed the overall stability and continuity of the macro-institutional context, from which the general range of options for sectoral adaptation can be derived. Otherwise it would make little sense to apply an institution-based perspective taking institutions as an independent factor in explaining political outcomes. To be sure, given the long-standing legitimacy as well as the strong lock-in and distributional effects generally associated with these arrangements, this assumption of stability is quite plausible, in particular when being linked or restricted to the macro-level or governing institutions. Moreover, it can be assumed that there are incremental rather than revolutionary developments of macro-institutional arrangements, since they generally allow for a broad range of sectoral choices. In this way, sectoral changes hardly imply pressures for corresponding adaptations at the higher institutional layer, in which sectoral arrangements are nested, but they might still be consistent with the broader scope of choices provided by the macro-institutional context.

However, while the macro-level arrangements might be characterised by a higher degree of institutional stability, this does not completely preclude constellations of 'institutional watershed' (Skowronek 1982) in which the logic of the political game changes from one in which 'institutions shape politics' to one in which 'politics shape institutions' (Thelen and Steinmo 1992: 15). Changes in governing institutions may occur as the result of external shocks (Krasner 1988) such as the political and economic transition we have recently witnessed in Eastern Europe. However, and more relevant for the cases examined in this book, such dynamics may also emerge from within the political-administrative system, without necessarily implying a complete overhaul of this system. To alter the scope of sectoral options, already less dramatic developments at the macro-level might be sufficient, which only partly but not completely depart from the path-dependent and incremental institutional history. Changes in the electoral system, for instance, might crucially affect the overall political structure of a country and create or abolish institutional veto points for policy-making, although this does not necessarily imply a departure from other traditions and the institutional peculiarities of the political-administrative system in question.

Against this background, one could argue that the analytical framework thus far developed runs the risk of explanatory openness – a problem that I explicitly wanted to overcome. How do we know if, and to what extent, changes in the general context of governing institutions take place, which for their part alter the scope of sectoral choices? I argue that, in contrast to the case at the sectoral level, this problem can be more easily captured by relying on general characteristics defining the macro-institutional reform capacity. In other words, it is argued that the opportunities inherent in the view that 'politics shape institutions' are an intrinsic feature of the macro-institutional context. The structural potential for such large-scale reforms is affected by the number of formal and factual institutional veto points that different actors have at their disposal for blocking and modifying reform initiatives. The number of these veto points is in turn defined by the macro-institutional context; e.g., by the strength of executive leadership, the number of constitutional safeguards, or the separation of powers between different territorial levels.

As such, the level of structural reform capacity can be viewed as indicating the 'contingency robustness' of institution-based explanations. It allows us to grasp the potential impact of changes in preferences, beliefs and the situational contexts for the configuration of governing institutions, although one can predict neither the timing nor the content of such changes. The concept of reform capacity therefore qualifies the validity of the institution-based predictions; i.e., in countries where the structural capacity for reforms is high, one needs to be aware of the fact that the institution-based assumptions regarding the sectoral changes might have to be modified as a result of macro-institutional changes.

2.3   Conclusion: institutions and institutional change

In conclusion, the review of the literature on the new institutionalism revealed that the varying theoretical approaches provide no unique and consistent framework. Ontological and theoretical differences exist not only with respect to the definition of institutions, but also with respect to the conception and explanation of institutional impacts, change and emergence. This theoretical and conceptual variation yields a dilemma when searching for an analytical framework to account for the impact of European policies on national administrations. More precisely, the different theoretical variants are characterised by strengths and weaknesses, which implies that each concept – taken by itself – is deficient.

The respective strengths and weaknesses of the different approaches are basically linked to the extent to which they are either institution-based (i.e., that they conceive of institutions as an independent explanatory factor), or agency-based (with strategic interaction in the context of institutional opportunities and constraints being the main explanatory factor). While institution-based approaches, such as sociological and historical institutionalism, allow for the development of *ex ante* hypotheses on institutional change, they suffer from determinism and conservatism and hence do not provide sufficient explanations for institutional dynamics. By contrast, while sufficiently accounting for such developments, rational choice institutionalism with its agency-based focus, faces the problem of explanatory openness which makes it difficult to develop clear expectations on institutional change. The crucial matter is therefore not to decide which approach is theoretically superior, but to link them in a synergetic way.

To establish a complementary linkage of institution-based and agency-based approaches, the framework of historical institutionalism served as a promising analytical starting-point. To reduce the deterministic and conservative bias inherent in institution-based approaches, two analytical modifications are proposed.

To address the problem of explanatory determinism, I distinguished between cases where institutional factors sufficiently explain patterns of institutional change and cases where additional factors need to be considered. Based on institution-based explanations, which assess sectoral changes from a more general perspective, it is possible to preclude certain options for sectoral change, namely adaptations which exceed the constraints defined by the macro-institutional context. The extent to which adaptations that remain within these constraints are actually achieved, however, cannot be inferred from a mere institution-based perspective; it has to be assessed on the basis of an agency-based explanation.

The institution-based perspective, from which the hypotheses on the potential occurrence of sectoral change are derived, necessarily assumes a stable macro-institutional context. Although this assumption, which is suggested by the framework of historical institutionalism, is plausible, it has to be taken into account that institutional changes cannot be completely precluded at the macro-level. The structural potential for such developments, however, is itself determined by macro-institutional peculiarities which define the existent reform capacity within a political-administrative system. To acknowledge that macro-level institutions might themselves be subject to change, therefore, does not imply completely falling back on *ex post* explanations, because the concept of national reform capacity allows us to identify different institutional configurations with varying potential for macro-level changes.

3 The analytical framework

To be sure, the above considerations are still very abstract and general in nature. However, further specification can hardly be achieved from a merely theoretical perspective; it has to take into account the peculiarities of the case under study. To do so, this chapter will clarify the scope of the underlying study and develop a more concrete framework for dependent and independent variables in order to specify the theoretical considerations in the light of the underlying research question.

3.1 The analytical scope of the study

This study is concerned with the impact of Europeanisation on national administrations. To what extent do national administrative systems change under European influence? To what extent do these changes imply patterns of administrative convergence across member states? Although one can think of numerous ways national administrative systems may become Europeanised, including, for instance, through the frequent interactions between supranational and national bureaucracies (Wessels and Rometsch 1996), the diffusion of policy ideas and mutual learning across member states' administrations, or legal implications associated with decisions of the Commission or the European Court of Justice (ECJ), I have already pointed out that the focus of this study is on the domestic impact of European *policies*. However, despite this initial restriction regarding the analytical focus, the particular type of policy under investigation still has to be clarified.

European policies and national administrations

Taking a national perspective on administrative reform, this question seems easy to answer, since *administrative policy* constitutes a policy field in its own right at the domestic level. As with other issues, there is a specific set of national policy programmes exclusively related to cross-sectoral aspects of administrative structures, processes, and practices.

However, in contrast to the member states, the EU does not pursue an administrative policy on its own; there are no European policy programmes with an exclusive focus on national administrations. Nothing equivalent to national administrative policy can be found at the supranational level.

In the absence of a European administrative policy *per se*, it could be argued that investigating the impact of European policies on national administrative systems does not necessarily make sense. Why should administrative styles and structures change when there is no corresponding European policy competence in these areas? On the other hand, such a statement overlooks potential administrative effects of European policies in other sectors, because in many instances decisions about policies imply decisions on corresponding administrative structures and the practices for proper implementation. Depending on the degree to which decisions 'couple' contents and administrative implications, European policies might have more or less far-reaching effects on domestic administrative arrangements.

The administrative impact of new regulatory policy

As the administrative impact of European legislation may vary from policy to policy, it is of particular analytical interest to focus on those areas where the impact of Europeanisation is most direct and pronounced. While most of the Community policies are regulatory in nature (Majone 1989: 167),[1] there are important differences with respect to the national impact of different regulatory policies. These differences are closely related to two broad types of regulatory policy: namely, *old regulatory policy,* which is concerned with the regulation of market processes by defining conditions for market access and operation; and *new regulatory policy,* which is directed at curbing negative externalities emerging from market activities. Classical fields of new regulatory policy are environmental protection, health and labour safety, consumer protection, and some areas of social policy.

In general, European market-regulation policies primarily exclude certain options from the range of national policy choices rather than positively prescribing distinctive policies to be enacted at the national level. The direct institutional impact of old regulatory policy on domestic administrative arrangements is basically restricted to the abolish-

---

[1] As Majone (1989) points out, the relatively limited room for financial manoeuvre, with the lion's share of financial resources going to agriculture and development, means that the EU Commission will tend to safeguard its vested institutional interests by extending its regulatory policy powers rather than its distributive ones (cf. Eichener 1996).

ment of domestic administrative arrangements which distort the functioning of the Common Market.[2] The European regulation liberalising
Community road transport, for instance, prohibits the member states to
exclude foreign hauliers from offering services in the domestic market.
However, it does not require the member states to change their national
market regulations; foreign competitors, as their national counterparts,
have to comply with relevant domestic rules. As will be shown in part IV
of this study, this, of course, is not to say that European market-
regulation policies have no domestic impact. However, this impact is
basically indirect: with economic integration altering the strategic
opportunities of domestic actors, the institutional equilibrium at the
domestic level might be challenged.

This picture contrasts with areas of new regulatory policy where
Community policies are explicitly directed at replacing existing domestic
regulatory arrangements, with corresponding provisions defined in
European legislation that imply that existing administrative provisions
really be re-shaped and re-formed.[3] Hence, in areas of new regulatory
policy there is generally a tighter linkage between European policy
provisions and domestic administrative arrangements. EU legislation
directly impacts upon national regulatory arrangements. Member states
have to bring administrative arrangements in line with a 'European
model', which is implicit to the supranational policy decision (Knill and
Lehmkuhl 1999). Protecting the environment by offering the public
access to environmental information or by defining emission standards
for industrial operations, for instance, makes a difference in corresponding administrative arrangements aimed at implementing these
policies at the national level. The definition of common-policy contents
at the supranational level therefore potentially has a more far-reaching
impact on domestic administrations than in areas of market regulation,
where administrative change might basically emerge indirectly as a by-
product of economic integration. Against this backdrop, new regulatory
policies are analytically better suited for the purpose of this study.

---

[2] It needs be emphasised in this context that market-making policies reveal a high variance
in the extent to which they prescribe institutional models for domestic compliance.
While this positive impact is rather limited for most of these policies, there are
nevertheless important counter-examples, such as the energy sector.

[3] The fact that the new regulatory policy has such a far-reaching influence on national
administrative provisions makes it one of the Commission's preferred policy types; this
coincides with the Commission's positional interest in strengthening its policy
competencies with respect to the member states.

Environmental policy as an empirical case

An important area of new regulatory policy refers to environmental issues, which, for their part, constitute a particularly appropriate case for the purpose of this study. First, the area is characterised by a high degree of Europeanisation. Especially during the last fifteen years, we have seen an impressive widening and deepening of European policy competencies. There are several environmental action programmes in which the Community has elaborated both the ambitions and the principles for developing its environmental policy. The development of an elaborated set of policy principles, norms and procedures for European environmental policy has been accompanied by a significant growth in policy activities (Weale 1996b: 602; Knill 1997b).

Second, European activities in the environmental area reflect a high degree of regulatory variety, which is obvious in different regulatory strategies and distinctive types of policy instruments. Besides classical approaches of 'command-and-control' regulation, which prescribe uniform and substantive objectives (such as emission standards, or the best available control technologies), we also find softer forms of intervention based on procedural regulation, self-regulation, public participation and voluntary agreements (Knill and Héritier 1996; Knill and Lenschow 2000a). Given the multiplicity of different policy instruments and approaches applied, when investigating national administrative changes in the context of supranational policy requirements it is particularly relevant to examine environmental policy. The broad range of different concepts implies varying implications for domestic administrations; hence it allows for the comparative assessment of transformation patterns across policies and countries.

Third, environmental policy is an area where the deficiencies in the implementation of European policies become particularly apparent. The Commission's own statistics on the implementation of Community legislation reveal serious deficits with respect to environmental legislation: in 1995 member states reported that only 91 per cent of the Community's environmental directives were being implemented, and that more than 20 per cent were not transposed in some member states. In the same year, based on complaints from the public, Parliamentary questions and petitions as well as cases detected directly by the Commission, the Commission registered a total of 265 suspected breaches of Community law. Over 20 per cent of all infringements registered by the Commission during that year were in the area of environmental policy. In October 1996 over 600 environmental complaints and infringement cases against member states were outstanding, with 85 of the latter awaiting determination by the ECJ (CEC 1996: 2). In view of these deficits in the formal transposition and practical application of EU environmental legislation in the member states, the environmental policy is a particularly interesting area for the purpose of this study, indicating that there is obviously no smooth and self-evident process of domestic adaptation to European requirements, but that the adaptation is subject to considerable difficulties and resistance (Knill and Lenschow 2000).

3.2   Dimensions of administrative change

To assess the impact of European legislation on national administrations, two analytical dimensions characterising sectoral administrative arrangements are distinguished: administrative style and administrative structure.

Administrative style

The dimension of sectoral administrative style includes not only patterns of regulatory intervention, but also dominant aspects characterising administrative interest intermediation. Administrative intervention relates to basic elements shaping the logic, type, content and flexibility of administrative instruments. The regulatory logic describes the extent to which administrative activities are based on inductive case-by-case specifications taking account of the peculiarities of the case in question, or by deductive approaches specifying regulatory requirements at a rather abstract and general level for a huge number of cases. The type of intervention describes whether sectoral instruments either reflect hierarchical patterns of command-and-control regulation or non-hierarchical patterns relying on self-regulatory and voluntary arrangements. Content refers to the extent to which intervention is based on substantive outcomes (i.e., the concrete numerical standards or technological standards to be achieved) or on procedural requirements (emphasising due process rather than specifying substantive outcomes). Finally, the degree to which sectoral intervention is based on detailed and highly specified regulatory requirements or on more open regulatory frameworks is referred to as regulatory flexibility.

The dimension of administrative style is not only affected by aspects of regulatory intervention which define the 'rules of the game' for public/private interaction, but also by institutionalised relationships shaping the interaction between administrative and societal actors; i.e., the patterns of administrative interest intermediation. The main questions in this context are: Is the relationship between public and private actors dominated by a general orientation of legalism emphasising rigid and uniform rule application or by a more pragmatic orientation which leaves room for bargaining in the light of individual circumstances? Are the relations between administrative and societal actors characterised by a more consensual or adversarial mode of interaction? To what extent do we find formal or informal interaction patterns? Are interactions between administrative and societal actors closed or open to third-party access? Do different societal actors have equal or privileged access to the implementation process (cf. van Waarden 1995)?

For analytical purposes, two ideal types of administrative styles are distinguished, namely intervening and mediating patterns of regulation and administrative interest intermediation. The *intervening* ideal type is characterised by deductive, substantive, hierarchical and detailed patterns of regulatory intervention. Administrative interest intermediation reveals legalistic, adversarial, formal and closed interactions, with access to regulatory process being restricted to those societal actors directly affected and addressed by administrative intervention. The *mediating* ideal type of intervention, by contrast, is characterised by more inductive, procedural, non-hierarchical and flexible patterns, allowing for a large degree of administrative discretion in defining regulatory requirements – which is done in the light of case-specific peculiarities. Administrative interest intermediation is based on pragmatic, consensual and informal interactions between administrative and regulated societal actors. Informality, however, does not exclude regulatory transparency, which provides third parties with equal access opportunities to the regulatory process.

Administrative structure

Referring to the dimension of administrative structure, the following factors are examined: firstly, the vertical and horizontal allocation of competencies between different public authorities will be considered. Does European influence lead to the centralisation or decentralisation (the vertical perspective) and to the concentration or dispersion (the horizontal perspective) of administrative tasks and competencies? Secondly, changes in interaction patterns between different administrative bodies are investigated. In this context both horizontal linkages (consultation and co-ordination) and vertical relations (patterns of legal, fiscal and practical control) are considered.

In contrast to the dimension of administrative style, where I have distinguished intervening and mediating ideal types (see table 3.1), this

Table 3.1. *The dependent variable: dimensions of administrative change*

Administrative Style	Administrative Structure and Organisation
Regulatory Intervention	*Competence Allocation*
deductive versus inductive	centralisation versus decentralisation
hierarchical versus non-hierarchical	fragmentation versus concentration
substantive versus procedural	
detailed versus flexible	
Administrative Interest Intermediation	*Co-ordination and Control*
legalistic versus pragmatic	patterns of vertical control
adversarial versus consensual	patterns of horizontal co-ordination
formal versus informal	
closed versus open	
privileged versus equal access	

analytical procedure seems to be less appropriate for administrative structures. This can be traced to the rather complex and highly diverging arrangements which are to be found across country borders. To be sure, one could certainly define particular clusters, as centralised versus decentralised structures, for instance. However, structural and organisational arrangements in general reveal so many peculiarities in various countries, that it might be difficult to avoid the problem of 'conceptual stretching' (Sartori 1984). Thus, the concepts that could most easily be applied to a broad range of cases would be so general that they would no longer bring into focus the similarities and contrasts among cases that are essential building-blocks for comparative analysis.

Having elaborated on the relevant dimensions and the criteria for the analysis of domestic administrative change, we will now turn to the factors which are relevant for explaining these transformations. Which aspects and conditions have to be taken into account when explaining the scope and the mode of national administrative changes under the impact of European policies?

3.3   Explaining administrative change: the concept of adaptation pressure

Following the theoretical considerations in the previous chapter, the domestic impact of European policies basically depends on the institutional compatibility of European policy requirements and national administrative arrangements. In the light of this, the degree of *adaptation pressure* which European legislation exerts on national administrative arrangements is conceived of as the independent variable. Assessing the explanatory scope of this variable requires a differentiated perspective on the institutional compatibility of European and domestic arrangements. To be specific, we have to distinguish between whether European policies require changes *within* – or *of* – the core of *national administrative traditions*, defined as general patterns of administrative style and structure which are institutionally strongly embedded in the broader context of a country's state tradition, legal system and political-administrative system.

Depending on the level of adaptation pressure, we are able to develop expectations about the extent to which domestic adaptations will be resisted (in cases of core challenges) or whether adaptations are generally possible (in cases where there are challenges within the core), albeit institutionally not determined. In other words, the explanatory scope of the concept of adaptation pressure varies with its institutional scope: to account for domestic change or the lack thereof when European requirements can be achieved without overthrowing the core of national administrative traditions, the institutional explanation has to be supplemented by an agency-based perspective.

The institutional scope of adaptation pressure, however, is – as developed in the previous chapter – not satisfactorily captured by a static comparison of European requirements and national structures. Administrative traditions are not static, but – depending on the national capacity for administrative reform – may be subject to more or less far-reaching developments, which can alter the scope of sectoral adaptation, and hence the institutional scope of European adaptation pressure. In view of this dynamic conception of adaptation pressure, national reforms can provide the basis for sectoral adjustments to external pressures which were previously viewed as core challenges to administrative traditions. To be sure, the concept of administrative reform capacity does not allow for predictions about if, when and how such macro-level changes will occur. It merely indicates the extent to which national administrative traditions are susceptible to contingent developments in view of preferences and beliefs of political and administrative actors.

In view of the above considerations, to account fully for the degree of European adaptation pressure we have to proceed in three steps. As a starting-point, it is necessary to consider whether European and national policies are in fact compatible. This 'simple' institutional assessment, based on how good the 'fit' between European and domestic arrangements is at the sectoral level, is not yet sufficient to grasp fully the institutional scope of the changes required by supranational legislation, however. It needs to be qualified by investigating the institutional embeddedness of the challenged national arrangements or how 'core' these are. Since the level of adaptation pressure is defined not only 'from above' by European requirements, but also by the national dynamics, the final step focuses on institutional factors affecting the potential for general national administrative reforms.

The sectoral dimension of adaptation pressure

To find out whether European policies imply pressures for domestic administrative change or not, it is necessary to assess the sectoral compatibility between European requirements and domestic arrangements. This 'simple' perspective on the 'sectoral fit' is based on the two dimensions of administrative style and structure specified above. In other words, we have to compare sectoral styles and structures at the national level with the corresponding administrative implications of the European legislation. However, a merely sectoral assessment tells us nothing about the institutional embeddedness of the challenged sectoral arrangements or whether they are 'core' institutions. It provides us with little insight into the extent to which European requirements remain within or exceed the range of options as defined by the macro-institutional context of the national administrative traditions.

The institutional dimension of adaptation pressure

How do we know when sectoral adaptation requirements reflect challenges to the core of a national administrative tradition? In the following I argue that the institutional scope, and hence the degree of adaptation pressure, increases with the extent to which challenged administrative arrangements are embedded in the macro-institutional core of national administrative traditions.

National administrative traditions can be defined as general characteristics shaping the administrative practices and structures within a country, which follow from the specific constellation of the macro-institutional context, including the state tradition, the legal system, as well as the political-administrative system (such as general aspects of the civil service and the state structure and organisation). National administrative traditions define the range of sectorally 'available' administrative styles and structures. In many studies, national administrative traditions are linked to distinctive national 'policy styles' (Jordan and Richardson 1982) or 'national styles of regulation' (Vogel 1986). However, such classifications have to be treated with caution. There are many authors who maintain that is impossible to speak of a single national style of regulation (cf. Jann 1983; Feick 1983; Keeler 1987; Atkinson and

Coleman 1989).[4] This argument is well in line with the assumption developed in our context; namely, that the macro-institutional background only delineates the range of options, and rarely determines the choices for particular sectoral arrangements. Hence, in our context: national administrative traditions are conceived of as regulatory patterns which are deeply rooted in legal, political and administrative institutions and which therefore show great stability over time (van Waarden 1995: 206). Rather than determining one single national regulatory approach, these patterns define a range of sectoral options.

Institutional embeddedness defines the degree of institutionalisation or institutional stability of sectoral administrative arrangements. The more embeddedness, the more existing arrangements represent core rather than peripheral parts of national administrative traditions. Following the propositions of historical institutionalism, embeddedness increases not only with the degree to which administrative arrangements are ideologically rooted in 'paradigms' (Hall 1993) affecting the beliefs and ideas of administrative actors, but also with the number of (inter-) institutional linkages and the tightness of these linkages, i.e., with the number of other changes that would have to be made if the institutions under observation were to be changed. Higher adaptation pressure emerges, the more EU legislation challenges such strongly entrenched patterns of administrative style and structure in institutions.

The extent to which sectoral styles and structures represent core patterns of national administrative traditions depends on their embeddedness in the general institutional context defined by the state tradition as well as the legal and political-administrative system. Thus, institutional embeddedness is greater the more sectoral arrangements reflect the basic conception of the state (state tradition). According to Badie and Birnbaum (1983) two broad paths implying different conceptions of the state can be distinguished: the 'state-led society' (France, Prussia) where the state has developed autonomous authority structures over society in order to lead the nation by active intervention and control; and the 'society-led state' (Britain) reflecting a network of elites and institutions which have national legitimacy in place of the state. In the latter model political influence is founded on social values and not on the forcible conquest of the state (Dyson 1980). The degree of the embeddedness of sectoral arrangements is also affected by the extent to

---

[4] Some authors claim that it is impossible to speak of a single national style, since the differences across policy sectors are more visible than the differences across nations (Feick 1983, Jann 1983). The neocorporatist literature has also cast some doubts on the appropriateness of characterising nations by a single type of state–industry relationship (Keeler 1987; Atkinson and Coleman 1989).

which they correspond with the particular characteristics of a country's legal system. Different legal traditions have led to different conceptions of how the law ought to lead and control administrative action. In the Continental states the separation between the state and society is reflected by the development of a comprehensive system of administrative law which contains detailed procedural and substantive provisions to authorise administrative intervention into society. Administrative action, therefore, is fundamentally related to legal rules defining possible courses of action. In Britain, however, administrative law and judicial review are comparatively less developed. Formal legal rules are less important for administrative activity than in Continental Europe. To distinguish whether elements of the sectoral structures reflect core or only peripheral aspects of national administrative traditions, we have to analyse the extent to which these elements are linked to the basic patterns of a country's administrative organisation and state structure. This includes an analysis of the dominant modes of allocating administrative competencies as well as well-established arrangements of administrative co-ordination and control.

The dynamic dimension of adaptation pressure

The above conception of adaptation pressure assumes a stable core of national administrative traditions. As a consequence, variation in the adaptation pressure is the result of differing European policies rather than changes in the domestic macro-institutional background. Although this conception might well be considered the 'normal case', given the general stability associated with macro-level institutions, we cannot completely preclude that the level of adaptation pressure may also be affected by national developments.

Following the considerations in the previous chapter, I argue that the extent to which the validity of institution-based predictions has to be qualified can be captured by the concept of administrative reform capacity. While this concept does not allow for predicting, if, when and how such reforms will occur, it indicates the structural potential for changes in the national administrative traditions, which may vary from country to country.

There might be countries where public administration enjoys a rather autonomous position, in which it is virtually impossible to impose politically motivated reforms on the administration. Under such circumstances, the only administrative reform is in the form of administrative self-adaptation. Consequently, there is a comparatively low potential for dynamic developments. At the other end of the spectrum, the position of public administration can be conceived of as being highly instrumental, implying that administrative arrangements can easily be adapted to political necessities and requirements.

Similar to the particular patterns shaping national administrative traditions, the capacity for changing these core features also has to be understood against the background of particular macro-institutional arrangements, namely the state tradition, the legal system, civil service traditions, as well as the state structure and organisation. To be precise, the structural capacity for national administrative reforms depends on the number of institutional veto points (Immergut 1992: 27) administrative actors have at their disposal for blocking and influencing political and societal reform initiatives.

In this context, I analytically distinguish three basic categories affecting a country's capacity for administrative reform: namely, the general capacity for executive leadership, the institutional entrenchment of administrative structures and procedures, as well as the influence of the bureaucracy on the policy-making process (Knill 1999). The number of veto points is, first of all, affected by aspects of the political system, including the party system (single party versus coalition governments) and the degree of political decentralisation (unitary and centralised systems versus federal systems with a strong interlinkage of policy-making at the federal and regional level). Second, the number of veto points increases with the extent to which administrative activity is based on legal and formal requirements. The need to go through formal procedures encourages participation and the open conflict of interests, and hence works against swift, single-handed institutional reorganisation. Moreover, the more comprehensive and fragmented administrative structures are, the more difficult it is to implement reforms 'from above' (Benz and Goetz 1996). Thirdly, I will consider the particular aspects which define the interaction between the administrative and political sphere, and hence the bureaucracy's influence on the policy-making process. To what extent is policy-making 'bureaucratised'; to what extent is the bureaucracy 'politicised', i.e., subject to political guidance and control?

> *Linking adaptation pressure and administrative change: three hypotheses*

The institutional and dynamic conception of adaptation pressure allows for the distinction of three levels of pressure (see table 3.2). Pressure is classified as high if EU policy is contradicting core elements of national administrative traditions. Moderate adaptation requirements, by con-

Table 3.2. *The independent variable: dimensions and levels of adaptation pressure*

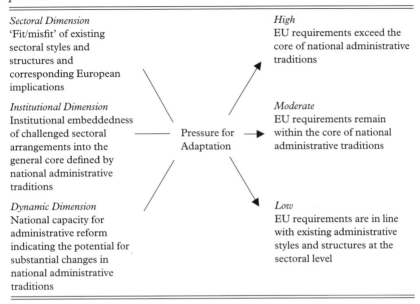

Sectoral Dimension 'Fit/misfit' of existing sectoral styles and structures and corresponding European implications		*High* EU requirements exceed the core of national administrative traditions
Institutional Dimension Institutional embeddedness of challenged sectoral arrangements into the general core defined by national administrative traditions	Pressure for Adaptation	*Moderate* EU requirements remain within the core of national administrative traditions
Dynamic Dimension National capacity for administrative reform indicating the potential for substantial changes in national administrative traditions		*Low* EU requirements are in line with existing administrative styles and structures at the sectoral level

trast, relate to cases where EU legislation is demanding only changes within the core of national administrative traditions and presents no challenge to these core factors themselves. In contrast to instances of moderate and high adaptation pressure, which both imply more or less far-reaching administrative changes, low pressure for adaptation exists if member states can rely on existing administrative provisions to implement European legislation. Given the dynamic conception, it is acknowledged that the level of adaptation pressure may shift as a result of national reforms, albeit as the exception rather than the rule, i.e., national reform developments may alter the institutional scope of European requirements. According to the three levels of European adaptation pressure, different paths of domestic transformation can be identified, where the theoretical and analytical considerations suggest either administrative change or persistence.

Hypothesis 1: contradiction of the core: administrative resistance

In cases where European policies imply contradictions of the administrative core, resistance to change is likely. As institution-based approaches suggest, well-established institutions and traditions do not easily adapt to exogenous pressures. Apart from the rare cases where there are external shocks or fundamental performance crises, institutions remain stable even in a changing environment. Hence, in cases of high adaptation pressure we expect only very limited and symbolic adaptations.

Hypothesis 2: change within a (changing) core: accepted or neglected adaptation?

Moderate pressure implies that the adaptations required can be achieved by sectoral changes *within* the general institutional framework without challenging that framework's core. Generally, the limited institutional scope of European requirements may be defined in a stable macro-institutional context with fixed core structures and principles. However, as pointed out above, we cannot completely exclude cases where initially high adaptation pressure – due to core contradictions between national and European practices – is reduced to moderate pressure in the context of national administrative reforms. National reform dynamics may alter the range of options for sectoral adaptation, hence implying that adaptation to EU requirements can be achieved *within* a self-changing core.[5]

With reference to the explanatory linkage developed in the previous chapter, I argue that it is in cases of moderate adaptation pressure, that an exclusive focus on institutional factors may render only insufficient results and where satisfactorily explaining adaptation performance may require a lower level of abstraction, namely the independent analysis of actor coalitions within the given institutional context. This hypothesis appears reasonable since moderate adaptation pressure, which gives rise to the 'institutionally more open' situations, is less able to 'determine' coalition formation and behaviour than in situations in which there is high or low pressure. Hence, in constellations of moderate adaptation pressure, the extent to which administrative change takes place – or not – cannot be completely captured by institution-based *ex ante* hypothesising; such hypothesising has to be supplemented by an agency-based approach in which institutions are conceived of as intervening factors rather than independent explanatory variables.

Hypothesis 3: confirmation of the core: compliance without change

If the constellation of European requirements and national administrative traditions implies no adjustments or only negligible ones, EU policy

---

[5] Of course, domestic core changes must not necessarily imply that the institutional scope of European adaptation pressure is reduced; they may have the inverse effect, even widening the institutional gap between national administrative traditions and the European statutes. However, since this latter scenario would not alter the initial constellation of high adaptation pressure, it will not be examined more closely in the context of this study.

can be seen as confirming national arrangements. This especially holds true in cases where national arrangements exactly reflect or even go beyond the supranational provisions. In these constellations no administrative adaptations are expected, as none is called for by European requirements.

Administrative change across member states: convergence or divergence?

One of the leading questions posed at the beginning of this chapter referred to the extent to which Europeanisation will bring about converging patterns in the sectoral administrative styles and structures across member states. So far, I have only elaborated on the conditions for administrative change from the perspective of single member states, without specifying the conditions under which potential changes might imply administrative convergence or divergence across Europe.

In general, one can think of three possibilities regarding how Europeanisation might affect the differences between national administrative systems. First, there is the possibility of administrative *convergence,* which is defined by the extent to which domestic styles and structures reveal similar characteristics because of the influence of European policies. Second, Europeanisation can have the opposite effect, causing administrative *divergence*, implying that administrative differences across member states are increasing. Finally, European policies might leave the difference between domestic administrative arrangements unaffected; hence implying the *persistence* of administrative differences across member states.

To elaborate on the three scenarios, let us take two member states, A and B, and assume that in each member state there are two possible ways that European requirements impact upon domestic administrative arrangements: namely, 'change' (i.e., adaptation to European requirements)[6] and 'no change' (including the above patterns of confirmation, resistance to core contradiction or neglected adaptation). This allows for the distinction between four constellations, which imply either administrative convergence, divergence or persistence (see table 3.3). As will be shown, the extent to which we observe the convergence, divergence or the persistence of administrative differences between two

---

[6] To be sure, change could also imply that domestic arrangements even drift further away from European requirements. This option, however, is not included in the conception of change as it is applied in this context. Change is understood as adaptation to European requirements; i.e., with making domestic sectoral arrangements compatible with European policy implications.

Table 3.3 *Patterns of administrative change across member states*

		Country A Change	No change
Country B	Change	Persistence Convergence	Convergence Divergence
	No change	Convergence Divergence	Persistence

countries is contingent upon two factors: namely, the initial constellation of sectoral arrangements in different member states (similar or different) and the different patterns of adaptation in the light of European requirements.

The persistence of administrative differences can be expected in all cases where European requirements do not result in corresponding sectoral adaptations; i.e., in each member state administrative arrangements are either confirmed by European policies or corresponding changes are resisted, given the challenges to existing core patterns of national administrative traditions or the lack of domestic support for changes within the core.

The picture is less clear, if we observe adaptation to European requirements in both countries. If initial sectoral arrangements are differing in both countries, this pattern will favour administrative convergence across member states. The persistence of administrative similarities can be assumed, by contrast, if both countries share similar starting points, i.e., identical sectoral arrangements.

The situation is similarly ambiguous in constellations of 'no change' and 'change'. The extent to which we observe administrative convergence or divergence again depends on how similar or different the starting-points of both countries were in regard to their sectoral arrangements. Assuming that sectoral arrangements were similar, and hence similarly confronted with European adaptation requirements, adaptation in one country and non-adaptation in the other implies administrative divergence. The same pattern reflects administrative convergence, however, if the starting position of both countries was different, implying that confirmation in one country is accompanied by patterns of administrative adaptation in the other.

3.4   Methodology and procedure

To recall, based on the analytical framework, I hypothesise that the mode and scope of domestic administrative transformation varies with the adaptational pressure exerted by European requirements. Adaptation pressure is based on two components: the administrative implications of European policies which are *similar* for every member state, and the administrative conditions at the national level (i.e., sectoral administrative arrangements, administrative traditions and administrative reform capacity) which might *differ* from country to country. The combination of similar EU requirements and varying national conditions for compliance implies that different member states are confronted with varying levels of adaptation pressure, and hence that there are distinctive patterns of administrative change and persistence *within* member states or convergence and divergence *across* member states.

The logic of comparison

Given this research design, the process of European integration offers almost ideal conditions for the comparative study of administrative change. In this context, comparisons can be drawn along two lines. First, one can compare how different national administrative systems cope with the identical requirements spelled out in supranational policies (*cross-country comparison*). The cross-country comparison can be organised along two different perspectives, controlling either European policies or the level of adaptation pressure. On the one hand, one could focus on the impact of the same European policy, and hence the identical administrative implications. On the other hand, it is also possible to start from identical levels of adaptation pressure that different administrations are confronted with. Taking this perspective, the comparison does not necessarily involve identical European policies, but identical differences between European implications and existing domestic arrangements. The question then is how national administrative systems respond to similar challenges. Since sectoral administrative arrangements may vary from country to country, identical administrative implications of the same European policy will not necessarily pose identical challenges to domestic administrations. The second possibility is to take different European policies as a starting point in order to analyse how varying levels of adaptational pressure impact upon administrative arrangements within the same member state (*cross-policy comparison*).

With respect to the cross-country comparison, two decisions have to be made, namely with respect to the number and nature of cases. In other words: how many and which member states shall be included in the study? Concerning the number of countries, the choice is basically between carrying out an 'extensive' study (including all member states) or doing an 'intensive' in-depth analysis of two or three countries (Ragin 1989). Each of these approaches faces its typical problems. Whereas extensive studies are often criticised for their level of conceptual abstraction and hence for ignoring case-specific peculiarities, choosing to study only a few cases poses the problem that more rival explanations are to be assessed than cases are to be observed (Lijphart 1971: 686). Despite the problems associated with a small number of cases, this study does just that, as the narrow gauge comparison of two countries makes it possible to test broad hypotheses against rich empirical materials (Rose 1991: 455). Moreover, there are several techniques based on the 'comparative method' (Lijphart 1971; Collier 1991) which help to overcome the methodological problems faced by analyses that are based on a small number of cases.

One way to partly overcome methodological problems concerns the selection of countries. Following the approach of 'most similar systems' (Przeworski and Teune 1970), the selected countries should have as many similar features as possible in order to reduce the number of intervening variables and varying parameters. At the same time, the differences with respect to the explanatory factors (in our case, administrative traditions and reform capacities which account for variance in the independent variable 'adaptation pressure') should be as strong as possible in order to allow for sufficient certainty when testing the different hypotheses on domestic change.

A cross-country comparison of Britain and Germany seems to be quite in line with the requirements of the 'most similar systems' approach. Both countries are characterised by rather similar socio-economic and political conditions, including economic and industrial development, education, population density, standards of living and social services, liberal-democratic politics with party and interest group participation in policy-making, as well as well-developed and effective administrative systems (Mény 1993; Allum 1995). Moreover, the particular parameters relevant in the environmental field (the policy area under study) reveal broad similarities in the two countries. Both Britain and Germany are characterised by the existence of severe environmental problems emerging from industrial pollution and road traffic, a high level of environmental awareness, as well as a huge number of environmental organisations with significant financial and personal resources at their disposal (cf. Héritier, Knill and Mingers 1996).

To be sure, it will always be possible to figure out parameters and data which reveal differences rather than similarities between both countries. On the other hand, when focusing on countries as cases it seems to be rather unrealistic to expect that the condition of complete similarity ever to be fulfilled (cf. Jann 1983). Hence, we have to make do with sufficient similarity, which these two member states certainly have. Furthermore, it is not apparent that the similarity requirement could have been fulfilled decisively better by selecting another combination of European member states.

On the other hand, the selection of Britain and Germany seems to be the best choice with respect to the requirement of differences in explanatory factors. Thus, administrative styles and structures in the area of environmental policy to be found in both countries have often been described as diametrically opposed to each other (Boehmer-Christiansen and Skea 1991; Weale, O'Riordan and Kramme 1992; Héritier, Knill and Mingers 1996). What is more, the institutional background in which sectoral arrangements are embedded reveals similarly diverging characteristics. This holds true not only for the state and legal tradition, but also for characteristics of the political-administrative system and the structure of the state; both countries are often considered as ideal type representatives of Anglo-Saxon and Continental systems (Dyson 1980; Damaska 1986). Given these differences, it is particularly interesting to investigate if and how the highly varying administrative arrangements of Britain and Germany are adapted to European requirements.

A second methodological means for dealing with few cases is to reduce the number of explanatory variables, either through combining variables or through employing a theoretical perspective that focuses on a smaller set of explanatory factors (Collier 1991). Both means are at least partly utilised in the context of this study. Thus, I have reduced the number of explanatory factors by introducing the concept of adaptation pressure as the basic independent variable for the explanation of administrative change or persistence at the national level. The concept of adaptation pressure combines three components: namely, a policy dimension (the sectoral compatibility of EU requirements and domestic sectoral arrangements), an institutional dimension (the link of the sectoral arrangements to the macro-context of governing institutions), and a dynamic dimension (referring to the administrative reform capacity as an indicator of the potential changes in national administrative traditions). Besides the reduced number of explanatory aspects which were combined in a single independent variable, a large number of the theoretical explanations were devoted to the development of a – still sufficiently – parsimonious theoretical framework that at the same time avoids the problem of oversimplification and determinism (cf. King, Keohane and Verba 1994: 20). To do so, the analytical framework was developed in such a way that more complex explanations which take account of actors, interests and strategies are only considered as long as the more abstract and parsimonious institutional approach provides no sufficient explanation for the case in question.

Thirdly, the reliability of studies focusing on a small number of cases can be improved by increasing the number of cases. In our context, this would first of all mean increasing the number of countries dealt with. However, the number of cases can also be increased with respect to the 'input side', i.e., the number of European measures under investigation. For this purpose, five distinctive pieces of European legislation from the area of environmental policy were selected. These five policies, which are related to air pollution, drinking-water protection, access to environmental information, environmental impact assessment and environmental management systems, reveal significant differences in the administrative implications that they have for the corresponding arrangements at the national level.

From the five pieces of legislation selected, the two measures on air pollution and drinking water come closer to existing sectoral arrangements in Germany, but at the same time they imply far-reaching challenges to administrative styles and structures in Britain. The policies on environmental impact assessment and environmental management systems, by contrast, contain less demanding requirements for the British, but put high adaptational requirements on the German administration. The legislation on access to information, on the other hand, similarly contradicted the existing sectoral arrangements in both countries.

In the light of this constellation of the varying administrative implications of European policies, two modes of cross-country comparison are conceivable. We can either compare how the same policy is complied with in different national administrative contexts. Or we can take different or similar policies which, however, imply an identical amount of adaptation pressure for the national administrations and compare corresponding compliance patterns at the domestic level. In this way, it is possible to find out whether national patterns of change and persistence are policy-dependent or adaptation-pressure dependent (as suggested by the institution-based hypothesis).

A final method to reduce the problems associated with a small number of cases refers to the use of what are known as within-case comparisons. As Collier (1991) points out, it is important to recognise that in many studies, the conclusions reached in the overall comparison of cases are also assessed – implicitly or explicitly – through within-case analysis. In our context, the within-case comparison is explicitly included, namely, by comparing the way different European requirements are complied with in the same member state (cross-policy comparison). In selecting distinctive European policies with varying administrative implications and hence adaptational pressures on domestic arrangements, it is possible to supplement the findings from the comparison between countries by a cross-policy comparison referring to individual member states.

Comparing public administrations

It has already been mentioned that the field of comparative public administration suffers from general theoretical and conceptual underdevelopment. A crucial factor contributing to this deficit is seen in the lack of concepts available for comparing bureaucracies across nations (Peters 1996; Rose 1991). Given the complexity and diversity of the phenomena under study, in many instances countries are used as nominal categories for describing systems of public administration, although this strategy may not offer the most efficient means of understanding *why* those systems function as they do (Peters 1988). In other words, the cross-country comparison of administrative systems requires concepts which allow for replacing the name of countries with analytical categories.

In order to address such problems of conceptualisation, two strategies are pursued. On the one hand, the classificatory schemes are built on relatively abstract concepts, such as national administrative traditions or national reform capacities which have to be specified in the light of the particular macro-institutional context given at the national level. In referring to these more abstract categories, the problem of using countries as nominal categories can be avoided. On the other hand, I have – at least where appropriate – specified the dependent variables by relying on the method of ideal types as a means to understanding the differences between actual administrative systems. Thus, two ideal types characterise the patterns of administrative style, namely mediating versus intervening administration. The method of employing ideal types has the virtue of providing a standard against which real-world systems can be compared and potential differences can be explained (Peters 1996: 29).

Procedure

The data needed for a qualitative analysis focusing on the impact of European policies on domestic administrative styles and structures were collected in intensive, exploratory interviews as well as document analysis. In order to cover all the relevant actors involved in the two countries under study, interviews were conducted with 23 actors in Germany and 27 in Britain. Furthermore, six interviews were conducted with representatives of the European Commission in order to balance the statements of national actors against the background of the supranational perspective on domestic implementation processes.

The focus of the exploratory interviews was on institutions, processes and subject-matters related to the implementation of the five policies under study in Germany and Britain, the specific adaptational problems emerging, the influence of supranational policies on domestic arrangements, as well as the role of different political, administrative and societal actors during the implementation process. The interviews were conducted over a period of one year (from June 1996 to May 1997) with members of the following institutions: the European Commission, competent government departments at the level of central government, specialist agencies and administrative authorities responsible for policy implementation, specialist institutes, expert bodies, commissions of enquiry, competent bodies at the state or regional level, local government authorities and local associations, industrial trade associations, polluting industries, representatives of scientific communities and the general public, i.e., citizens' action groups. The interviews were tape-recorded and subsequently subjected to a qualitative analysis in relation to the topic of investigation.

Structure of the following chapters

The previous theoretical and analytical reflections have led me to expect domestic administrative adaptation to European requirements only as long as these changes could be achieved within the macro-institutional context of the national administrative traditions. To understand patterns of sectoral change or resistance to European adaptation pressure, we therefore need a background understanding of the specific patterns characterising these traditions as well as the factors defining the structural potential for changes in this general institutional background. These two aspects are the central focus of the following part of this book, which will provide a comparative analysis of German and British administrative systems. In chapter 4, I will identify the background factors and typical components of administrative traditions in Britain and Germany. The focus is thus on the macro-institutional context (including the state tradition, the legal tradition, the civil service tradition, as well as the structure and organisation of the state) which defines the basic range of options for sectoral styles and structures, i.e., the national administrative traditions. Since the macro-institutional context affects not only the basic characteristics of the national administrative structures and practices, but also the extent to which the latter might be subject to more or less dynamic path-dependent developments, chapter 5 analyses the specific conditions defining the degree of the administrative reform capacity in both countries under study.

Following these general considerations, the empirical findings of the five environmental policies under study are presented and analysed in part III. While chapter 6 provides an overview of the administrative implications of the different measures under study, their domestic impact on administrative arrangements in Germany and Britain is analysed in chapters 7 and 8. Part IV provides conclusions in the light of the empirical and theoretical findings. While chapter 9 offers a comparative assessment of the theoretical and analytical considerations, chapter 10 examines the general validity of these findings. In this context, I distinguish three logics of Europeanisation and corresponding adaptation patterns at the national level. I also briefly illustrate the applicability of the model for other policy areas, namely European road-haulage and railways policy.

II

Administrative traditions in Germany and Britain: opposing patterns and dynamics

In the analytical framework developed in the previous chapter the institutional scope of European adaptation pressure was identified as the primary factor to account for patterns of administrative transformation at the domestic level. The level of adaptation pressure can be inferred from the institutional compatibility of European requirements with the macro-institutional context of national administrative traditions. Although not determining the occurrence and form of sectoral adjustments, national administrative traditions confine the scope for sectoral choices. This way we are able to exclude certain options for domestic adjustment. The explanation of sectoral patterns of administrative change and persistence therefore requires a background knowledge of national administrative traditions. To capture the institutional dimension of adaptation pressure, we need to know if and to what extent European pressures for sectoral adaptation reflect challenges to administrative core patterns or not.

As pointed out in the analytical framework, the level of adaptation pressure varies not only with European policy requirements, but may also be affected by national administrative reforms which alter the macro-institutional context, and hence the range for sectoral choices. To grasp this dynamic conception of adaptation pressure, we need to have a closer look at the capacity for administrative reform, as it can be derived from the constraints and opportunities defined in the macro-institutional background.

4   The institutional foundation of German and British administrative traditions

National administrative traditions reflect general patterns of administrative styles and structures which are strongly embedded in the macro-institutional context of the state tradition, the legal system, and the political-administrative system (including characteristics of the civil service as well as the state structure and organisation). As these macro-institutional factors vary considerably across the two countries under study, fundamental differences with respect to the core patterns of national administrative traditions can be observed.

4.1   Germany: consensual intervention within comprehensive structures

The traditional elements characterising administrative intervention and interest intermediation in Germany come closer to the ideal type of intervening rather than mediating administration, as is illustrated in particular by the dominant patterns of interventionism and legalism. On the other hand, the tradition of corporatism as well as the preference for consensual rather than adversarial interaction patterns between administrative and societal actors implies important departures from the interventionist ideal type specified in the previous chapter. With respect to the structural dimension, German administration is traditionally characterised by rather comprehensive and segmented arrangements which are not only shaped by the federal structure of the state, but also by long-standing traditions of hierarchical administrative organisation at the regional level.

The German state tradition: semi-sovereign authority

Although from a comparative perspective, Germany represents the Continental tradition of a 'state-centred society', the evolution of the German state followed a particular path. This development gave rise to a distinctive separation of state and society which is found neither in the

Anglo-Saxon nor in the French tradition (Grimm 1991: 128). The conception of the German state is shaped by different institutional layers which in part counterbalance each other. The ideological conception of a *state of authority* viewing the state as superior to society is mediated by several aspects strongly rooted in the historical development of German statehood, namely the rule of law, federalism and corporatism.

In France, the 1789 Revolution reversed the absolutist dominance of society by the state. The state did not lose its monopoly of coercion, but society itself determined the use of state power. Parliament, the elected representation of society, thus built the linkage between individual and common interests. The citizen's equal share in political decisions guaranteed, as explained by Rousseau, that state power could not serve other purposes than the common interest. This development is in fundamental contrast with Germany, where the dominant position of the state was a crucial characteristic even in the late nineteenth century when the German nation-state was founded. In German thinking, the common best remained a value above particular societal interests to be ascertained autonomously by the state. A dual conception of state and society emerged, with society reflecting the accumulation of particular interests and the state representing all higher values of human life (Grimm 1991: 128–9).

Whereas in France, the old monarchical system was overthrown by a successful revolution establishing democracy, state formation in Germany was shaped by a situation where absolutism could no longer be preserved by the princes and democracy could not yet be reached by the people. The state could preserve its exclusive responsibility for the common best by introducing certain constitutional modifications. The *Obrigkeitsstaat* (state of authority) intervening into societal developments 'from above' was constrained by the rule of law (*Rechtsstaat*). The *Rechtsstaat* protecting the private sphere against autocratic state intervention was the compensation for the lack of democracy (Hellstern 1986: 669; Ellwein 1993b: 31; König 1996: 25). As a further substitute for the lacking democratic structures, cities were granted the institution of local self-government (*kommunale Selbstverwaltung*), under the supervision of government but with considerable autonomy (Ellwein 1985: 43).

Although the principle of the *Rechtsstaat* was central to German political thinking even before the achievement of German unity in the 1870s (Böckenförde 1991), its basic principles – the supremacy of law, full state liability for illegal public actions, comprehensive rights of appeal against administrative acts – were only fully and effectively realised in the Federal Republic (Derlien 1995: 85; Benz and Goetz 1996: 15). Hence, the role of the state in the Federal Republic is far removed from the authoritative model of the *Obrigkeitsstaat* as it was predominant in Imperial or 'Wilhelminian' Germany (1871–1918) with its foremost architect Bismarck (Lehmbruch 1997). Although the state remains a crucial actor, its power and potential to intervene in society 'from above' have been fundamentally counterbalanced by the *Rechtsstaat* principle.

The authoritative position of the German state is further mediated by two other principles, which played a crucial role in the formation of the German state: federalism and corporatism, which together with the rule of law contributed to the emergence of the 'semi-sovereign state' (Katzenstein 1987). The basic principles of the German *executive federalism* were established as a part of a historical compromise allowing for the establishment of the German nation-state in the nineteenth century. The core of this compromise was that the subnational states accepted the centralisation of legislative powers, but retained the executive power, and hence their administrative domain. In addition, the states participate in federal rule-making through the *Bundesrat* (Federal Council). Legislative rule-making in Germany therefore involves elaborate bargaining mechanisms between the federal and state governments.

The necessity to compromise can be traced to the fact that in Germany the formation of bureaucratic states at the subnational level emerged before the nation-state. It was no longer possible to simply supersede this decentralised power structure by centralised arrangements. In seventeenth-century France monarchical absolutism appeared as the prototype of the modern state achieving domestic stability after a long period of religious conflicts, implying the formation of a centralised and unified statehood. In England, on the other hand, political centralisation was achieved by vesting sovereignty in Parliament instead of the monarch, with Parliament being the principal representation of territorial interests. Neither the French nor the English path of state formation, however, was realistic in the German case. In Germany, kings and emperors had always to rely on political accommodation with the powerful regional rulers, the *Fürsten* (princes) of the major *Territorien*. Given the strong autonomy of the *Territorialstaaten*, the German emperors remained at the (formal) top of a fragmented power structure. In contrast to France, the modern (continental) state, with a professional administration and a standing army, did not develop at the national level, but at the subnational level of the territories, i.e. in Prussia, Austria, Bavaria, Saxony or Württemberg (Ellwein 1994; 1996).

The tradition of the German state, however, is not only shaped by the influence exerted by the powerful territories, but is also based on the accommodation of interests of corporate societal actors. Institutionalised systems of conflict accommodation among corporate actors with (corporate) equality have a long tradition in Germany and played a crucial role in the resolution of the religious conflicts in the seventeenth century. The basic elements of these arrangements – (limited) corporatist self-administration as well as a (legal or *de facto*) representational monopoly guaranteed by the state, which oversees the functioning of these systems of conflict management – have a strong affinity to the arrangements found today in the domains of labour relations, social policy and education (Lehmbruch 1997).

Given the tradition of *corporatism*, the development and expansion of the German welfare state took place without driving out the market-based private sector. Rather than intervening into market processes in order to cope with the deficiencies of the market, Germany relied on corporatist arrangements which allow for the co-existence of market ideals such as free enterprise and individualism, with a positive evaluation of the welfare state.

Corporate arrangements are reflected in a whole range of intermediary organisations that partly assume public functions and partly represent private interests. They include paragovernmental associations such as chambers of commerce and industry; public and private banks which play an important role in industrial policy; employers' associations; trade unions; and non-profit organisations active in social service provision. (Benz and Goetz 1996: 17)

The conception of the German state as *Rechtsstaat* therefore does not automatically imply that problems created by the market are addressed by hierarchical intervention. Given the corporatist tradition, which also makes up an important component of the German state development, problems are often dealt with through public–private co-operation or by non-governmental organisations. These patterns are of particular relevance with respect to the accommodation of diverging objectives of the welfare state and a free-market economy.

The legal system: binding the administration to the law

The German legal system is based on the continental legal tradition of the Roman Law, whose principles enhanced and facilitated the differentiation of the absolutist state out of society. Compared to the British Common Law tradition, several peculiarities of the system of Roman Law can be identified. First, Roman Law is based on a deductive and substantive philosophy as opposed to the inductive and procedural approach of the Common Law. Roman Law is characterised by the definition of abstract and general principles, which are applied to individual cases. The high degree of codification implies that legal specification is not restricted to procedural requirements for the individual interpretation of particular cases, but contains substantive provisions by defining concrete legal consequences for different case constellations. Given the highly codified character and the deductive approach, Roman Law is secondly characterised by a hierarchically organised system of courts and professionally trained lawyers and judges. Thirdly, the basic function of the Roman Law is described as that of an instrument of the state for intervening in society rather than serving as a means of conflict resolution between different societal actors. Accordingly, Roman Law was 'conceived of and developed as the articulation of the state, as a distinctive, binding, and enforceable system' (Dyson 1980: 42). Finally, the Roman Law facilitated the separation of the state and society by making an explicit distinction between public and private law, i.e. relations between the citizens and the state and relations among private citizens (Badie and Birnbaum 1983; Damaska 1986; Hellstern 1986; van Waarden 1995).

It was especially this latter principle together with the strong emphasis put on the development of the public law, that played a crucial role in the formation of the German state. The principle of the *Rechtsstaat* becomes apparent by two particular aspects which are of relevance for governmental and administrative activities: the binding of the administration to the law (*Gesetzesbindung der Verwaltung*) and a very comprehensive and coherent system of administrative control by judicial review (Hellstern 1986: 676).

The binding of the administration to the law implies that, as a general rule, the scope and mode of administrative activity is specified by law. Public administration serves the application of the law rather than policy-making, and hence possesses comparatively little flexibility and discretion when implementing legal provisions (Ellwein and Hesse 1989: 392; Peters 1995: 137). It is a consequence of this general approach that we observe a hierarchically structured and rather dense system of public law guiding administrative activity in Germany.

The legal hierarchy relevant for administrative activity consists of constitutional law, statutory law (enacted by Parliament) and regulations (*Rechtsverordnungen*) which specify the content of Parliamentary legislation. Government is only allowed to enact regulations if the statutory law contains a corresponding authorisation. In addition to these different forms of regulatory rules, there exists a broad range of administrative circulars and technical guidance notes (*Verwaltungsvorschriften* and *technische Regeln*) which, in general, are only internally binding for the administration (Schwarze 1996: 128).[1] These internal rules have the purpose to specify further the regulatory content of statutory law and regulations in order to support unique and equal implementation. Compared to laws and regulations, *Verwaltungsvorschriften* allow generally for a quicker and more flexible adaptation of regulatory requirements in the light of situative changes, such as technological developments (Mayntz 1990). It has to be emphasised in this context that the legal specification of administrative activities is not only related to the substantive implementation of different policies, but also refers to procedural aspects. Comprehensive provisions for administrative procedures are cross-sectorally specified in federal and regional Administrative Procedures Acts (*Verwaltungsverfahrensgesetze*).[2]

The generally high level of regulatory density, on the other hand, does not imply that the administration has no discretion when implementing legal requirements in individual cases. It has been recognised for a long time that the legislator can only regulate complex matters by using indefinite legal concepts and general clauses (*Generalklauseln*).[3] This holds true especially for areas characterised by a high degree of scientific uncertainty, such as nuclear safety, for instance. This way, regulatory responsibility for decision-making is transferred to the administration, which has certain leeway for the definition of appropriate requirements in individual cases. The action-space for administrative activity, however, is narrowed by a set of principles subject to judicial review which were developed for specifying the use of administrative discretion, including the prohibition of arbitrary decisions (*Willkürverbot*) or the proportionality principle (*Grundsatz der Verhältnismäßigkeit*) (Hellstern 1986: 677).

Besides the binding of the administration to the law, the principle of the *Rechtsstaat* implies a comprehensive system of judicial review of state activity. Judicial review is not only related to the legality of administrative activity, but encompasses also statutory legislation enacted by the Parliament. This can be traced to the fact that that the institution of the *Rechtsstaat* preceded the introduction of Parliamentary democracy. In Britain, by contrast, the supremacy of Parliament logically excludes judicial review of statutory law (Heady 1979; König 1996).

Hence, in Germany there exists a constitutional jurisdiction (*Verfassungsgerichtsbarkeit*), which has extensive rights to consider the constitu-

---

[1] There are, however, some court decisions assuming that internal circulars under certain circumstances are also externally binding for the administration, hence having similar effects as regulations (Schwarze 1996: 128).

[2] Federal and regional laws contain very similar provisions.

[3] General clauses become apparent in the use of terms as, for instance, *Gefahr* (dangerous risk) or *öffentliche Sicherheit* (public safety).

tional validity of any federal or regional statute, as well as to rule on disputes among the branches of government. Moreover, any person can directly complain to the Constitutional Court, if he or she feels violated in his or her basic rights (Ellwein and Hesse 1989: 440–6). For the judicial control of the administration a separate system of courts exists. The main task of the administrative jurisprudence (*Verwaltungsgerichtsbarkeit*) is the protection of individual subjective rights, which might have been violated by the implementation, refusal or omission of an administrative act (Hellstern 1986: 677).

The civil service: servants of the state

In contrast to the late development of a professional civil service in Britain, a modern and professional German civil service (*Berufsbeamtentum*) already emerged during the eighteenth century. Administrative modernisation went along with the centralisation of absolutist state power in the German territories. In Prussia an institutionalised education system for civil servants was established around 1720. Officials received a distinctive form of training in 'cameralism', a practical 'science of the state' which involved a number of disciplines including, most predominantly, economics. The emergence of the *Rechtsstaat* implied a general shift in the professional education of officials. With the importance of the rule of law, legal training became the basic requirement for entrance into the higher civil service (Mayntz 1978: 4; Raadschelders and Rutgers 1996; Kickert and Stillman 1996). Given the further development of the *Rechtsstaat* and the binding of the administration to the law, it comes as no surprise that the pattern of the predominantly juridically trained higher civil service remained more or less unchanged. Other specialist groups besides the jurists, including economists, engineers and scientists are a minority in the general administration and instead cluster in specialised authorities. Combined they comprise not more than 20 to 30 per cent of the civil service in the federal and *Länder* ministries (Derlien 1995: 69; Page 1992: 47).

A second legacy left from the early emergence of the institution of the *Berufsbeamtentum* is the particular status of the civil servants, which basically can be explained against the background that, given the traditional conception of the *Obrigkeitsstaat*, German civil servants are 'servants of the state', acting on behalf of the state in order to achieve the 'common best'. This contrasts with the British conception of officials serving civil society (König 1997). German civil servants have a particular 'service and trust' relationship (*Dienst- und Treueverhältnis*) with the state, since they exercise functions that only can be exercised by the state. This traditional concept is embodied in the Federal Constitution (the Basic Law) (Derlien 1995: 69). The distinctive relationship between the state and its servants is expressed in a particular body of public law regulating aspects of civil service recruitment, education, examination, organisation, status and career. Given the particular status of German civil servants, we find a dominance of closed internal careers. In addition, internal mobility is, compared to the British system, at a rather low level, since the transfer of a civil servant to another position occurs occasionally rather than automatically and is dependent on the fulfilment of certain legal requirements (van Waarden 1995).

Against the background of the legal specialisation of the civil service and the binding of the administration to the law, formal rules and regulations governing public action and their stability and predictability are highly valued within the civil service (Aberbach, Putnam and Rockman 1981). This implies a legalistic orientation to policy-making and a formalistic and legalistic approach to policy implementation. In general, German civil servants are used to having a low level of discretion and flexibility. They are trained to 'go by the book'; hence, vaguely phrased law, especially procedural standards without a concrete, substantive basis causes great discomfort (van Waarden 1995; Page 1992; Peters 1995). The cautious attitude of risk-aversion is illustrated by the fact that administrators, in cases of only vaguely defined general clauses, in many instances prefer to wait for court decisions which allow for the concretisation of the law (Hellstern 1986: 677).

Despite the predominance of legal and formal intervention, however, the relationship between administrative and societal actors is generally based on consensual rather than adversarial interactions. German public administration is capable of integrating and co-ordinating societal interests relatively independent from legislative and governmental guidance (Lehmbruch 1987). Hence, the dominance of legalistic patterns of intervention is not only mitigated by the long tradition of corporatist arrangements, which emphasise the self-regulation of corporate actors by delegating responsibility to private interest organisations for certain, legally clearly defined areas (van Waarden 1995). The fact that legalism coincides with consensual rather than adversarial relationships can also be traced to the fact that consensual and informal patterns of bargaining, albeit under 'the shadow of the law', are preferred by both administrative and societal actors. This preference can in turn be explained by mutual resource dependencies. On the one hand, the correct application of the law by the administration, in many instances, is hardly possible without the detailed information and knowledge provided by societal actors. On the other hand, the position of societal actors is crucially affected by the concrete way the administration uses and applies its resources provided by the legal system.

Moreover, implementation research carried out during the 1980s revealed that interaction between administrative and societal actors is characterised by a good deal of pragmatism and informal flexibility which exists alongside the legalist tradition. The rule of law has to be reconciled with the conditions of an efficient administration, and the potential tension between the two is usually resolved through informal routines (Benz 1990; Ellwein 1990; Seibel 1996: 78). This became particularly obvious with respect to environmental regulation. Given the complex nature of environmental problems, informal administrative action emerged as a consequence of missing or insufficient legal specification (Bohne 1981). In contrast to Britain, however, informal administrative action in Germany takes place under the 'shadow of the law', i.e., the leeway for informal interaction is restricted by substantive and procedural requirements (Ellwein and Hesse 1994: 17–18).

According to the German tradition of the state, the civil service is accountable to the state and to the law rather than to society. Hence, we can understand the quite restricted possibilities for societal actors to get access to administrative documents (Ellwein and Hesse 1989: 387). This attitude is in particular a result of the distinctive character of legal administrative control, which places its emphasis on the protection of subjective individual rights rather than the participation of the public in administrative decision-making. Hence, in Germany access to official files has traditionally been restricted to persons whose individual substantive rights might be affected by an administrative decision. Access to administrative decision-making therefore is limited to these cases, which are – given the legalistic approach – exactly specified by administrative law (Winter 1996).

The structure of the state and patterns of administrative organisation

The structure of the German state as well as corresponding patterns of administrative organisation imply a comprehensive framework for the allocation of administrative competencies and related mechanisms of administrative co-ordination and control. This can first be observed when considering the functional division of competencies between the federal and the regional level. A basic characteristic of the German federalist tradition is the concept of executive or administrative federalism (*Verwaltungsföderalismus*). From this concept it follows that the federal level has the primary competence with respect to policy formulation. However, apart from certain limited cases,[4] at the federal level there exists no administrative framework concerning the implementation of these policies.[5] Rather, the implementation and administration of federal law lies generally with the regions which participate in federal rule-making through the *Bundesrat*.

As a result of this basic division of labour, the exclusive rule-making powers of the regions are rather limited. Exclusive policy-making competencies of the regions are restricted to culture and education, police, as well as the definition of the legal framework for local self-administration and the legal specification of federal framework legislation (*Rahmengesetzgebung des Bundes*). Furthermore, in areas of competing legislatory powers (*konkurrierende Gesetzgebung*), the regions have policy-making powers as long as the federal level does not make use of its competencies. However, nearly every area in this field is covered by federal law, hence underlining the dominant and coexistent patterns of legislatory centralisation and administrative decentralisation (Mayntz 1978).

The functional division of responsibilities with respect to policy formulation and implementation implies a rather independent position of the *Länder* when deciding upon the appropriate administrative arrangements for implementing federal legislation. Apart from the law, the federal level generally has no competencies for intervening and guiding administrative activities at the regional level. Federal administrative guidance and control of the regions is restricted to a low number of constitutionally defined cases. Article 85 of the Basic Law defines the possibilities for federal guidance in certain cases where the regions are acting on behalf of the federal level and the latter assuming complete financial responsibility for the policies in question (*Bundesauftragsverwaltung*). In addition to the administrative discretion of the regions, they enjoy – depending on the degree of specification of federal laws – considerable legal discretion for defining the concrete requirements of federal legislation.

A second general aspect that characterises administrative structure and organisation in Germany refers to the hierarchical division of competencies at the regional level. This can be understood against the historical background of administrative development in the German states which, as indicated above, preceded the establishment of the German nation-state. During the nineteenth century, a process of

---

[4] Examples for such exceptional cases are PTT, transport and labour.
[5] This contrasts with the federal system in the US, where the federal and state level are responsible for both policy formulation and implementation with respect to the policy areas under their jurisdiction.

administrative modernisation took place in the German states, which was inspired by both the Prussian reforms and the French model of a hierarchical bureaucratic organisation (Ellwein 1993a; Lehmbruch 1997). In contrast to Britain, a comprehensive framework of administrative organisation emerged which is basically still in place today.

At the core of this framework is a three-tier hierarchical structure in most regions,[6] including the regional ministries, the county administrations (*Regierungspräsidien* or *Bezirksregierungen*), and the lower state administration (*Untere Verwaltungsbehörden*). The ministries are at the top of the regional administration and have overall responsibility for deciding upon appropriate organisational arrangements and legal specifications for the implementation of federal policies, but are in general not involved in practical implementation. The county administrations have a twofold function, including both the control of the lower authorities and the practical implementation of more complex policies not appropriate to be dealt with at the local level. The major locus of practical implementation, however, lies with the lower administrations, which consist of both general authorities (basically the local districts and cities without district – *Kreise* and *kreisfreie Städte*) and special agencies (*Sonderbehörden*). The activities of the special agencies are related to areas where special expertise is required, such as health and safety, air pollution control, water protection and management, structural engineering, and forestry. As the general administration, these special agencies in many instances were established in the process of administrative modernisation during the nineteenth century. The creation of specific factory inspectorates responsible for the control of air pollution from industrial plants, for instance, dates back to the mid-1800s (Boehmer-Christiansen and Skea 1991: 160).

Whereas the federal level – apart from its competence in policy formulation – has no means to hierarchically intervene in regional implementation processes, the hierarchical structure at the regional level implies that subordinate authorities are subject to both legal and administrative (i.e., practical) guidance from the superior level. Superior authorities can directly intervene in the operations of subordinate authorities by both individual instructions and the issuing of administrative circulars (Mayntz 1978: 95). As implementation research has pointed out, however, subordinate authorities in many instances still have considerable discretion and flexibility for adjusting their activities

---

[6] Exemptions are the smaller states such as Schleswig-Holstein, Saarland, Brandenburg, Hamburg and Bremen, which established only a two-tier structure consisting of the ministerial and the county level.

in the light of particular requirements (cf. Mayntz *et al.* 1978; Mayntz 1983).

The final aspect characterising the organisation of German public administration in general refers to horizontal fragmentation and segmentation. The emphasis on hierarchical structures coincides with the emergence of horizontally segmented administrative arrangements. Hence, there exists a broad range of separate vertical lines of authority, implying, in many instances, the horizontal division of administrative units within the same authority.

This pattern of horizontal differentiation becomes particularly apparent in the administrative segmentation at the ministerial and lower level of the regional administration. At both levels, organisational arrangements are based upon specific policy areas, with mechanisms of horizontal co-ordination between different areas being rather limited. Basically co-ordination between different units and divisions follows the principle of 'negative co-ordination' (Scharpf 1973), implying that co-ordination efforts are restricted to avoiding potential interference with the activities of other units rather than developing integrated policy solutions. Although the county administrations are organised in a more integrated way for the purpose of strengthening administrative co-ordination (Mayntz 1978: 104), this effect is limited in practice and restricted to cases where conflicts between different lower authorities are resolved by their common superior authority.[7]

To summarise, the analysis of the particular characteristics of the state tradition, the legal system, the civil service tradition as well as the structure and organisation of the state points to several core features shaping national administrative traditions in Germany. To begin with the dimension of administrative style, national administrative traditions are characterised by four crucial principles of administrative intervention and interest intermediation, namely interventionism, legalism, corporatism and consensualism. The combination of these aspects is not only a consequence of the distinctive path of German state formation, but is to be understood also in the light of the legal system and the characteristics of the civil service. According to these core aspects of administrative intervention, patterns of administrative interest intermediation generally tend to be rather legalistic, formal, allowing for third-party access only in legally specified cases. On the other hand, the tradition of corporatism, as well as the mutual resource dependencies characterising the relationships between administrative and societal

---

[7] Given this limited co-ordinative impact, administrative institutions at the medium level between the ministries and the lower authorities are often seen as being superfluous (Ellwein 1985; 1996: 16).

actors provide the basis for rather informal and consensual patterns of administrative interest intermediation. This constellation is in contrast with the more adversarial interaction patterns to be found in the United States, where legalism coincides with pluralist rather than corporatist arrangements.

With respect to administrative structures, the macro-institutional context of the state tradition and state structure indicate a rather comprehensive and rigid picture which is characterised by three basic patterns. First, we find a general division of competencies between the federal level taking responsibility for policy formulation and the regional level enjoying rather autonomous powers with respect to the implementation of federal programmes. Second, at the regional level administrative competencies are allocated on the basis of a multi-tier hierarchical organisation. This hierarchical structure is, thirdly, accompanied by patterns of horizontal segmentation along policy sectors, with co-ordination being fairly restricted.

4.2   Britain: mediating tradition within flexible structures

In the British state, legal as well as civil service traditions favour patterns of administrative intervention and interest intermediation which come quite close to the mediating ideal type. Rather than being an instrument of hierarchical state intervention, public administration is conceived as a means of mediating between societal interests. While the macro-institutional context thus indicates a clear direction with respect to sectoral administrative styles, it is relatively open with respect to administrative structures, hence allowing for a high degree of structural flexibility. Nevertheless, one general pattern can be identified, namely the traditional absence of hierarchical control between different administrative levels which is particularly evident with respect to central–local relations.

The British state tradition: government by civil society

The mediating tradition of public administration in Britain is closely related to the historical evolution of the state which reflects 'an aberrant case' (Dyson 1980: 36), compared to the developments in Continental Europe. In Britain no ideological boundary developed between the state and society as it did in the Continental European tradition. Little credence has been given to the idea of the state as an abstract identity bearing inherent responsibility for the performance of public functions or as a collective actor representing the nation as a whole (Grimm

1991). Britain has frequently been described as a 'stateless society' (Nettl 1968: 562) or in terms of 'government by civil society' (Badie and Birnbaum 1983: 121). The lacking development of the state as a political and legal concept also becomes apparent in the fact that the term 'state' was and still is only used at the level of international relations or in the terms of 'welfare state'. Instead, reference is made to 'government', 'country', 'people', or 'nation' (Dyson 1980: 37; Abromeit 1991, 295; Richardson 1994b: 179).

The distinctive development of the British state conception is basically a result of diverging political developments in Continental Europe and Britain from the seventeenth century onwards. In contrast to the Continent, where absolutist regimes emerged as a consequence of the confessional civil wars, in Britain a concentration of political functions in the hand of the king and a distinction between state and society cannot be observed. Although also in Britain political power was centralised, sovereignty became vested in Parliament instead of the monarch. The struggle between monarch and estates ended in the victory of the latter. The Glorious Revolution of 1688 established the supremacy of Parliament (Grimm 1991).

Already in the sixteenth century, the political process was based on bargaining between the Crown and the great land magnates, and unlike its Continental counterparts, Parliament had acquired a basis of territorial representation and was the principal location for the articulation and aggregation of territorial interests. In this context, the 'monarch was not above or outside the community but was a member of the "community of the realm"' (Dyson 1980: 38). Against this background, the Glorious Revolution was a conservative settlement which safeguarded the traditional rights of Parliament, the courts and local communities against the claims of a centralising monarchy.

As a consequence of the Glorious Revolution, a monarchical executive, with a private, secretive and personalised conception of government was made to coexist with the increasing political claims of Parliament. Public action was made relatively unobtrusive and amenable to Parliamentary and local control (Badie and Birnbaum 1983: 122):

The subsequent gradual extension of public activity, legitimated by Parliament and local government, was not justified by reference to the notion of an autonomous state acting to realise certain inherent purposes. It took the form of a maze of statutes, the complex form of contending political groups seeking to realise their versions of the general interest through representative institutions. (Dyson 1980: 39)

In contrast to the Continental development, public activities did not emanate from an autonomous state, but from the competition of different societal interests represented in Parliament. This emphasis on societal initiative and self-regulation favoured the emergence of representative forms of government and the importance of the market. On the other hand, this development not only inhibited the emergence of a 'strong state', but made it superfluous:

Whereas in other countries such as France and Germany it was economic backwardness that led to the creation of a strong state, in Great Britain it was the very rapid growth of capitalism and the market that resulted in the backwardness of the state, with civil society maintaining its position of dominance. (. . .) In Great Britain the market reigns supreme, not the state. (Badie and Birnbaum 1983: 123–4)

The tradition of the 'stateless society' also becomes apparent in the fact that – despite the early industrialisation – the development of the welfare state occurred rather late in Britain. Self-organisation and self-responsibility remained the basic characteristics of social policy in Britain until the early twentieth century (Esping-Andersen 1990). It was only then that a strengthening of the British welfare state could be observed, which was reinforced by the Labour Party after the Second World War. In the context of a Keynesian economic policy, the state – as in other European countries – intervened more strongly in private markets. Many industries (including the railways and energy supply) were nationalised.

Despite these developments towards a more active and interventionist state, basic elements of the 'stateless society' could always be observed (Abromeit 1991: 298). Thus, in contrast to Continental Europe, the nationalised industries never became state agencies or part of the public administration, but had the status of private companies in public ownership. Although being confronted with the restrictions of public budgeting, nationalised industries were managed in commercial terms, i.e., private sector principles (cf. Abromeit 1991: 314; Knill 2001). Moreover, the concept of a 'residual welfare state' implies that the provision of social services is restricted to a so-called 'flat-rate', with additional services being subject to private initiatives and insurance systems (Esping-Andersen 1990).

Notwithstanding these persisting traditions of the 'stateless society', however, the sheer number of nationalisations taking place after the Second World War indicates the high potential for national reform dynamics, which will be further analysed in the following chapter. The amplitude with which national reform developments oscillate around institutional trajectories is much higher in Britain than in Germany, where nationalisations occurred at a much lower scale. The particular dynamics given in the British case are further illustrated by recent developments in the opposite direction, i.e., the large-scale privatisation programme initiated by the Conservative government under Margaret Thatcher.

The legal system: law as mediating social development

The development of the legal system in Britain is closely linked with the distinctive tradition of the state. The English legal system is based on the medieval tradition of an evolutionary judge-made Common Law and a legal profession that did not evolve the idea of the state as a legal institution. The Common Law 'was based largely on the observation of the traditional practices prevalent in civil society and much less attention was paid to the definition of a separate public sphere' (Badie and Birnbaum 1983: 90–1). The English law system emerged bottom-up in society and had gradually become integrated into a body of valid law rather than being 'created' by autonomous institutions separated from and standing 'above' society. Furthermore, typical of the English law tradition is the absence of hierarchy between different judges and courts and a preference for lay-functionaries and amateurs.

While the Roman Law tradition facilitated the separation of state and society and the development of public law principles, the British legal tradition implied a less clear distinction between both spheres. In contrast to the Roman Law, which Damaska (1986: 18) classifies as a 'hierarchical ideal', with the function of law being that of leading the society as an instrument of policy implementation, the Common Law reflects the 'coordinate ideal' (ibid.: 23). Law is seen as a means of mediating social developments, i.e., as instrument for the resolution of conflicts arising in civil society. According to Damaska, English law serves a state which assumes a passive and reactive role. Its primary function is to settle conflicts in society when society cannot solve these conflicts itself. The legal form is that of the contest (as opposed to the form of inquest given in the Roman Law tradition) between private parties, with the state mediating and adjudicating as a third party (cf. Dyson 1980: 42).

In so far as law is used for policy implementation, it should be 'yielding law'. It should yield, give priority to regulation of civil society itself. Private contracts, market solutions, and self-regulation by societal associations take priority. (. . .) Policy implementation should preferably take place without the use of law, that is, through informal rather than formal regulations. (van Waarden 1995: 234)

Typical characteristics of the Common Law are its inductive and procedural philosophy. The inductive logic implies that legal requirements are decided and interpreted in light of a particular case. Instead of deciding if certain abstract and general rules apply for a particular case, the Common Law is case law, with each case being a new case. Accordingly, the degree of legal codification is rather low. Legal specification is restricted to a narrow concept expressing a procedural philosophy rather than substantive criteria for reaching decisions (Dyson 1980; Badie and Birnbaum 1983; Hellstern 1986; Jowell and Birkinshaw 1996: 297).

Given the missing distinction between a public and private sphere, the British legal system developed no particular body of public law principles, when the Common Law was replaced by Statute Law as an expression of parliamentary supremacy (Dyson 1980: 42). As a consequence, in Britain there evolved neither a system of administrative or public law nor an administrative jurisdiction for guiding and controlling administrative activity comparably to the arrangements found in Continental Europe. Although there exist over 2,000 administrative tribunals in Britain, their competencies are much more restricted than those of Continental administrative courts. The tribunals play an important role as a kind of arbiter between citizens and the administration, but they have no competencies for developing legal principles of public law (Budge and McKay 1988: 170f.; Spoerr 1991; Mény 1993: 336–7).[8]

The fact that the decisions of the administrative tribunals are subject to judicial review by the High Court of Justice does not significantly increase the degree of legal control of administrative activities. This can be traced to several reasons. First, judicial review is restricted by the principle of Parliamentary supremacy and a lacking written constitution. Hence, it is not possible for courts to declare unconstitutional statutes passed through the formal processes of Parliamentary approval (Page 1992: 135). The focus of judicial review is therefore basically directed at resolving disputes about the application of the law to particular events (Rose 1989: 138). Second, even in this limited sense judicial review rarely produces challenges to administrative decisions and actions. Administrative bodies enjoy wide discretion to decide in the light of the particular circumstances. The courts may require the body to act within its conferred powers, but they have only limited competencies to legally control the administration's evaluation of the fact situation. Thus, the courts are allowed to intervene only in cases of 'procedural unfairness'

---

[8] The establishment of the administrative tribunals coincided with the development of the British welfare state after the Second World War. The public should be enabled to use these 'quasi-courts' as a means of putting through their statutory rights with respect to the provision of social services (Budge and McKay 1988: 170).

or 'unreasonable or irrational decisions', i.e., decisions that are 'so unreasonable that no reasonable body could so decide' (Jowell and Birkinshaw 1996: 277; Boynton 1986).

Jowell and Birkinshaw (1996: 322), however, point to developments during the past 30 years indicating the beginnings of a separate system of public law principles. This becomes obvious in an increased application of the principle of proportionality for controlling the use of administrative discretion. Nevertheless it has to be emphasised that the scope and pace of these developments is restricted in the light of Parliamentary supremacy and the missing written constitution (ibid.; cf. Sterett 1994).

The civil service: servants of civil society

With respect to the British civil service system, basically three aspects have to be mentioned in order to characterise its peculiarities in relation to Continental systems. First, the rather late development of a modern civil service has to be emphasised. For a long time British administration was based on local dignitaries, the local Justices of the Peace. The inadequacies of this 'government by gentlemen' or *Honoratiorenverwaltung* (Weber 1972: 561), involving patronage, corruption and inefficiency, only became obvious during the nineteenth century when the 1854 Northcote-Trevelyan Report provided the basis for the establishment of a highly qualified, permanent and politically impartial modern civil service, relying on a system of appointment and promotion based on merit (Kingdom 1989: 13; Page 1992: 22–4).

Second, an important legacy left from these nineteenth-century reforms is the low degree of professional specialisation. As in the legal system, there is a preference for generally educated and intelligent amateurs: civilised gentlemen, groomed in the fine educational institutions of society, the independent universities of Oxford and Cambridge. This implies that civil servants are coming from civil society and are supposed to 'serve' that society rather than some abstract state, as is the case in Germany (van Waarden 1995; Peters 1995; Kingdom 1989).[9] Given the dominance of generalists and the low importance of the law in guiding administrative activities, there is a general preference for pragmatic rather than scientific solutions. Accumulated experience is seen as more important than scientific knowledge (Bulmer 1988). Accordingly, in Britain no distinctive administrative sciences developed, as opposed

---

[9] Although it has never been formally defined, the term 'civil servant' is usually reserved for those working in the civil service itself and, as opposed to the German *Beamte*, does not include employees in the large range of other public agencies (Kingdom 1989: 23).

to those in Germany and the United States (Thomas 1978; Christoph 1993).

The preference for generalists does not imply, on the other hand, that specialists play no role within British administration. Rather there exist two separate hierarchies with generalists being basically involved in policy formulation whereas specialists have advisory functions or are in charge of policy implementation (Judge 1981). Despite reform proposals to strengthen the specialisation in public administration (as spelled out in the Fulton Report 1968) and an increased reliance on special advisers and think-tanks by the Conservative governments of Thatcher and Major, the generalists still hold the key cards. Attempts to increase specialist influence had only a limited influence in tempting the traditional neutralism and generalism of the British civil service (Bulmer 1988; Peters 1995).

A third aspect characterising the British civil service is the combination of high internal and low external mobility. Civil servants are recruited at an early age and subsequently transferred regularly, in order to prevent them becoming specialist in any one policy area or 'captured' by a specific clientele (Heady 1979: 204). This policy of internal rotation as well as the low degree of external fluctuation (with respect to both the political system and the private sector) has enhanced the image of neutrality of British civil servants. Both this image of neutrality and the high status British civil servants enjoy within society explain that the British public perceives governmental officials as having sufficient integrity and competence to be able to represent its interests reasonably well (Vogel 1986: 257; Peters 1995: 72).

The high level of societal trust in the civil service explains not only that administrative law, i.e., legal control over the civil service and possibilities of citizens appealing against decisions of the administration, is comparatively underdeveloped. It also accounts for the large discretionary authority of the civil servants and their opportunities for practising secrecy. Administrators have greater leeway in dealing with private interests. They are less fearful of co-operating with them, providing some with privileged access or engaging in informal and closed relations (van Waarden 1995). On the other hand, the missing framework of administrative law provides administrative actors with rather limited legal resources when interacting with society. Hence, engaging in consensual, informal relations with societal actors becomes a reasonable operational option guiding administrative behaviour (Vogel 1986: 83). A further reason allowing for an informal and secretive administrative practice is the supremacy of Parliament, which within the British conception of the state is a societal rather than a state institution. Since the executive power is subject to Parliamentary control, administrative accountability towards society is seen as being sufficiently guaranteed (Burmeister 1990).

The structure of the state and patterns of administrative organisation

In contrast to Germany, the British structure of the state leaves a rather broad range of options with respect to sectoral administrative structures and organisation. This holds true especially for the allocation of competencies between different administrative units and levels, where, in sharp contrast to the German case, no specific options are excluded or favoured by the macro-context of national administrative traditions. There is only one general core aspect characterising administrative structures and organisation in Britain, namely the general absence of hierarchical control between different administrative levels.

To begin with competence allocation, there are no strongly entrenched arrangements with respect to the functional division of labour between and within different levels of central and subcentral administration. Rather the distribution of administrative competencies seems to be quite flexible, with shifting competencies and administrative reorganisation taking place frequently, at least when compared to Continental European countries. Structural flexibility can be traced to two factors.

First, the unitary structure of the British state implies that the overall responsibility for policy formulation and implementation lies with central government. Central government enjoys wide discretion when deciding on the allocation of administrative competencies within and between the central and local level. The constitutional position of local government is inferior to that of central government. Although there exist also elected representations at the local level, local authorities in Britain – as opposed to Germany – lack constitutionally guaranteed competencies and responsibilities, but are subject to *ultra vires*, empowered to undertake only those functions deliberately granted to them by Parliamentary statute (King 1993: 217). Central government has therefore not only powers to reduce administrative competencies given to the local level, but also can reorganise the entire structure of local government as well as its finances (Page 1992: 69; Peters 1995: 138).

Against this background of British central–local relations, the low institutional stability of local authorities' competencies and organisation can be understood. Given the unitary structure of the state and the dominance of the centre, however, it seems at first glance surprising that it is also difficult to identify stable patterns of administrative organisation at the central level. A basic reason for this phenomenon lies in the distinctive evolution of public administration in Britain, the second factor explaining the absence of comprehensive patterns of administrative structure and organisation.

In contrast to the administrative development in Continental Europe, British administration has evolved over centuries by accretion with relatively little planning and without a central organisational format which would make the system more comprehensible (Peters 1995: 138). According to this pattern, the increase in civil service functions, which was basically a result of nineteenth-century industrialisation and the welfare state development, led to the creation of new administrative bodies on an *ad hoc* basis, rather than allocating new functions to already existing authorities and within existing structures (Gray and Jenkins 1985: 11–12; Kingdom 1989: 19).

In view of this particular evolution, a complex, but little coherent administrative structure can be observed, including different types of organisation, such as executive departments, executive agencies carrying out implementation activities separated from the sponsoring department, local government, the health services, and a large number of non-departmental bodies. With respect to the latter type a further distinction can be made between nationalised industries and the so-called quangos (quasi-non-governmental organisations) which are either public bodies hived-off from their sponsoring department (as, for instance, universities) or publicly financed private bodies exercising public authority (cf. Greenwood and Wilson 1989; Peters 1995: 138–40).

On the other hand, the general lack of structural coherence concerning the allocation of administrative competencies has important implications for administrative co-ordination and control. It is a basic feature of the British administrative system, that authorities responsible for a certain area enjoy a significant degree of autonomy. Besides the limited mechanisms developed for horizontal co-ordination within the fragmented system, there exists no multi-tier system allowing for detailed hierarchical supervision of subordinate administrative levels and units, as is the case in the German regions. Hierarchical guidance and control by the central government departments occurs only with respect to general rather than policy-specific aspects, such as the definition of a broad legal, operational and financial framework. Within this framework, administrative authorities and agencies at both the central and local levels enjoy far-reaching discretion for specifying the generally vague regulatory provisions defined by Parliamentary statute.

The general lack of hierarchical control structures can first be observed within the context of local administration. Although there exists a two-tier organisational structure of local authorities,[10] both levels are responsible for different tasks and fulfil their functions rather independently from each other. In contrast to the German arrangements, there exist no mechanisms of hierarchical guidance and control of the district level by the county administration.

Second, the lack of detailed hierarchical guidance and control becomes obvious with regard to the relations between central and local government. Although there exists a two-tier structure of British administration (consisting of central government and local government), hierarchical guidance of the local level by the centre is basically restricted to questions of financial resources, but leaves broad leeway for the local authorities' day-to-day activities. While the constitutional constellation implies that both administrative competencies and structures at the subcentral level are contingent upon decisions of central government, a second important characteristic of central–local relations lies in the fact that, within these constitutional constraints, local authorities enjoy considerable freedom in the ways they structure their own organisation and fulfil their tasks. Local authorities carry out their functions without being subject to legal and administrative guidance and control by central government. Depending on the concrete level of legal, administrative and financial discretion given to local authorities, their activities are therefore characterised by wide variations in standards and practices throughout the country (Page 1992: 74; Peters 1995: 139).

The main reason for these arrangements lies in the traditional separation of national and local politics in Britain. In contrast to France, where an interpenetration of central and local political elites can be observed and the central government influences regional and local politics by the prefects, i.e., central agents (Ashford 1982), in Britain the local and central spheres of government are completely separated:

Central and political elites have traditionally been insulated from each other. A dual polity has prevailed whereas the centre has distanced itself from sub-central governments, giving them operational autonomy in matters of 'Low Politics' (. . .) in order to enhance their autonomy in matters of 'High Politics' (. . .). (Budge and McKay 1988: 136)

According to this constellation, the central and local levels are to some extent interdependent. Local government requires central government

---

[10] In Britain the local government system consists of 515 counties, districts, London boroughs, the City of London, the Scottish regions, districts and islands, to which may be added a series of boards to run the services formerly carried out by the seven metropolitan authorities (including the Greater London Council) which were abolished in 1986 (Page 1992: 68).

statutes and money to be able to provide local services; and central government depends upon local government to deliver a substantial portion of state services. Due to the authoritative decision-making power of central government, however, this exchange relationship is rather asymmetric. Initiatives to reduce local government spending of both the 1974 Labour government and the Conservative government since 1979 have shown that central government has the capacity to take unilateral decisions without giving much away in bargaining with local authorities (Rhodes 1991: 85; Page 1992: 75; Knill 1995: 304).

In conclusion, the analysis of the macro-institutional background revealed that pursuing a mediating administrative style reflects a strongly embedded core aspect of British administrative traditions. The conception of the state, according to which public policies emerge from the interaction of societal interests, indicates the participation of societal actors during policy formulation and implementation. The state should not impose any policies on society. The mode of state intervention is therefore based on non-hierarchical, less interventionist regulatory instruments. 'Britain is best characterised as emphasising consensus and a desire to avoid the imposition of solutions on sections of society' (Jordan and Richardson 1982: 81).

Moreover, the inductive and procedural rather than substantive character of regulatory activity can be traced to the characteristics of the British legal system which developed no principles of administrative law in order to guide and control administrative activity comparable to the Continental tradition. Hence, pragmatic and informal bargaining between administrative and societal actors is more important than legalistic and formal relationships. Law has the function of mediating social developments rather than intervening in societal activities from above. Pragmatic, consensual and informal relationships are furthermore facilitated by typical characteristics of the British civil service, namely the dominance of generalists, the combination of high internal and low external mobility as well as the high societal trust into the civil servants' neutrality and loyalty in serving the public interest.

Turning to general patterns of administrative structure, the macro-institutional context indicates a broad range of sectoral options with respect to the allocation of administrative competencies. Neither the allocation of administrative responsibilities between different levels of government nor the patterns of administrative organisation at each of these levels reveals a consistent and comprehensive picture. As a consequence, we observe a wide variation of organisational arrangements not only with respect to different local authorities, but also when it comes to administrative structures at the central level.

The only general pattern, which is closely linked to the lack of structural coherence, has to be seen in the traditionally wide discretion of administrative authorities when carrying out their functions. This lack of hierarchical mechanisms for administrative co-ordination and control is particularly pronounced in the case of central–local relations. Given the traditional separation of 'high' and 'low' politics in Britain, local administrations carry out their tasks with relatively little hierarchical oversight by central administration. The same picture holds true with respect to different administrative layers at the central and sub-central level.

In sum, the comparison of administrative traditions in Germany and Britain points to fundamental and partly opposing patterns of administrative styles and structures. In Germany, national traditions indicate a hierarchical and legalist style enriched by consensual and corporatist arrangements, while the corresponding arrangements in Britain come close to the mediating ideal type of administrative style. Turning to administrative structures, the macro-institutional context also indicates important differences. We find comprehensive structural arrangements in Germany, with clear patterns of administrative competence allocation, considerable administrative autonomy of the regions, and hierarchical guidance and control within the regional multi-tier structure. Moreover, hierarchical differentiation is accompanied by horizontal segmentation across policy sectors. In Britain, by contrast, administrative traditions leave more leeway for the allocation of administrative competencies at the sectoral level. The only core pattern characterising structural arrangements refers to the considerable autonomy of administrative authorities at the central and local level with respect to operational activities which coincides with a general lack of detailed hierarchical control and guidance.

5   Administrative reform capacity in Germany and Britain: autonomous versus instrumental administration

The analysis of basic characteristics of British and German administrative traditions, as they are defined by the distinctive macro-institutional context given in both countries, provides us with the necessary background knowledge in order to assess the institutional scope of European adaptation requirements. In other words, we are able to identify whether European requirements for sectoral adjustments imply challenges *of* the core or remain *within* the core of national administrative traditions.

I have argued, however, that, notwithstanding the general stability and continuity of administrative traditions, exceptional changes in these core arrangements cannot be fully precluded. Although not putting into question the validity of our institutional explanation (based on the concept of adaptation pressure), such developments reduce its predictive reliability. As pointed out in chapter 3, this problem can partly be captured by identifying the structural potential for administrative reforms, which is itself an institutionalised feature of the macro-institutional context and hence might may vary from country to country (Knill 1999). The concept of national administrative reform capacity serves as indicator for the overall reliability of the institution-based hypotheses on domestic administrative adjustments in the light of European requirements, although we can predict neither the occurrence nor the timing of administrative reforms.

The national capacity for administrative reforms depends on the number of formal and factual institutional veto points administrative actors have at their disposal in order to influence and resist political reform initiatives. The number of these veto points is crucially affected by specific macro-institutional provisions, namely the state tradition as well as the legal and political-administrative system. For analytical purposes, we can group the factors affecting national reform capacity into three broad categories: (1) the general strength of executive leadership; (2) the institutional entrenchment of administrative structures and procedures; and (3) the influence of the bureaucracy on policy-making.

The general strength of executive leadership is related to the centralisation and concentration of political power; i.e., the government's general ability to enact political reforms. The number of institutional veto points with respect to administrative reforms is secondly affected by the degree to which administrative structures and procedures are entrenched or tightly linked to a broader institutional framework. The difficulties of implementing administrative reforms from above by swift, single-handed reorganisation increase with the extent to which administrative activity is based on legal and formal requirements as well as comprehensive and fragmented structures. Finally, the political influence of the bureaucracy refers to the extent to which administrative actors are able to shape the outcome of policy formulation and implementation in line with their interests.

Given the far-reaching differences in their macro-institutional context, the two countries under study are not only characterised by rather opposing administrative traditions (as analysed in the previous chapter). They also reveal a highly varying potential for administrative reform. In Germany, low reform capacity coincides with a quite autonomous position of public administration within the political system. In Britain, by contrast, administrative styles and structures are less static; public administration is instrumental to rather than autonomous from the political sphere.

5.1   Germany: incremental self-adaptation of an autonomous bureaucracy

Notwithstanding the frequent emergence of 'reform rhetorics' in German politics, large-scale innovations hardly occur in political reality. This general statement, which is to be understood in light of the limited capacity for executive leadership provided by the German political system in general, holds true in particular when it comes to administrative reform. This can be traced to the traditionally influential position of the German administration on policy formulation and implementation as well as the strong institutional entrenchment of administrative structures and procedures. As a consequence, administrative change takes generally the form of an ongoing process characterised by incremental self-adaptation of the bureaucracy in the light of changing environmental demands (Böhret 1982; Ellwein 1994, 1996; Benz and Goetz 1996).[1] The 'intelligence of the German bureaucracy', i.e., the

---

[1] It was against the background of such gloomy assessments of the likelihood of comprehensive reform that some academic analysts began to stress the virtues of permanent administrative modernisation which would be at the core of a continuous administrative policy (Hesse and Benz 1990).

fact that German administration tends to adapt to perceived incontingencies through self-generated reforms rather than being pushed and bashed by politicians and reformers (Derlien 1996a; Seibel 1996), therefore implies a high stability of administrative core arrangements. Change takes place *within* the core of existing administrative traditions rather than altering these traditional arrangements, an aspect which becomes obvious when considering the history of administrative reform in Germany.

Executive leadership in a fragmented system

The first factor which accounts for the limited capacity for administrative reform lies in the restricted scope for executive leadership. The German political system is characterised by both fragmentation and decentralisation of political power, implying fundamental limitations on the government's ability to successfully formulate and implement comprehensive policy innovations. Institutional veto points restricting the potential for executive leadership emerge from basically five sources: the federal structure of the state; the role of party competition; the *Rechtsstaat* principle; the corporatist tradition; as well as the organisation of government.

An important characteristic of the German federal system is the existence of strong interlinkages of policy-making between the central (federal) and subcentral (*Länder*) levels (Scharpf, Reissert and Schnabel 1976). Since the federal government, as a general rule, has no hierarchical administrative authority over the *Länder* executives, intergovernmental co-ordination has to be obtained by negotiations between autonomous bureaucracies. In these relationships, the leading role of the federal level is counterbalanced by the regions' experience in field administration and implementation. Such a structurally and procedurally interlocked system is not favourable to comprehensive reforms and institutional innovations. In this light, the interlocking of federal and regional executives was identified as a key factor explaining the only incremental changes occurring in Germany during the 1970s and 1980s, whereas other Western governments reacted to new challenges with ambitious reform projects (Hesse and Benz 1990; Lehmbruch *et al.* 1988).

Despite these limitations, the decentralised structure of the federal system also provides certain opportunities for innovation. The interlinked decision-making system impedes comprehensive reforms, but, at the same time, facilitates the diffusion of innovative ideas and experience that emerge from the multiplicity of political arenas at the subcentral level (Dyson 1992: 14; Czada 1993: 93). However, at the subcentral level too, large-scale change typically requires a lead from above and is often factually restrained by the centrally set legal framework (Benz and Goetz 1996: 17).

In view of the institutional fragmentation of the German state, party competition has not become the dominant mechanism of political leadership. In contrast to the Westminster model with its tendency for strong party governments, a German government supported by a *Bundestag* majority finds itself tied into a complex network of institutions and organisations where decision-making by bargaining is often the norm. Consequently, in Germany party competition is to a lesser extent a vehicle of political leadership than a co-ordination mechanism in the fragmented institutional structure, namely with respect to the relationships between the federal and regional governments as well as between different regions. The mediating role of political parties becomes particularly apparent when the opposition holds a majority in the Federal Council (Lehmbruch 1976).

The impact of party competition in promoting strong executive leadership is furthermore restricted by the German electoral system which is based on proportional representation slightly modified to allow an element of personal election (Ismayr 1992). In contrast to the British relative majority system, which favours the emergence of strong single-party governments, the German arrangements foster a more diverse party landscape, which, in many instances, leads to the establishment of coalition governments. This way, the scope for comprehensive reform decisions is additionally reduced, given the need for compromise and bargaining between the governing parties. On the other hand, one could argue that the German electoral system facilitates policy innovation by enhancing the scope for effective political action by the opposition, which can consider a range of different coalition options. However, without denying the potential dynamics emerging from this constellation, these opportunities are generally not sufficient to outweigh the limited reform capacities stemming from the fragmented institutional structure and the need for co-ordination between governing parties.

A third institutional veto point restricting the scope for executive leadership, emerges from the *Rechtsstaat* principle which implies that Parliamentary legislation is subject to judicial review by the Federal Constitutional Court as to the constitutionality of the legislation in question. The Court offers an important possibility to modify or block governmental reform initiatives even after they have been accepted by the Parliament. Although only a small number of constitutional complaints have resulted in statutes being declared void, lower court decisions being reversed or administrative acts set aside, the effect of the constitutional jurisdiction should not be underestimated, since the mere prospect of an action often induces the legislator to modify or drop a project (von Beyme 1991, 375).

Fourth, the German tradition of corporatism implies important institutional and factual veto positions. The multitude of co-operative arrangements between public and private actors as well as the delegation of powers to private associations increases the government's need for bargaining and accommodating various societal interests when formulating and implementing political reforms. The relevance of these corporatist patterns is further enhanced by the emergence of representational monopolies, i.e., the existence of strong peak associations which are able to rely on the broad political support of their members and the strong linkages between associations and political parties (Schmitter and Lehmbruch 1979; Dyson 1982). Although the corporatist mediation of diverse interests allows for considerable adaptational flexibility and ample opportunities to adjust political strategies in the light of differing problems, such adjustments are unlikely to imply radical reforms, given the variety of preferences of the numerous actors involved (Benz and Goetz 1996: 18).

Finally, the organisation of government at the ministerial level contributes to the reduced scope for executive leadership. Although the chief of government is constitutionally entitled to fix the 'guiding principles of policy' (*Richtlinien der Politik*), this competence is closely circumscribed in practice. Besides the necessities stemming from Parliamentary coalition-building, the *Ressortprinzip* (departmental principle) plays an important role in this context. According to this principle, ministers, albeit bound to the 'guiding principles', are the autonomous hierarchical heads of their departments. Given the strong tendencies towards administrative segmentation favoured by this autonomy, exerting powerful executive leadership is much more difficult for the federal chancellor than for a British prime minister, who can rely upon the principle of ministerial responsibility (Peters 1995: 215). Although administrative segmentation is to some extent counterbalanced by horizontal routines of consultation across ministerial bureaucracies, this co-ordination, more often than not, occurs only in a 'negative' way: this means that ministries strive to have their viewpoints and interests taken into account, hence reinforcing the need for bargaining and accommodation (Lehmbruch 1997).

To conclude, the potential for strong executive leadership is restricted by several institutional factors, namely the structure of the state, aspects of party competition, the *Rechtsstaat* principle, the impact of corporatist arrangements, as well as the internal organisation of government. These factors provide numerous institutional veto points which generally restrict the government's ability to formulate and implement comprehensive political and institutional reforms. These limitations on the governmental reform capacity, however, should not be confused with a restricted capacity to resolve political problems for which the institutional characteristics provide distinctive opportunities based on bargaining and consultation. But whilst these mechanisms might prove to be appropriate to deal with emerging problems, they constitute significant barriers to fundamental institutional reforms.

As will be shown in the following, this general statement is of particular relevance when it comes to *administrative* reform. The scope for political leadership in this case is further reduced by the strong institutional entrenchment of administrative structures and procedures. The capacity for administrative reform is restricted by additional veto points emerging from both constitutional, legal and organisational peculiarities of the German administrative system. Besides these high institutional hurdles for comprehensive administrative changes, its influential position with respect to both policy formulation and implementation allows the German bureaucracy to prevent political reform attempts by absorbing and integrating them into existing structures and procedures.

A rigid backbone: the stability of administrative structures and procedures

In contrast to the Anglo-Saxon model of the 'civic culture' administration, where the emergence of Parliamentary democracy preceded the development of public bureaucracies, the German administration represents a type that is commonly referred to as Continental or 'classical' administration (Heady 1979: 170). An important characteristic of this type is the fact that the identity and stability of statehood are based on the administrative rather than the political system: administrative modernisation preceded political modernisation (König 1996: 23; Olsen and Peters 1996: 17). As revealed in particular by the German development, administrative continuity was an important counterbalance to political instability. Even when political regimes broke down completely, as was the case in 1918 and 1945, public administration never ceased to work more or less regularly (Ellwein 1996: 16; Seibel 1996: 74). As opposed to the arrangements in Britain and the United States, the German administration from the very beginning was 'made to last' (Ellwein 1994: 52). That this attempt was quite successful is demonstrated by the strong institutional entrenchment of administrative structures and procedures, which pose high hurdles for comprehensive reforms.

Institutional stability first emerges from the constitutional status of important administrative characteristics. Constitutional changes require a two-thirds majority in the *Bundestag* and the Federal Chamber, and hence a broad consensus including the government and opposition. Thus, the traditional principles of the professional civil service are embodied in the German Basic Law. They have long been criticised for being no longer appropriate (as, for instance, the distinction between different status groups of workers, employees, and civil servants proper). However, corresponding reform attempts constantly failed as a result of a missing party-political consensus. In a similar way, attempts by the federal government to redraw regional boundaries by merging the city states of Hamburg and Bremen were doomed to fail (Derlien 1996a: 152). On the other hand, as revealed by the privatisation of the railways and telecommunications, the constitutional hurdle for public-sector change is not always insuperable (Lehmkuhl 1996; Schmidt 1996).

Second, administrative stability emerges from the *Rechtsstaat* principle. Administrative principles, procedures and structures are defined by a comprehensive system of public law. Given its systematic character, the public-law system provides a rigid backbone which restricts the opportunities for swift and single-handed institutional reorganisation. The different rules and regulations are systematically linked (e.g., by distinguishing the 'general administrative law' and the 'particular administrative laws' which are built on the former). Hence, only minor adaptations in one area might require corresponding adaptations in other areas, as a result of the tight coupling of the legal system. The institutional conservatism inherent in this constellation is further enhanced by the fact that administrative reform is required to go through formal procedures; a process which encourages participation and open confrontation of conflicting interests (Peters 1995: 221; Benz and Goetz 1996: 16). What is more, the highly developed public-law system associated with the *Rechtsstaat* means a reduced scope for public-sector reforms which aim at deregulation and output-oriented guidance and control. The German model, which emphasises legalism as the basic principle of administrative 'rationality', can hardly be transformed into a model based on managerial and economic efficiency (Klages and Löffler 1996; König 1996, 1997; Lüder 1996).

The third characteristic explaining the strong institutional entrenchment of administrative arrangements is related to the patterns of administrative organisation. In this context, two effects have to be distinguished. On the one hand, institutional inertia is a consequence of a highly differentiated, but at the same time tightly coupled administrative structure at the regional level. As analysed in the previous chapter, regional administration is vertically divided into several tiers which are tightly linked by the principle of hierarchical control. Moreover, the division of labour at the lower level between general authorities and special agencies means also that in a horizontal dimension tight linkages between different administrative branches exist. This way, even minor structural changes might be rather costly, since they require subsequent adaptations within the comprehensive administrative arrangements at the regional level. On the other hand, structural stability can be traced to a rather opposite phenomenon; namely, the fragmentation of administrative responsibilities. Fragmentation implies only a loose coupling between different administrative units and levels, hence significantly increasing the difficulties of introducing administrative reforms 'from above' (Benz and Goetz 1996: 16). Administrative fragmentation is basically a result of the German state structure. The principle of administrative federalism leaves only limited opportunities to the federal level for guiding and controlling the administration of federal programmes at the *Länder* level. The same holds true for activities of the municipalities in the context of local self-administration.

In sum, the conception of the German administration as a durable and stable system provides significant obstacles to comprehensive reform. The strong institutional entrenchment of basic administrative principles creates a rigid backbone which cannot easily be changed. This holds true especially in light of the rather limited scope for political leadership given generally within the German political system and the strong political influence of public administration to which will now turn.

Inevitable power: the political influence of the German bureaucracy

The German administration was not only conceived as a stable and enduring system, but also as a rationalist machinery which is purely instrumental to politics. In this Weberian ideal type conception, a strict division is made between the political and administrative sphere, i.e., between programme formulation and implementation. According to this division, the administration is completely 'programmed' by legal rules, including the programmes to be implemented as well as a whole range of detailed procedural and organisational rules which politically determine administrative activity (Ellwein 1993b: 32). However, this rationalist and instrumental view of public administration, which is constitutionally grounded in the German Basic Law,[2] is actually far from reality. Instead of being strictly separated from politics, the administration is crucially affecting the way it is programmed, since the political and administrative spheres are partly overlapping (Peters 1995: 137; Ellwein 1996: 13). Moreover, as programming is often open or incomplete, administrative actors enjoy considerable influence to further shape the programme during the implementation stage.

Interestingly, and as already predicted by Weber (1972: 1061), the political power of the German bureaucracy emerges as a functional necessity, as the difficulties for completely programming the administration by legal rules increase with the number and complexity of state activities. Under such circumstances, political leaders become more and more dependent on the specialist knowledge provided by their administration. In other words, the autonomy of an instrumentally designed bureaucracy emerges as the inevitable consequence of an ideal-type model incompatible with a complex reality. As we will see later in this chapter, this picture clearly contrasts with the British case. Whereas in Germany, the power of bureaucracy is inherent to the model, and hence absolute, the political influence of its British counterpart is contingent, i.e., defined by the political leaders. This confirms earlier observations, that the political influence of the administration may vary as a consequence of differing legal, administrative and political traditions (Suleiman 1984).

Overlapping spheres: the interlinkage of politicians and bureaucrats
The interaction between administrative and political actors during the process of policy formulation is characterised by two complementary tendencies which both contribute to the stability rather than reformability of the German administration. On the one hand, the emphasis traditionally placed on bureaucratic expertise in policy-making as well as the particular role understanding of top-level ministerial bureaucrats contribute to the bureaucratisation of politics, i.e., political initiatives are significantly affected by bureaucratic suggestions. On the other hand, there is a trend towards politicising the administration, which has increased over the past two decades, implying that bureaucratic expertise is supplemented by a more political role understanding of top-level bureaucrats. The combination of both tendencies allows for the integration of bureaucratic and political 'rationalities' in the overlapping context of the 'political administration'.

The fact that in Germany bureaucracy preceded democracy had a

---

[2] Article 20 of the German Basic Law defines a clear division of power between policy formulation and implementation and binds the executors to the law.

lasting impact on the importance attributed to bureaucratic expertise in policy-making (Derlien 1995: 89). Although the formal decision-making competence lies with the political level, the procedural and specialist knowledge (*Dienstwissen* and *Fachwissen* in Weber's terms) of the civil service is a crucial factor shaping political programmes, especially with respect to more comprehensive or long-term decisions (Ellwein and Hesse 1989: 390; Peters 1995: 229–30). This is further enhanced by the fact that, as opposed to Britain, German civil servants are not regularly changing their positions, and hence are able to accumulate expert knowledge over time; an aspect which is of particular relevance given the generally shorter office terms of ministers. Moreover, the legalist culture emerging from the *Rechtsstaat* principle increases the importance of procedural knowledge in policy-making (Ellwein 1985; van Warden 1995).

This aspect explains not only the dominance of jurists in the German civil service, but also the minor reliance on specialist knowledge provided by external 'think tanks'. Whereas in the United States and Britain specialist 'think tanks' outside the government machinery tend to play an increasingly important role in policy-making, German policy reforms are generally developed in institutionalised, closely knit circles of top-level bureaucrats and scientific advisers formally linked to the government. Rather than being driven by politicians, administrative reforms are defined and prepared by the bureaucrats and their scientific advisers (Lehmbruch 1997; Derlien 1996a: 178). Administrative reform therefore generally means *self-reform* favouring incremental adaptations rather than radical change.

Given the importance of specialist knowledge in policy formulation, the accumulation of expertise in the bureaucracy as well as the limited opportunities to by-pass bureaucratic advice in relying on external sources, the political power of the German bureaucracy significantly reduces the scope for political leadership. The only way to tame bureaucratic power in such a constellation is to strengthen the scope for political leadership by politicising the administration. This occurs basically in two ways. First, administrative positions at the very top of the hierarchy, i.e., state secretaries and division heads in the ministries, are filled with so-called 'political civil servants' who have no life-time tenure, but can be temporarily retired. This mechanism is especially applied to streamline the federal civil service politically after a change of government (Derlien 1988).[3] A second trend is the increasing party-politicisation of the civil

---

[3] From a comparative perspective, the politicisation of the German higher civil service therefore takes a middle position between the British and US systems. While the first can be said to maximise permanency and expertise and takes political loyalty of the

service. Mayntz and Derlien (1989: 397) observe a clear rank correlation with membership in the governing party within the federal bureaucracy, significantly reducing advancement opportunities for non-party members and those with the wrong party book.

The attempts to politicise the bureaucracy contribute to the integration rather than the separation of the political and administrative spheres. This becomes particularly evident when considering the role understanding of German higher civil servants at the federal level, which reflects the hybrid pattern of a fully professionalised and semi-politicised decision-maker (Mayntz and Derlien 1989).

These findings indicate two conclusions: first, expertise as the most distinct role characteristic of the administrative elite has not suffered from politicisation, but was 'enriched' by a more widespread acceptance of the political context in which the bureaucracy operates. Second, this acceptance and the common party-political affiliation of bureaucrats and ruling politicians provides the mechanism for integrating party politicians and civil servants whose most strongly accepted role is still that of the problem-solver, policy initiator and policy executor. The integration of both spheres is further facilitated by the growing professionalisation of politicians, as well as their frequent legal training and civil service background (Derlien et al. 1988: 14; Derlien 1995: 89).

A major consequence of this co-ordination and integration is the interlinking of politics and administration, which in turn significantly reduces the political scope for administrative reforms, since this would at the same time imply the need to 'reform the reformers' (Ellwein 1994: 121). While securing an, albeit limited, scope for executive leadership, this interlinkage at the same time reduces the political capacity for administrative reform.

The autonomy of a 'centrifugal' bureaucracy

The political influence and hence limited reformability of the German administration, however, emerges not only from the distinctive relationship between bureaucrats and political leaders during policy formulation. It also becomes apparent when considering the implementation stage. Contrary to the instrumental model of a legally completely 'programmed' administration, civil servants enjoy considerable flexibility and autonomy when applying, implementing and enforcing political programmes. These processes strengthen the position of the

---

impartial civil service for granted, the US system of having political appointees with high intersectoral mobility is obviously to maximise political loyalty at the expense of expertise (Derlien 1995: 76).

administration towards its political leaders, since they are hardly subject to political or legal guidance (Ellwein 1993a: 59).

On the one hand, administrative flexibility is a functional necessity for the applicability and enforceability of many programmes. Given the number, nature and complexity of many policy issues, complete 'programming' of administrative behaviour by legal rules is, more often than not, neither possible nor practicable. Moreover, the legislative programme might turn out to be rather inappropriate for practical application and has to be made enforceable by the implementing administration; a process during which the initial programme is modified or specified by the administration (Mayntz 1978: 74). As social science research has pointed out, these modifications and specifications often occur in the context of informal contacts and bargaining between administrative authorities and societal interests (Mayntz 1983; Ellwein 1994).[4] This way, the position of the administration may not only be strengthened by its capacity to make federal programmes suitable for implementation, but also by integrating societal interests independent of legal or governmental guidance (Lehmbruch 1987: 35).

This dependence of the political leadership on administrative implementation capacities becomes particularly pronounced in the context of the German state structure. As we have seen in the previous chapter, the federal division of labour between *Bund* and *Länder* as well as the principle of local self-administration imply that decisions on policies and corresponding implementation structures are taken at different levels of the political system. Besides the problems of legally programming administrative activities at the subordinate levels (which is no German peculiarity), the German 'centrifugal' administrative system therefore indicates an even broader scope for administrative autonomy, namely, the decision on appropriate administrative resources, procedures and structures (Ellwein 1993a: 59).

To conclude, in contrast to the constitutional conception of the public administration as instrumental to and separate from politics, the constitutional reality (*Verfassungswirklichkeit*) reveals a rather different picture of overlapping spheres and significant administrative influence on policy-making. As a consequence, the scope and probability for comprehensive administrative changes is further reduced by two factors characterising the German political-administrative system: the interlinking

---

[4] It should be emphasised that this phenomenon is nothing new, but could already be observed during the nineteenth century. As Thomas Ellwein's research shows, administration already at that time engaged in negotiations with industry and was remarkably successful in achieving durable institutional arrangements with respect to the regulation of technological risks emerging from industrial plants (Ellwein 1989).

of political and administrative 'rationalities' during policy formulation and the decentralised implementation in a fragmented system.

Taken together, the limited scope for executive leadership, the strong institutional entrenchment of administrative structures and procedures as well as the political influence of the German administration complete the picture of an *autonomous administration*. Autonomy does not imply that the German administration is completely independent from its political and societal environment. Rather the administration is capable of independently reacting to environmental changes (Luhmann 1972: 154). In other words, the German administration cannot be reformed 'from outside' by deliberate political attempts. Administrative change can only be expected in the form of self-adaptation to environmental challenges. Accordingly, 'administrative reforms are typically initiated by top-level bureaucrats (at least never enforced against them) and then smoothly organised by the rank-and-file professionals' (Seibel 1996: 34).

Bureaucratic autonomy and the correspondingly limited political reform capacity should therefore not be confused with administrative rigidity. But the dominant pattern of self-adaptation suggests that administrative adjustments take place *within* existing traditions and principles (Ellwein 1993a: 58). This has significant implications for the scope for administrative change: adjustments are generally incremental and patchy rather than radical and comprehensive. As Benz and Goetz (1996: 20) point out:

Administrative change in Germany is not inspired by a broad reform design that encompasses different parts of the public sector, extends to different levels and has a reasonably coherent set of reform objectives. Instead, a range of external adaptive pressures have an impact on the public sector and combine with political motivations, bureaucratic politics and a legal-administrative inheritance to produce a highly variegated patchwork of adaptations and permutations.

Administrative reforms in Germany: incremental changes within a static logic

This picture of continuity is confirmed when considering the post-war development of the German administration. Notwithstanding the fact that, at the time they occur, adjustments are often praised as thorough and ground-breaking, administrative change in Germany basically reveals a patchwork of incremental adaptations. In this context, three crucial developments can be distinguished, namely: the technocratic approach to reform the machinery of government from the 1960s onwards, the global wave of public sector reforms since the mid-1980s, as well as the historical event of German unification.

The primary objective of the technocratic approach was to modernise the 'machinery of government' at all levels in order to increase the effectiveness of internal administrative operations, including reforms of the civil service, territorial organisation as well as co-ordination and planning within the ministerial bureaucracy. Notwithstanding numerous adaptations in the light of these varying reform pressures, traditional principles characterising the operation, structure and practice of the German administration remained basically unchanged. Both the civil service reform and the attempts to improve planning and co-ordination within the ministerial bureaucracy (Mayntz and Scharpf 1975) were major failures, notwithstanding numerous adaptations (cf. Derlien 1996b). Also the territorial reforms were only partly implemented. The regions succeeded in putting through a comprehensive reorganisation of local self-government by forming larger units of local government, but the decentralisation of administrative competencies from the regional to the local level – the second objective associated with the reorganisation of local government – turned out to be cumbersome and not altogether successful (Derlien 1996b: 29).

A similar picture of only incremental changes can be observed in the context of the international 'reform wave' from the mid-1980s onwards, which is closely linked to catchwords like deregulation, privatisation and new public management (Wright 1994: 102). In assessing the overall effects, 'it is difficult to avoid the impression, that, compared to the radical transformation in the administrative systems in some other Western industrial countries . . . Germany was a backwater of adminis-trative development' (Benz and Goetz 1996: 9).

Deregulation efforts were restricted to simplifying rather than chang-ing administrative activities and procedures (Seibel 1986; Busse 1996). Attempts to 'roll back the state' through privatisation, contracting-out and competitive tendering remained on a very modest scale with almost no progress at the regional and local level (Benz and Goetz 1996: 5). However, it has to be taken into account that, in contrast to Britain, France or Italy, the public-enterprise sector in Germany was consider-ably smaller. Hence, denationalisation was less likely to form a core element of public-sector change (Ambrosius 1994). With respect to public management reforms, moderate changes have so far been limited to the local level (Banner 1994; Reichard 1994). Notwithstanding the increasing use of the managerial rhetorics, the complex legal framework in which the German administration operates imposes significant re-strictions for the introduction of private-sector management concepts.

As Derlien (1996: 156) concludes, any parallels of the German changes with the large-scale reforms in other (mainly Anglo-Saxon) countries would be superficial and rhetorical.

While the diffusion of these international 'megatrends' triggered no significant departures from well-established administrative structures and practices, many observers anticipated profound changes in the German political and administrative system as a result of the German unification (Lehmbruch 1990). Some administrative scientists talk of the emergence of a 'Third Republic' (Czada 1994) whose institutional arrangements differ decisively from the old Federal Republic. However, as far as the public sector is concerned, stability and continuity seem to have prevailed. Despite numerous constitutional amendments, their overall significance remained very limited. In particular, the federal and regional governments could not agree on decisive changes in intergovernmental relations, despite widespread calls for radical change (Benz 1995). Moreover, the established structures and procedures within the federal and regional bureaucracies seem to have been largely preserved. Instead, the Western models of administrative organisation were exported in the East through the establishment of West–East 'partnership agreements', hence restricting the scope for institutional innovation in the new *Länder*. The same picture holds true in principle for the local level, although certain adaptations to specific circumstances given in the Eastern regions took place (Eisen 1993; Derlien 1996a: 160; Benz and Goetz 1996: 12).

To conclude, this short review of the developments in the German public sector indicates a picture of high continuity. On the one hand, continuity relates to the ongoing process of administrative adaptation, which intensified in the context of international reform trends and German unification. However, none of these changes, not even the successful territorial reform of local government, can be characterised as fundamental or comprehensive, but remained within the scope of existing administrative traditions. Hence, administrative continuity refers not only to the pattern of ongoing adaptation, but also to the persistence of long-established structures and procedures.

Stability is basically the result of the rather autonomous position of the bureaucracy within the German political system, implying that administrative change in general takes the form of an ongoing self-adaptation rather than reflecting a deliberately designed political reform. Administrative autonomy is favoured by the generally limited scope for executive leadership within the fragmented German polity, highly institutionalised patterns of administrative procedures and organisation, as well as the influential role played by the bureaucracy in policy-making. As a consequence, administrative development hardly implies departures from well-established core principles; the structural potential for administrative core changes is very low.

5.2   Britain: dynamic transformations of an instrumental bureaucracy

Compared to Germany, the term 'administrative reform' in Britain, especially in recent years, implied more than pure rhetoric, but had fundamental factual consequences. Large-scale changes and developments in British public administration are nothing impossible, as revealed by the far-reaching public sector reforms initiated by Conservative governments from 1979 onwards. To be sure, high capacity for administrative reform does not necessarily imply that British politicians always achieved their objectives associated with administrative change and that such changes have always been the order of the day. However, in contrast to Germany, there is a significant *potential* to transform administrative structures and practices, assuming that there is a government committed to do so. This potential for administrative reform is basically a consequence of the strong position of executive leaders within the British political system, the malleability of administrative structures and procedures, as well as the contingent rather than absolute influence of British bureaucrats in policy-making.

Executive leadership in an integrated system

In contrast to Germany, the British political system facilitates strong executive leadership. Given the concentration and centralisation of political power, which is typical for the Westminster model, British governments are to a lesser extent confronted with institutional veto points when advocating their policy proposals. The potential for more radical and comprehensive policy innovations is much higher than in the context of the German *Verhandlungsdemokratie*.

The most important factor which contributes to strong and integrated executive leadership is related to the constitutional principle of Parliamentary supremacy. Since the British Parliament is the sole representative of political power, it is the only formal institutional veto point which may potentially restrict the scope for executive leadership. Apart from the democratic control and legitimisation of the executive by the Parliament, there are no further constitutional and institutional constraints for governmental activities (Burch and Holliday 1996: 10).

In view of the role of Parliament as the sole authority to adopt or avoid laws,[5] and the missing written constitution, Britain knows no judicial reviews subjecting the laws passed by the legislature to scrutiny as to their constitutionality. Constitutional law is composed of statutes and conventions which have no different status from other laws. This means that they can be modified by a simple Parliamentary majority (Peele 1993). Whereas in Germany Parliamentary legislation is subject to judicial review by the *Bundesverfassungsgericht*, in Britain the Parliament is regarded as the highest court in the land (Jennings 1966; Johnson 1977; Campbell and Wilson 1995: 7); a function which is formally fulfilled by the House of Lords. Hence, the opportunities to block governmental activities through the courts are rather slim in Britain.

A second consequence following from Parliamentary sovereignty is the centralisation of political power within a unitary state structure. In contrast to the federal separation of powers in Germany, there is no territorial assembly in Britain which enjoys a coequal status to that of the Westminster Parliament (Dunleavy 1993: 3). Although there exist elected representations at the local level (district and county councils) and, since 1997, at the level of the regions of Scotland and Wales, these representations are constitutionally subordinate to the Westminster Parliament. Their existence, powers and competencies depend directly on statutory enablement by Westminster (Allum 1995: 423). Since Britain knows no constitutionally entrenched guarantee of local self-government or regional autonomy, local authorities and regions can at any time have their powers rescinded by a simple Parliamentary statute. Furthermore, there is no second chamber comparable to the German *Bundesrat* which may serve as a channel for the regions and the local authorities to advocate their interests in the policy-making process, as the legislatory competencies of the second chamber, the House of Lords, are fairly restricted. Given its membership based on hereditary and life peers and its high reputation, the political influence of the House of Lords basically emerges from its role as policy adviser (Knill 1995: 298). Against this background, the scope for executive leadership is less dependent on intergovernmental bargaining between different autonomous levels of government, than on the extent to which the government is backed by a Parliamentary majority.

In the absence of any other formal limits on governmental activity (as they are provided by the *Rechtsstaat* and the federal separation of powers

---

[5] The supremacy of Parliament is, however, to some extent restricted by the effects of Britain's EU membership. Many European rules have direct effect and become British law independent of their transposition by the national Parliament (Peele 1993: 26; Knill 1995: 311).

in the German case), party competition is the single mechanism for the legitimisation and control of executive leadership (Campbell and Wilson 1995: 7). The scope for executive leadership therefore depends almost exclusively on the extent to which a government can rely on the support of its Parliamentary majority. The existence of strong majorities is, on the other hand, facilitated by the electoral system which is based on the relative majority principle. This favours the emergence of stable and powerful one-party governments. In view of the close linkages between the Parliamentary majority and the government, the sovereignty of the Parliament has become the synonym for the sovereignty of executive leadership in Britain (Sturm 1995: 192):

Britain has 'the fastest law in the West', with the fewest formal or codified restrictions on government action of any liberal democracy. Governments with secure Commons majorities can short-circuit or ignore public consultation, guillotine parliamentary debate, over-rule unfavourable judicial rulings by retrospective legislation, and even bulldoze through patently unimplementable policies for a time, as happened with the poll tax. (Dunleavy 1993: 5)

The strength of executive leadership in Britain is not only facilitated by the concentration and centralisation of political power at the level of central government, but also by patterns of the governmental organisation, namely the British doctrine of collective responsibility. The emphasis on collective decision-making rather than departmental autonomy reflects not only the constitutional requirement that the government stand united in Parliament. It also reflects the belief that the work of government can be carried out effectively only if it remains united and well co-ordinated (Campbell and Wilson 1995: 12).[6] Given the dominant role of the prime minister as *primus inter pares*, the capacity for strong executive leadership is great, especially in cases where effective political leaders such as Churchill or Thatcher actually have 'presidentialised' the office (Peters 1995: 215).

Although there is a long tradition in Britain to involve societal associations in the formulation and implementation of policy programmes, this aspect does not significantly reduce the scope for executive leadership, as is the case with the corporatist arrangements in Germany. This difference can be explained by two factors. First, the structure of British interest groups is essentially pluralist. In contrast to the more coherent organisational structures in Germany with the major sectoral interest groups united in a national peak association, interest group organisation in Britain is generally more fragmented (Holliday

[6] Although the doctrine of collective responsibility has sometimes been violated in practice, it is an important operational code of governmental activity in Britain (Burch and Holliday 1996: 11).

1993: 309). Given the missing capacity of the weak peak associations to bind their members to certain collective agreements, corporatist arrangements are highly unstable (cf. Hall 1986: 254). This way, there exists no solid institutional basis for the incorporation of societal interest groups into the policy-making process. Second, there hardly exist any institutionalised linkages between interest associations and political parties (notwithstanding the particular interlinkages between the Labour Party and the trade unions) (Schmid 1993: 184). Hence, the opportunities of interest groups to influence political decisions by making use of party political channels are restricted.

As opposed to Germany, where interest associations can affect political decisions by a number of channels and arenas, the political influence of British associations is basically dependent on the extent to which they are able to rely on informal contacts to the political-administrative system (Knill 1995: 312). This implies, at the same time, that their opportunities for access are dependent on the motivation of the political leaders. Notwithstanding the general preference for bargaining and consultation (as pointed out by Jordan and Richardson 1982), the British government appears to have considerable discretion in deciding not only which groups are included and excluded, but also in defining issues which exclude any substantial group involvement or negotiation (Jordan 1981: 121; Page 1992: 118). This picture is in clear contrast to Germany, where the idea of non-negotiable policies has been less apparent. As became apparent in particular with the Conservative Thatcher government from 1979 onwards, the initiative for changes in political styles (from consensual to adversarial) rests with the government far more clearly than in Germany (Dyson 1982: 45). Interest group pluralism has not prevented a strong government putting through its reform proposals against far-reaching societal and political opposition.

To summarise, as a result of the centralisation and concentration of political power at the level of central government, the potential for strong executive leadership is very high in Britain. The powerful role of the executive is to be understood in the light of the particular institutional factors, including the unitary state structure, Parliamentary supremacy, the role of party competition, the internal organisation of government as well as the pluralist rather than corporatist patterns of interest intermediation. Given the low number of institutional veto points the executive is confronted with when advocating its policy proposals, the potential for comprehensive and encompassing reforms is considerable, assuming a corresponding motivation of political leaders. As will be shown in the following sections, this general statement also holds true for the particular case of administrative reform.

A missing backbone: the malleability of administrative structures and procedures

The political and administrative development in Britain and Germany reveals inverse patterns. In contrast to Germany (and France), the political development in Britain was characterised by stability and continuity from the seventeenth century onwards. Political modernisation and the establishment of a stable democratic system preceded administrative modernisation. The identity and stability of statehood were based on the political system rather than a rational and comprehensive administration, as was the case on the Continent. Consequently, public administration took shape feature by feature in a way that reflected the political development and was consonant with the latter (Heady 1979: 198–9). The bureaucracy must be prepared to fit into its proper niche in the political system. Major political innovations or transformations are not likely to have a bureaucratic source. According to the instrumental rather than autonomous design of the British bureaucracy, the institutional entrenchment of administrative structures and procedures is comparatively low, broadening the scope for 'politically designed' administrative reforms.

The first reason explaining the lower institutional entrenchment of administrative arrangements in Britain emerges from the supremacy of Parliament and the lack of a written constitution. As explained above, this implies that any administrative changes requiring Parliamentary legislation can be achieved by a simple majority. Hence, there are no particular institutional hurdles preventing public-sector reforms, as, for instance, the two-thirds majority requirement for changes of the German constitution (Kingdom 1989: 12).

A second factor, which could potentially contribute to an increased institutional stability of administrative arrangements, is the existence of a comprehensive system of legal rules guiding the organisation and operation of public administration. However, given the British legal system, which developed no particular body of administrative law for the guidance and control of administrative activities, such a dense and tightly coupled framework of rules and procedures is lacking. This holds true not only for the regulation of the internal organisation and working conditions of the civil service, but also for the general rules guiding administrative activity.

Whereas in Germany the internal structure as well as the particular rights and obligations of the *Berufsbeamtentum* are defined in a particular body of administrative and constitutional law, such a framework of civil-service law is missing in Britain. Although the particular characteristics of the civil service (such as lifetime tenure, a merit system, neutrality and loyalty) are the same in both countries, these principles are not legally defined in Britain. Apart from certain guidelines issued by the Treasury and the Civil Service Commission, the civil service law is basically defined by informal, continuously changing internal circulars. This way, government has considerable flexibility to adapt these conditions when advancing administrative reforms. A further factor contributing to this flexibility lies in the fact that there is a great variety in the arrangements across the civil and public service. Since there is no unique and overall pattern across the whole scope of public administration, single adaptations are even easier to achieve (Johnson 1994: 196–7).

Moreover, the lack of detailed and tightly coupled rules guiding administrative practice and procedures significantly reduces the institutional costs of administrative change. Whereas in Germany legal changes in only one area of administrative law may require widespread adjustments in other areas as a result of the comprehensiveness of the legal system, the legal system in Britain allows for more flexibility. Given the lower level of legal specification, administrative reform attempts require less comprehensive and encompassing efforts.

However, the lack of a rigid institutional backbone to the British administration is not only the result of a missing constitutional and legal entrenchment of administrative structures and procedures. It is also a consequence of the particular patterns of administrative structure and organisation. In the German case, we have identified two organisational patterns which contributed to the stability of administrative structures, namely the existence of a highly differentiated but tightly coupled administrative structure at the regional level as well as the absence of coupling between the administrative structures at the federal and regional levels. Neither of these characteristics is present in the case of Britain, hence reducing the institutional stability of administrative arrangements.

As explained in the previous chapter, the organisation of public administration evolved on an *ad hoc* basis and only to a limited extent reflects a comprehensive and systematic structure. Despite highly differentiated and complex administrative structures, we find tight linkages between different administrative units neither at the central nor at the local levels (Page 1992: 57; Gray and Jenkins 1985: 92–3). In the absence of structural comprehensiveness, administrative reorganisation at both the central and local levels to a lesser extent requires subsequent adjustments affecting large parts of the administrative system as would be the case in Germany.

A further contrast to the German arrangements lies in the fact that, notwithstanding the traditional separation between central and local government, the administrative autonomy of the British local authorities is not entrenched by the constitutional guarantee of administrative competencies. In view of the constitutional inferiority of local government, local administrative structures can easily be changed by the central government. Although the local authorities enjoy considerable freedom with respect to their activities and internal organisation, this freedom is contingent upon the decision of central government.

The limited constitutional, legal and structural entrenchment reflects the conception of the British administration as a flexible system which is subordinate and instrumental to political requirements and priorities. Contrary to the German administration whose stability emerges from a rigid institutional backbone, comprehensive administrative innovations are less difficult in the British context, given the missing institutional backbone as a factor of administrative stability. Hence, the combination of strong executive leadership and the lacking institutional entrenchment of administrative structures and procedures suggests that the capacity for administrative reform is rather high in the case of Britain. This impression is further confirmed when considering the bureaucracy's position in the policy-making process.

Contingent power: the political influence of the British bureaucracy

At first glance, one would hardly find any major differences with respect to the political influence of German and British bureaucracies. As with the German ministerial bureaucracy, the British civil service is well known for its rather political role. Moreover, as a result of the limited role of detailed legal rules, the British administration enjoys considerable autonomy during the stage of implementation. From this perspective, the British administration seems to be even more politically influential than its German counterpart.

However, the picture looks quite different, if we consider the sources of administrative influence in each country, i.e., the institutional foundation of bureaucratic power. As we have seen in the German case, bureaucratic power emerges as inevitable consequence. It is a functional necessity to bridge the gap between a system designed as purely instrumental and the challenges of increasing complexity. In Britain, on the other hand, instrumentality and bureaucratic power were never seen as exclusive. Rather the instrumental character of public administration refers to the fact that the degree of bureaucratic influence is actually defined by the political leaders. Hence, instrumentality refers to the contingency of administrative influence in Britain, whereas the autonomy of the German administration means that bureaucratic power is functionally necessary and therefore politically unavoidable. To elaborate on the specific factors defining the position of the British administration, we have to consider more precisely its role in policy formulation and implementation.

Separate spheres: the crucial difference between politics and bureaucracy

The fact that the political influence of the British bureaucracy during the process of policy formulation is contingent rather than absolute depends on one crucial characteristic that distinguishes the British from the German bureaucracy: the clear separation between politics and administration (Heady 1979: 204; Campbell and Wilson 1995: 14). In contrast to the German constellation of overlapping spheres, the main characteristic of the British system are the caste-like differences between politicians and officials (Bulmer 1988: 47). It is exactly this remaining distance between both spheres that provides political leaders with sufficient independence to define the political weight of the civil service.

At first glance, this separation is not at all obvious. Although the core element of the Whitehall model is the reliance of elected politicians on a non-partisan, permanent civil service, whose neutrality and legitimacy are based on its relative preparedness to act on behalf of any duly elected government (Campbell and Wyszomirski 1991: 15; Christoph 1993: 523),[7] it would be quite wrong, however, to think that civil servants are separated from politics. The Whitehall model demands not that civil servants be non-political but that they be politically promiscuous (Rose 1987). In fact, many of the classical activities of the civil service are essentially political in the context of the British system, implying a high political responsiveness of civil servants (Heady 1979: 209; Hennessy 1989):

British governments are institutionally free to do what they wish. External economic pressures may block a government's programme, but the courts and the legislature are unlikely to. Ministers in consequence have no institutional hiding-place from policy problems in their areas. . . . British ministers face a constant political imperative and the help they need is essentially political in character. . . . The higher civil service in Britain has therefore worked in a situation where the need for highly technical ability has been low and the

---

[7] This expectation can produce rather strange situations: 'The same civil servant who helped a Conservative minister draft replies to parliamentary questions or speeches refuting the criticisms of the Labour Shadow Minister may find after an election that the Shadow Minister is now the minister for whom the civil servant drafts responses to the criticisms of the Conservative opposition' (Campbell and Wilson 1995: 17).

demand for politically attuned advice high and frequent. (Campbell and Wilson 1995: 28–9)

One could therefore conclude that the political influence of the civil service is even higher than that of the German ministerial bureaucracy. British civil servants, with their complete political independence, are better able to 'speak truth to power' than eager-to-please political appointees with less job security. From this perspective, British civil servants potentially constitute an even more independent source of political influence than their partly politicised German counterparts. The picture is reinforced by what Heclo and Wildavsky (1974) called 'village life in civil service society', referring to the goldfish-bowl-like world in which officials work in close co-operation with ministers, insulated from public scrutiny.[8]

The fact that a politically powerful civil service was always an important characteristic of the British political-administrative system does not automatically imply, however, that the degree of this influence was absolute. Thus, especially the Conservative governments under Thatcher and Major demonstrated that the political influence is nothing to be taken for granted, but is contingent upon the preferences of political leaders.

While previous political leaders almost exclusively relied on the political advice provided by the civil service, in crucial areas this factual advisory monopoly has been broken from 1979 onwards. 'British ministers have become used to the idea that, although civil servants can produce good ideas, there is no reason to listen *only* to civil servants' (Campbell and Wilson 1995: 294). On the one hand, this move away from dependence on bureaucratic advice becomes evident by the emergence of 'think tanks' as a permanent part of the British political scene. Although 'think tanks' have a long tradition in Britain, their influence has significantly grown from the 1980s onwards (Stone 1996: 677–8).[9]

A further instrument which reduced the influence of bureaucratic advice can be seen in the creation of a politicised counter-bureaucracy, including a small group of external advisers in foreign and economic policy as well as the Policy Unit. The latter serve not only as an antidote to advice from government departments, but also to reach over the heads of ministers to intervene in the details of departmental policy

---

[8] The 1980s BBC TV satire on Whitehall *Yes, Minister* developed humorously suspicions of the political power of the civil service.

[9] Most important in this context were the so-called 'New Right think tanks', including the Centre for Policy Studies, the Institute for Economic Affairs and the Adam Smith Institute (Stone 1996: 678).

formulation (Campbell and Wilson 1995: 295).[10] Although bureaucrats still play an important part in policy-making, this part has been reduced in order to make room for politically sponsored policy entrepreneurs and analysts. Accordingly, the role of the civil service has tended to shift from advising the minister to implementing ministers' wishes, no matter how poorly considered they were (ibid.: 65).

The main reason for the government's ability to independently modify the political role of the civil service lies in the fact that – despite the, until recently, close co-operation between ministers and civil servants – both professions remained within separate careers and role understandings. There never existed any interlinkage between the two spheres of politics and administration, as is the case in Germany. This distance allows the politicians to decide to what extent they intend to rely on the neutral and loyal advice offered by their civil service.

The maintenance of a completely separated system is facilitated by several factors which are not given in the German case, namely the civil servants' generalist rather than specialist background, the high internal mobility of the civil service as well as the minor importance of procedural and technocratic knowledge in policy-making. These factors indicate that the advice that can be both required from and provided by the civil service can be more easily substituted by other sources, given its more political and general character. Hence, British politicians are to a lesser extent dependent on their bureaucracy than German ministers. There is a lower potential for the bureaucratisation of politics and therefore a lower requirement to counterbalance this trend by politicising the bureaucracy. Thus, as opposed to Germany, the growing professionalisation of politicians contributed to an increasing distance rather than convergence of both spheres. Career politicians are eager to associate themselves with initiatives for radical change, and hence rely to a lesser extent on the 'institutionalised scepticism' (ibid.: 297) of their civil servants.

The fact that British politicians are able to define the extent of bureaucratic influence in policy-making suggests that they are much more able to initiate and implement large-scale administrative reforms despite bureaucratic resistance. This clearly contrasts with the German case, where the close interlinkages between bureaucracy and politics almost excludes the politically designed reform of public administration.

---

[10] The Policy Unit was already established under the Wilson government, but further developed under Thatcher. Although the Unit is composed of a mixture of civil servants and outsiders, past experience shows that the civil servants became too politicised and were not always able to return easily to their former occupations (Campbell and Wilson 1995: 54).

The long shadow of the centre

The political power of the British bureaucracy depends on the preferences of its political leaders not only during the process of policy formulation, but also when it comes to the implementation of these policies. Again, this might be surprising, given the absence of detailed legal guidance (which is typical for the British legal tradition) and the considerable autonomy both central and local implementation authorities are generally assumed to have with respect to their day-to-day activities. But again it has to be emphasised that this autonomy is contingent rather than absolute.

This is to be explained against the background that, as opposed to the federal division of labour in Germany, the overall responsibility for policy formulation and implementation lies with the central government. Hence, all administrative units involved in policy implementation, either at the national or local level, act as agents of central government. There is no constitutional guarantee with respect to administrative structures and the allocation of administrative competencies between different authorities and levels of government (Rhodes 1991: 85).

Notwithstanding the far-reaching leeway implementation authorities might enjoy in the absence of detailed legal guidance and control, this autonomy has to be seen in the context of the government's potential to easily intervene into existing structures and arrangements. Hence, assuming corresponding preferences of political leaders, subsequent authorities have limited opportunities to influence administrative reform programmes during their implementation.

In conclusion, the analysis of the institutional factors affecting the national capacity for administrative reform reveals a comparatively high potential for more radical and comprehensive innovations. The macro-institutional context of the legal, political, and administrative system provides the basis for a far more dynamic development of administrative structures and procedures than is the case in Germany. Taken together, these factors contribute to the picture of an *instrumental bureaucracy* in the sense that its structural, procedural and political autonomy is defined by the political sphere. In contrast to the German case, the power and stability of the administration are therefore contingent, not absolute. Given the much higher potential for British politicians to advocate and implement administrative change, reforms can be expected to be rather dynamic and comprehensive. In contrast to Germany, change must not necessarily remain within the core of administrative traditions, but may imply changes of this core.

Administrative reform in Britain: innovation within a dynamic logic

In comparing the changes in the British public sector during the last three decades with corresponding developments in Germany, the above statement is confirmed. Although the scope and mode of administrative changes developed along similar lines during the 1970s, from the 1980s onwards we observe an increasing gap between dynamic processes in Britain and the ongoing process of incremental self-adaptation in Germany. Given the high structural potential for administrative reform in Britain, the neo-liberal programme of a 'strong, directive, and above all, persistent executive leadership' (Rhodes 1996: 4) of the Conservative government led to radical public-sector reforms. These reforms were not restricted to changes within the core of administrative traditions, but crucially affected these traditions. This clearly contrasts with the German case, where despite similar political conditions (a persistent conservative government), the patterns of administrative development remained unchanged.

Before the Conservative takeover in 1979, the scope and mode of administrative change were similar to the German development. Major reform attempts concentrated on modernising the 'machinery of government' and, as in Germany, the impact of these attempts was modest. Changes remained within the core of well-established administrative traditions. The most important changes occurred at the level of local government, where – for similar reasons as in Germany – administrative structures were rationalised by the 1972 Local Government Act (Greenwood and Wilson 1989: 143). The 1968 Fulton Report contained several proposals to rationalise the activities of central government. It favoured a more technocratic approach, the implementation of new management techniques, as well as the creation of specialised sub-departmental implementation agencies. However, subsequent governments only partly implemented the proposals (for instance, by creating a civil service college and establishing a particular civil service department charged with the improvement of managerial techniques throughout the service) and the success of these attempts was rather limited (Gray and Jenkins 1985: 44–6; Kingdom 1989: 29; Butler 1993: 396–7; Campbell and Wilson 1995: 43–5).

As in Germany, administrative change therefore was incremental rather than fundamental. Given the limited commitment of the then political leaders to make use of their capacity to put through administrative reforms, the civil service was capable of resisting most of the reform initiatives (Kingdom 1989: 23). This general picture changed significantly, however, with the takeover of the Thatcher government in

1979. To improve efficiency and effectiveness of the public sector, policies concentrated on three issues: namely, privatisation, management reforms and administrative reorganisation; with all of these elements putting potential challenges to existing administrative traditions.[11]

Among the most important changes that took place in the British public sector are those related to public enterprises. An initially tentative and low-key programme of privatisation beginning in the late 1970s developed into a massive transfer of public utilities into the private sector, including, for instance, telecommunications, British Airways, the energy, gas, and water suppliers as well as the railways (Kay, Mayer and Thompson 1989; Gamble 1988; Foster 1992; Knill 2001). Along with privatisation went the growth of a new 'light rein' style of utilities regulation by separate agencies operating completely independent of governmental control (Massey 1992; Hood 1996: 37).

Besides privatisation, far-reaching changes in the management and the structure of the public service took place (Hood 1991: 5; Pollitt 1993). Referring to public-sector management and operation, policies were first directed at the introduction of private-sector management concepts in the public sector, emphasising explicit standards, measures of performance and managing by results. Besides the introduction of departmental efficiency scrutinies, the Financial Management Initiative identified departmental aims, costs and performance indicators and divided the departments into 'cost centres'. Moreover, performance-related pay schemes in the civil service were introduced from 1985 onwards (Hood 1996: 41). In addition to the introduction of private-sector management, managerial reforms stressed the establishment of market competition and the improvement of public services not suitable to market mechanisms. Corresponding activities started already in 1980 with the statutory compulsion for local authorities to put areas of service provision out to competitive tender rather than retaining in-house provision.[12] In 1991, civil service work was opened up to outside contractors, requiring government departments to identify 30 per cent of their business that could be subcontracted. To improve the quality of

---

[11] It is not the intention of this section to document the nature of British public-service changes over that period in fine detail, since most of them have been described and commented on elsewhere (Hood 1995; Metcalfe and Richards 1987; Pollitt 1993, 1996; Stewart and Walsh 1992). Rather my concern here is to elaborate on the impact of these reforms on well-established administrative traditions. Accordingly, the content of the main changes involved is given only a relative compressed and allusive treatment.

[12] The areas for compulsory competitive tendering were steadily extended and included not only virtually all blue-collar work, but also large parts of white-collar professional work (Hood 1996: 38–9).

those public services not suitable for market testing or contracting-out, the 1991 Citizen's Charter introduced a 'consumerist' programme aiming for transparent service standards, full and accurate information about running services as well as methods of complaint and redress (Campbell and Wilson 1995: 243; Knill 1995; Rhodes 1996; Hood 1996).

However, the changes associated with NPM were not only restricted to public-sector management and operation, but also affected administrative structures. Important changes were introduced with the Next Steps initiative. It implied the creation of semi-autonomous agencies responsible for operational management, separating these management functions from policy-making functions which remained the responsibility of the relevant departments. The objectives and performance targets of these separately managed units are defined in contract-like framework documents agreed with ministers. The agencies, which by April 1995 were already employing 67 per cent of the civil service, cover a diverse group of organisations, including welfare services, public services, regulatory, production and leisure agencies (Ridley 1995; Rhodes 1996: 8; Flynn 1996: 51).

At the local level, the existing system of uniform and inclusive local authorities was steadily changed by processes of restructuring (including the abolition of the Greater London Council and the English metropolitan councils in 1986); the introduction of institutional routes for state schools and housing estates to 'opt out' from local authority control; the limitation of local authority powers to decide spending and taxing levels (culminating in the disaster of the 'poll tax'); as well as the steadily extended areas for compulsory competitive tendering (see above).

Given the structurally high capacity for administrative reform in Britain and the emergence of executive leaders who were strongly committed to administrative change, the developments in the British public sector imply important changes in administrative core characteristics. In contrast to Germany, where administrative adaptation follows a static logic, the British reforms reflect a more dynamic pattern. Administrative change remained not within the existing logic, but implied important modifications in what previously had been considered as core characteristics of administrative styles and structures.

Thus, the tradition of 'informal bargaining' tends to be replaced by patterns of 'transparent regulation' (Knill 1995: 314; Jordan 1997). As a result of the establishment of performance-oriented regimes and the creation of independent and semi-autonomous regulatory agencies, we saw a shift towards more formal, legalistic and open patterns of administrative interest intermediation. These shifts in regulatory style can also be associated with changes in intra-administrative relations. The relation between the new agencies and their sponsoring department is defined in formal contract-like documents. Moreover, the establishment of independent agencies implies a formalisation of intra-administrative co-ordination, which, in turn, may reduce the leeway for informal interaction between administrative and private actors, at least in cases where the latter are now regulated by different (e.g., economic and environmental) agencies (Weale 1996a; Rhodes 1996).

Moreover, the emphasis placed on output and performance favours the emergence of more substantive rather than purely procedural patterns of administrative intervention, hence reducing the scope for administrative discretion during policy implementation (Baggott 1989; Stewart and Walsh 1992: 507). This is further enhanced by the value attributed to a managerial and specialist perspective in the running of the agencies, which contrasts with the tradition of generalism, amateurism and pragmatism that had dominated policy implementation previously (Campbell and Wilson 1995: 299; Ridley 1995).

Finally, both privatisation and agencification have far-reaching structural implications, leading to a 'trimmed down' but increasingly fragmented public sector. Whereas only policy formulation and co-ordination remain within the core of the strongly reduced political-administrative system, policy implementation and the provision of public services are contracted-out to a broad range of executive agencies and private organisations (Rhodes 1996).

Many commentators emphasise that the reforms in Britain should not be exaggerated. Thus, we can still observe many patterns reflecting traditional patterns of administrative styles and structures. For instance, informal bargaining between societal and administrative actors is still an important factor that characterises administrative interest intermediation (Knill 1995). Moreover, the tendency towards opening-up government has not affected the traditional secrecy of governmental processes itself, particularly with regard to political decision-making. Transparency is restricted to 'low politics', i.e., to areas where it serves the public-choice perspective of 'consumerism' (Tant 1990). In addition, it is still open to question to what extent the creation of semi-autonomous agencies reduces the scope for the traditional politics of central (departmental) control (Jenkins 1993: 95; Massey 1995: 12–13).

However, even when accepting the view that administrative change in Britain reflects no complete departure from past traditions, the reforms significantly altered the context in which British administration operates. Notwithstanding the question whether the reforms will work as they were intended or not, the scope of the changes has crucially modified the basis for administrative activity in Britain. Thus, agency creation, contracting-out and privatisation are linked to institutional change and the creation of new institutions and, as such, 'they changed the structure of the Whitehall game' (Campbell and Wilson 1995: 301).

In conclusion, the review of recent developments in the public sector reveals the high structural potential to reform administrative structures and practices given in Britain. This is to be understood against the background of the powerful position of central government within an integrated system, the low institutional entrenchment of administrative structures and procedures, as well as the contingent rather than absolute influence of the bureaucracy in the policy-making process. In view of these conditions, the position of the administration within the British political system is instrumental rather than autonomous. There are hardly any constraints that sufficiently committed political leaders face in order to put through potential reform initiatives. There is a higher capacity for dynamic changes of national administrative traditions.

In this context, high capacity for national reforms should not be confused with a high frequency of such reforms. Also in Britain, far-reaching administrative changes are the exception rather than the rule. Given the high costs and conflicts involved when promoting fundamental institutional changes, the actual occurrence of such developments requires not only strong governmental commitment, but also enduring efforts to realise political objectives, as was the case during seventeen years of Conservative government. It is against this backdrop that we can understand that both Olson (1982) and Dunleavy (1993) emphasise the stasis and sclerosis characterising the British institutions before the Conservative takeover in 1979.

III

Domestic change and persistence: the implementation of EU environmental policy

Having elaborated on characteristics and dynamics of administrative traditions in Germany and Britain, it is the objective of this part to assess and illustrate the validity of our analytical assumptions on the change and persistence of national administrative styles and structures. To do so, the focus is on the implementation of EU environmental policy. For analytical purposes, five pieces of European legislation are considered which reflect the broad regulatory variety to be found in the environmental field and therefore cover a broad range of different administrative implications. Moreover, the five policies are selected in such a way, that their institutional adaptation requirements are 'symmetrically' distributed between the two countries under study.

6   The administrative implications of EU environmental policy

The selection of EU environmental policy as an empirical case is of particular analytical advantage for the purpose of this study. On the one hand, environmental policy reflects an area where supranational policy competencies are broadly developed; there exists a comprehensive framework of European regulations confronting the member states with considerable requirements for administrative adjustment. On the other hand, comprehensiveness coincides with regulatory variety. EU environmental policy reflects no single coherent and consistent regulatory concept and approach, but reveals a regulatory patchwork of different instruments, principles and strategies. This allows for the selection of varying cases which are characterised by differing requirements with respect to administrative styles and structures.

6.1   The nature of EU environmental policy

The basic aspects characterising EU environmental policy, namely its comprehensive development as well as its considerable regulatory variety can only be understood in the light of the particular factors which shape the decision-making context at the supranational level.

Comprehensiveness and regulatory variety

From the institutional and legal perspectives, EU environmental policy differs from other policy fields such as trade, agriculture or transport primarily in that it is not explicitly mentioned in the 1957 Treaty of Rome that established the Community. This was certainly due to the lack of awareness of the issue at the time, likely to have been particularly extreme in the case of a community like the EU designed primarily to promote economic co-operation (Johnson and Corcelle 1989: 1). Despite these institutional and legal limitations, however, EU environmental policy gradually developed into a policy area in its own right, rather than constituting a mere appendix to economic integration.

The starting point for this development can be seen in the establishment of an environmental task force group within the Commission in 1972, which was later to develop into the Directorate General XI Environmental and Consumer Protection and Nuclear Safety, and the subsequent adoption of the Community's first action programme on the environment. The environmental action programmes of the EU specify the focal areas of EU legislation for the coming years and determine the fresh strategic directions in environmental policy, and hence constitute a policy framework to be filled in by appropriate directives. Following the basic objectives and strategies developed in subsequent action programmes,[1] a fairly comprehensive and complex framework of European environmental regulation emerged. The last 10–15 years especially have witnessed a widening and deepening of supranational competencies and activities in the environmental field (Rehbinder and Stewart 1985; Bongaerts 1989; Knill 1997a).

The emergence and increasing importance of EU environmental policy was both accompanied and motivated by corresponding legal and institutional changes. Given the initial absence of a legal basis, environmental policy had to be based on the general clauses of articles 100 and 235 of the Treaty which allow for Community action for the purpose of harmonising legal and administrative provisions with a view to completing the Common Market. In other words, environmental policy had to be legitimated in terms of economic integration. The importance of environmental policy relative to other Community fields of action, concerned primarily with economic integration, increased markedly during the 1980s. This development has become particularly apparent in recent institutional innovations at the European level: the 1986 Single European Act (SEA) and the 1992 Maastricht Treaty. Within the framework of the SEA, environmental policy was for the first time explicitly embodied in the EU Treaties. The significance of the SEA is that it recognises the need not only to link the goals of free trade with a 'high level' of environmental protection, but also to pursue environmental objectives as a legitimate goal in itself. The enhanced standing of environmental policy is especially evident in the changes the Maastricht and Amsterdam Treaties introduced in Council decision-making procedures. In contrast to the former principle of unanimity required for the adoption of environmental policies, Council voting is now by qualified majority[2] (Haigh 1996; Knill and Héritier 1996).

---

[1] The latest development in this area, the Community's fifth environmental action programme was adopted in 1992.

[2] However, the unanimity requirement is retained for important areas, in particular tax matters, regional planning, land use (with the exception of waste management), as well

Notwithstanding the development into a comprehensively regulated policy area, EU environmental policy is not characterised by a single coherent and consistent approach, but by a broad variety of concepts and instruments. The patchwork character of EU environmental policy can be illustrated with respect to several dimensions.[3] First, there is a variance in regulatory principles, including both reactive and preventative approaches to environmental protection. Second, the regulatory concepts applied at the European level reach from single-media approaches (focusing on the emissions into or the quality of either air, water or soil) and cross-media approaches (viewing environmental protection from an integrated perspective). Third, we find a multitude of regulatory instruments, including (1) numerical standards concerning the state of the environment (quality standards), the maximum emission of pollutants at point sources (emission standards), the control or construction of products (product standards), limits for all emissions irrespective of origin (emission 'bubbles'), the application of control technologies (technological standards); (2) procedural requirements concerning the authorisation of industrial processes or other projects as well as public participation; and (3) voluntary agreements and industrial self-regulation (cf. Haigh 1990, 1996).

This general picture holds true, although one can distinguish different stages of EU environmental policy, with certain approaches and instruments playing a more or less dominant role. Initial attempts of the Community to control environmental pollution were largely based on a reactive approach relying on quality-based instruments and were directed at single environmental media. During the 1980s, the Commission abandoned this strategy in favour of emission-based instruments and placed greater emphasis on the preventative character of EU environmental policy. From the late 1980s onwards, a further stage of EU environmental regulation can be observed. As pointed out in particular in the Community's fifth environmental action programme, the focus is on so-called 'new instruments', emphasising regulatory transparency, participation, self-regulation and voluntary agreements, as opposed to classical forms of hierarchical top-down regulation (Knill and Lenschow 2000b). However, the emergence of new regulatory stages characterised by the dominance of certain approaches increased

as water management and measures substantially affecting the choice of energy sources by member states and the general structure of national energy policy.

[3] Of course, one could think of many other analytical dimensions in order to grasp the patchwork character of EU environmental policy. For our purpose, however, it is sufficient to illustrate this variety rather than developing a complex framework for the classification of different EU policies.

rather than reduced the regulatory variety of EU environmental policy, as new regulatory concepts were generally added to existing approaches rather than replacing the latter. Moreover, the dominance of certain approaches only implied the reduction rather than the exclusion of concepts that were still associated with approaches dominant during earlier regulatory stages.

The supranational decision-making context

The analytical relevance of comprehensiveness and regulatory variety of EU environmental policy becomes particularly apparent when taking into account that in this field, as an area of new regulatory policy, direct institutional pressures for domestic adjustment is most explicit. As pointed out in chapter 3, it is an important characteristic of new regulatory policy that European impacts are not restricted to excluding certain domestic policy choices (as is more the case with market regulation), but positively shape institutional and policy choices at the national level. It is especially in the light of this high interference with domestic arrangements, that legislatory progress in areas of new regulatory policy is generally considered as being less dynamic than in areas of market regulation or negative integration (Scharpf 1994). In this light, the comprehensive developments in the environmental field require explanation. Why did the member states accept supranational policies that challenge well-established administrative arrangements at the national level?

To answer this question, we need to have a closer look at several aspects characterising the policy-making context at the European level. A first reason why member states might accept European policies despite their far-reaching requirements for domestic adjustment refers to political pressure. High political pressure, emerging from both the international, European and national levels may significantly reduce the opportunities for national governments to legitimise their resistance to European policy proposals during the negotiations in the Council. Political pressure is particularly high, when a country finds itself in an isolated position at the European level. Britain, for instance, found itself in such a position during the negotiations on European clean air legislation in the 1980s. Being internationally accused of being the 'dirty man of Europe' and facing increasing pressures from the domestic level, the British finally gave up their resistance in the Council (Knill 1995; Héritier, Knill and Mingers 1996). The emergence of high political pressure in the environmental field is favoured by the trans-boundary nature of many environmental problems calling for international solutions as well as the high visibility and public awareness with respect to many problems of environmental pollution.

Second, member states might accept European decisions as these measures are the 'lesser evil' compared with alternative proposals on the agenda (Knill 1995: 137; Schmidt 1997b). Thus, Britain accepted the 1980 Directive on air quality standards for sulphur dioxide and particulates only, because the Commission would otherwise have proposed an alternative policy concerning the definition of product standards for the sulphur content of fuel oil. Since this alternative proposal would have implied even higher pressures to adjust domestic arrangements, Britain gave up its resistance to the 1980 proposal (Knill 1995: 135). The Commission, which formally controls the process of supranational policy formulation, therefore has important strategic opportunities to increase the support for European policies by setting the agenda, and hence defining the content and issues of Council negotiations (Schumann 1991: 50; Eichener 1996).

A third reason facilitating the acceptance of institutionally demanding European policies is the offer of compensation. Compensation can take many forms, including financial support for member states in order to increase their technological capacities for compliance, regulatory exemptions (e.g., with respect to standards or implementation deadlines), as well as package deals. Compensation 'sweetens' the acceptance of institutionally challenging policies for the member states, but does not reduce the actual pressure for administrative adjustment.

A fourth factor explaining the extent to which member states agree on European policies despite their domestic challenges refers to wrong assumptions over the factual impact of these policies on domestic arrangements. In such cases, national negotiators misinterpret the national consequences of European legislation, assuming that compliance is possible without changing existing administrative arrangements. Wrong assumptions are likely in cases of high scientific and technological uncertainty, an aspect which is particularly relevant for the environmental field. During the negotiations on the 1980 Drinking Water Directive, for instance, many member states were not fully aware of the administrative and economic consequences of the strict standards proposed and wrongly assumed that compliance could be achieved without any legal or administrative changes (Richardson 1994a; Haigh 1996). Misinterpretations are also likely when European policy proposals are characterised by an open and vague texture, leading national negotiators to underestimate the still demanding implications of European legislation. Germany, for instance, accepted the 1985 Directive on Environmental Impact Assessment and realised only afterwards that the

Directive required considerable changes in existing administrative structures and procedures (Héritier, Knill and Mingers 1996: 296).[4] Moreover, wrong expectations with respect to the domestic impact of European policies can emerge when the exploitation of ambiguously formulated European legislation is restricted from *ex post* by subsequent rulings of the ECJ specifying the regulatory content of European policy.

In addition to the above-mentioned factors, national governments might accept institutionally demanding European policies in order to gain support for putting through domestic reforms against strong political and societal resistance; European policies serve as a resource for national governments to increase and legitimate domestic pressures for change. In such cases, one could certainly argue that it makes no sense to speak of European adaptation pressure, since the European requirements are basically in line with the objectives of the national government. However, the parallelism of European and domestic policy objectives does not exclude the emergence of adjustment pressures for national administrative styles and structures which are the basic concern of this study.

A final aspect, which facilitates not only the comprehensive character of EU environmental policy, but also its regulatory variety, refers to the regulatory contest between member states in order to influence European policy-making. As earlier research on the making of EU environmental policy has revealed, the diverging interests of the member states play an important role in promoting the regulatory variety of EU environmental policy. In general, member states pursue two objectives with respect to the formulation of EU environmental policy. On the one hand, they strive to avoid potential costs of institutional adaptation emerging from the implementation of supranational policies at the national level. On the other hand, they seek to minimise competitive disadvantages for their economies which might emerge from regulatory changes triggered by supranational policies.

To avoid potential costs of institutional adaptation and economic disadvantages for the national industry, member states, in many instances, are not relying on a passive strategy of blocking supranational policy proposals not favoured by them. Rather, they pursue a pro-active strategy to influence the European policy-making process by advocating innovative proposals which are in line with their domestic arrangements. The Commission, which is itself interested in advancing its interests by

---

[4] In many instances, wrong expectations and misinterpretations concerning the adaptational requirements of European legislation can be traced to co-ordination problems between domestic actors involved in Council negotiations and those actors in charge of subsequent implementation (Richardson 1994a).

developing new policies, thus gains additional resources from the regulatory contest between the member states. It can rely on the active support of certain member states when advancing its proposals. Institutional differences at the national level hence provide the basis for supranational policy dynamics which emerge from a regulatory contest between the member states.

The dynamics emerging from the regulatory contest between the member states are of twofold relevance for the formulation of EU environmental policy. On the one hand, the striving of the member states to actively influence supranational policy-making favours the comprehensive nature of EU environmental policy. Policy initiatives rely not only on the activities of the Commission, but to a large extent emerge from national proposals. As regulatory and institutional arrangements differ from member state to member state, the regulatory contest favours the emergence of EU environmental policy as a regulatory patchwork. Not only within a single policy area but sometimes within one and the same directive, divergent approaches can be on parallel offer if it has proved impossible to negotiate a consensus (Héritier et al. 1994; Héritier, Knill and Mingers 1996). On the other hand, the regulatory contest favours an equal distribution of adaptational requirements between different member states, given that regulatory competition is unlikely to always favour the same 'winner' (Knill 1997a). As a consequence, member states are generally more prepared to accept adaptations in one area as long as their interests are sufficiently taken into account when other measures are decided.

The potential impact of the above-mentioned factors in the making of EU environmental policy, and hence the likelihood that European legislation interferes with domestic administrative arrangements, increased with changes in the formal decision-making procedures at the European level. As we have seen above, the environmental field was characterised by a significant increase in supranational decision-making powers from the mid-1980s onwards. Most important in this respect are the explicit legal reference in the Treaty as well as the, at least formally, less demanding qualified majority voting in the Council. These changes contributed to an intensified regulatory contest between the member states, given their reduced opportunities to rely on a veto position in Council negotiations.

In sum, EU environmental policy is characterised by a comprehensive, but hardly consistent patchwork of different regulatory approaches and instruments. As we will see in the following section, this multitude of policy concepts and instruments is reflected in varying administrative implications. Domestic administrative arrangements, which vary from country to country, are therefore confronted with different levels of adaptation pressure.

6.2   The policies under investigation

In order to analytically benefit from the regulatory variety given in EU environmental policy, we have selected five pieces of European legislation which cover a broad spectrum in terms of their administrative implications, namely the Directives on combating air pollution from large combustion plants (LCP Directive),[5] the quality of water intended for human consumption (Drinking Water Directive),[6] freedom of access to environmental information (Information Directive),[7] environmental impact assessment (EIA Directive),[8] as well as the Regulation concerning a Community Eco-Management and Audit Scheme (EMAS-Regulation).[9]

Policy content and development

The 1988 *LCP Directive* has to be seen in the broader context of its 1984 Framework Directive on the combating of air pollution from industrial plants, the first important reaction from the EU to the problem of forest dieback and acid rain. The 1984 Directive lays down fundamental procedures that are to be observed in authorising industrial plants. The Directive does not itself fix emissions limits, but specifies various industrial sectors for which limits for certain – also listed – pollutants are subsequently to be set by so-called 'daughter' Directives. The industrial sectors mentioned in the Directive include energy supply, production and processing of metals, manufacturing of non-metallic mineral products, chemicals, and waste disposal. The Directive requires that all plants listed in the schedule require authorisation to operate. Authorisations may be issued only if (1) the best available technology not entailing excessive cost (BATNEEC) is applied to reduce and prevent emissions, (2) set limit values will be not exceeded, (3) the applicable air quality limit values are taken into account (Haigh 1990: 224).

---

[5] Directive on the Limitation of Emissions of Certain Emissions into the Air from Large Combustion Plants (88/609/EEC).
[6] Directive Relating to the Quality of Water Intended for Human Consumption (80/779/EEC).
[7] Directive on the Freedom of Access to Information on the Environment (90/313/EEC).
[8] Directive Regarding the Assessment of the Effects of Certain Public and Private Projects on the Environment (85/337/EEC).
[9] Regulation No. 1836/93 allowing Voluntary Participation by Companies in the Industrial Sector in a Community Eco-Management and Audit Scheme.

The LCP Directive was the first 'daughter' Directive based on the 1984 framework legislation. It attempts to tackle one of the principal causes of acid rain by limiting emissions of sulphur dioxide and nitrogen oxides from fossil-fuelled power stations and other large combustion plants, such as oil refineries. Different requirements were set for new and existing plants. Existing plants (those authorised before 1 July 1987) are subject to total emission limits, so-called national emission 'bubbles' – a new tool of EU environmental legislation at its time of introduction. The national 'bubbles' are based on phased reductions with different limits for different member states.[10] Member states were required to draw up programmes for the progressive reduction of total annual emissions. These programmes were to include timetables and implementing measures. For new plants (plants authorised after 1 July 1987) emission limits applicable to individual authorisations were defined (Haigh 1996: 6.10).

Although the application of the 'bubble concept' left it to the member states to select appropriate means in order to achieve the limit values, the leeway for national decision-making was in fact quite restricted. Given the dependence of domestic energy generation on high sulphur coal in most member states (except from the nuclear-dominated industries in France and Belgium) as well as the considerable reduction rates required by the Directive, the 'bubble concept', in many instances, required the installation of the rather expensive technology of flue gas desulphurisation, the only solution available and feasible at that time (Boehmer-Christiansen and Skea 1991). This way, European legislation not only prescribed emission limits to be achieved at the national level, but, albeit only implicitly, also the technological means of how to fulfil European standards.

In view of these requirements, negotiations in the Council turned out to be particularly difficult. Britain especially, which feared high costs of institutional adaptation and the loss of competitive advantages for its less strictly regulated industry, turned out to be the major opponent of the Directive. Britain was supported by Spain which claimed that the high costs for upgrading existing control technologies would hamper its economic development. It was after five years of negotiations when a final agreement could be achieved by breaking up the British–Spanish alliance. Being offered financial compensation and significantly

[10] Britain was required to reduce its total emission of sulphur dioxide by 20 per cent in 1993, 40 per cent in 1998, and 60 per cent in 2003, whereas the corresponding figures for Germany were 40, 60 and 70 per cent. Concerning nitrogen oxides, Britain had to reduce its emission ceilings by 15 per cent in 1993 and 30 per cent in 1998, whereas the requirements for Germany amounted to 20 per cent in 1993 and 40 per cent in 1998.

watered-down control requirements, Spain no longer resisted the Directive. Britain, which found itself in an isolated position, was confronted with increasing pressure from both the supranational and domestic levels and finally gave up its opposition. However, an agreement was only possible after certain concessions were made to both countries, including lower reduction rates with respect to their total emissions and certain derogations from emission limits for plants burning indigenous solid fuel (Knill 1995).

Despite its similarly demanding implications, the negotiations on the 1980 *Drinking Water Directive* turned out to be less problematic. The Directive defines standards concerning the quality of water intended for drinking or for use in food and drink manufacture in order to protect human health.[11] The Directive has the additional effect of protecting the environment, as drinking water sources must be sufficiently free from contamination to allow for appropriate water treatment. The Directive covers all water for human consumption including public and private water supplies. It lays down over sixty water quality standards and guidelines for water quality monitoring. Three types of standards are used: the guide level, the maximum admissible concentration, and the minimum required concentration. Member states must set national values in order to comply with the standards defined in the Directive. Detailed monitoring requirements are specified in Annex II of the Directive defining analytical measurement methods as well as minimum monitoring frequencies (Haigh 1996: 4.4–2).

However, despite these highly specified requirements the provisions of the Directive are characterised by certain inconsistencies. Besides doubts raised on the scientific soundness of certain quality standards, deficits exist in particular with respect to the monitoring requirements. Thus, the measurement technologies prescribed for some values were already outdated when the Directive came into force and were found incapable of performing the measurement of some fine values called for in the Directive (Haigh 1996: 4.4–4; Knill and Lenschow 1998).

Compared to the LCP Directive, the Drinking Water Directive faced a lower degree of national opposition during the negotiations in the Council. A major reason for this difference has to be seen in the high

---

[11] In an attempt to harmonise the existing EU water legislation, the Commission has proposed a Water Framework Directive regulating principal issues of water quality and its monitoring and control (COM(97) 49 final). This Directive is intended to replace some specific quality-oriented water legislation such as the Groundwater and Surface Water Directives. The member states seem to agree that the – substance-oriented – Drinking Water Directive shall not be subsumed under this Framework Directive, however (although the Drinking Water Directive will be affected through the interaction with the Framework Directive).

degree of technological and scientific uncertainty surrounding the concrete values of the proposed quality standards. In other words, at the time of decision-making, member states were not fully aware of the domestic consequences of the standards they accepted in the Council (Kromarek 1986; Richardson 1994a: 141).[12]

The objective of the 1990 *Information Directive* is to ensure free access to the information on the environment held by public authorities or national bodies with public responsibilities for the environment. It lays down the basic conditions under which such information is to be made accessible. Information on the environment within the meaning of this Directive includes all data stored in written, visual, sound or electronic form on the state of bodies of water, air, soil, animal and plant life, as well as natural habitats. All activities that influence this state are also subsumed under the Directive's information concept.

Information must be made available to any person, regardless of the nature of the requester's interest, citizenship or residency. Refusal or failure to provide it can be followed up by an appeals procedure. A reasonable charge may be asked for the information. The Directive permits certain exemptions (such as for national defence, public security, cases under judicial enquiry, commercial and industrial confidentiality, personal data, material supplied by third parties without being subjected to a legal obligation to do so, unfinished documents and internal communications, and where disclosure of the information may damage the environment).

Since the disclosure of environmental data was (and still is) a highly sensitive issue in most member states, the Information Directive was only accepted after the Commission had significantly revised its previously more ambitious policy proposals. It was only after the content of the Directive was significantly watered down by relying on a rather open and vague texture, that an agreement in the Council could be achieved (Kimber 2000). Germany and Britain, in particular, took a rather sceptical position towards the Commission proposal. During the negotiations, however, Britain, surprisingly to many observers, gave up its opposition and supported the Directive. Germany, finding itself isolated, only voted for the Directive in order to avoid losing its reputation as a 'front-runner' in environmental policy (Héritier, Knill and Mingers 1996: 238).

The 1985 *EIA Directive* can be thought of an embodiment of the preventative approach to environmental protection. Projects (construc-

---

[12] One reason for this lacking awareness was the intensification and industrialisation of agriculture which led to increasing use of nitrate-based fertilisers and pesticides (Rüdig and Kraemer 1994: 68).

tions, installations, interventions in the natural surroundings) likely to have significant effects on the environment by virtue *inter alia* or their nature, size or location are to be made subject to an assessment of their environmental effects before consent may be given. In this context, the Directive distinguishes projects where an EIA is mandatory,[13] given their far-reaching environmental impacts, and projects where the need for an EIA has to be decided by national authorities in the light of the particular situation[14] (Haigh 1996: 11.2–1). In addition to its preventative approach, the Directive takes an integrated, cross-sectoral perspective on environmental protection. Thus, environmental impacts have to be assessed with respect to four categories, including (1) human beings, fauna, flora; (2) soil, water, air, climate and landscape; (3) the interaction between the first two groups; and (4) material assets and cultural heritage.

The following stages are specified as part of the impact assessment procedure. (1) The developer of the project in question is obliged to provide information on the nature of the project, its environmental impacts, and the measures envisaged in order to avoid, reduce and remedy damaging effects on the environment. (2) This information must be made available to authorities concerned by the project (given their environmental responsibilities) and to the public in order to give them the opportunity to express their opinion before the project is started (consultation procedure). The specific characteristics of the consultation procedure are at the discretion of the member states, e.g., the determination of 'the public concerned', the form the consultation will take, and its precise timing. (3) Finally, the information provided is taken into consideration – as one of several factors – by the competent authorities during the authorisation procedure.

Council negotiations on the EIA Directive turned out to be extremely protracted. Although there was agreement in most member states that EIA was a useful concept, the positions concerning the specification of

---

[13] These projects, which are specified in Annex I of the Directive, refer to the construction or operation of oil refineries, large installations for the gasification and liquefaction of coal, thermal power stations and other combustion installations, nuclear power stations and reactors, installation for the permanent storage and final disposal of radioactive waste, work for the initial melting of cast-iron and steel, installations for the extraction of asbestos, integrated chemical installations, construction of motorways, express roads, long-distance railway traffic and airports, trading ports, inland waterways and ports, waste disposal installations for the incineration, chemical treatment or landfill of toxic and dangerous waste.

[14] Directive 97/11/EEC introduced certain amendments clarifying the 1985 Directive with respect to existing project classes and specified selection criteria which clarify the way member states have to determine whether non-mandatory projects require impact assessments or not.

the EIA procedure differed highly across countries. Similar to the Information Directive, an agreement in the Council was only possible by broadening the margins for smooth domestic implementation, as becomes apparent in the rather open wording of the Directive (Cupei 1994). An agreement in the Council was furthermore facilitated by the fact that the German negotiators had underestimated the administrative consequences of an, albeit watered-down, EIA Directive on domestic administrative arrangements. Given the initially widespread Council opposition with respect to corresponding policy proposals of the Commission, the German government, surprised by the 'sudden' consensus emerging in the Council, was not sufficiently prepared to evaluate the domestic adjustment requirements of the Directive (Héritier, Knill and Mingers 1996: 296).

In contrast with the Directives on EIA and Information, the 1993 *EMAS-Regulation* was adopted by the Council after a comparatively short period of negotiations. The major reason for this was the voluntary nature of the measure which is intended to offer incentives for firms and enterprises to introduce an environmental management system. The regulation represents the Commission's current attempt to accompany regulatory (command-and-control) policy instruments with 'new instruments' relying on self-regulation and economic incentives. EMAS presents a potential economic incentive for firms or enterprises who may find economically and environmentally more efficient management solutions or use the EMAS certificate for marketing purposes. The key features of EMAS are: (1) adoption of a company environmental policy (determining environmental objectives and the management system intended to ensure the achievement of these objectives; (2) the verification of the public environmental statement; a task to be carried out by an officially appointed, independent and accredited environmental verifier (Haigh 1996).

Germany was the only country opposing the Regulation. On the one hand, the German Environment Ministry argued that the voluntary character and the procedural rather than substantive and technological control requirements would contribute to lower its high level of environmental regulation. Resistance also came from the Economics Ministry, criticising the additional regulatory burden on German industry, which was already subject to stringent standards. However, given its isolated position in the Council, Germany gave its approval after having ensured that the Regulation defines the principle of the best available technology as a performance indicator for environmental management systems (Héritier, Knill and Mingers 1996: 256–7).

Administrative implications for domestic adjustment

As a consequence of the variety of approaches and instruments under-lying the five policies under study, they imply rather different require-ments with respect to the adjustment of sectoral administrative styles and structures. To begin with the dimension of administrative style, the LCP and Drinking Water Directives correspond to the interventionist ideal type, while the Information Directive and the EMAS-Regulation point to the mediating ideal. The EIA Directive, by contrast, lies some-where between these two poles.

The interventionist character of the LCP and Drinking Water Direc-tives becomes apparent in the hierarchical definition of substantive emission or quality standards emphasising the precautionary principle and the use of the best available technologies. Given the detailed and uniform specification of these requirements, the potential for adminis-trative discretion and flexibility is significantly restricted. It is only with respect to the national 'bubble' targets specified in the LCP Directive, that member states have a certain leeway in deciding on appropriate means in order to achieve the reduction limits. However, even in this case, flexibility is reduced by the fact that the prescribed targets, in many instances, could only be achieved by relying on certain control technologies. The characteristics shaping regulatory intervention in the case of the two Directives favour formal and legalistic patterns of interactions between administrative actors and the regulated industry. Given the narrow gauge for administrative discretion, informal and pragmatic negotiations seem to be difficult to uphold in the context of the European requirements.

The administrative impact of the Information Directive and the EMAS-Regulation, by contrast, basically reflects characteristics of the mediating ideal type, with patterns of administrative activity being based on procedural rather than substantive requirements. In promoting regulatory transparency and public participation, the Information Directive implies more open patterns of administrative interest inter-mediation, with different societal interests having equal opportunities for the access to administrative decision-making. The mediating admin-istrative style is even more pronounced in the case of the EMAS-Regulation, which emphasises industrial self-regulation by defining procedural requirements considering the voluntary introduction of an environmental management system. Similarly to the Information Direc-tive, the EMAS-Regulation emphasises regulatory openness and trans-parency, given the publication of the industrial attempts to improve their environmental performance.

The EIA Directive is characterised by both mediating and interventionist elements. On the one hand, the cases where an EIA is required for the authorisation and operation of projects is specified in a hierarchical way; i.e., the EIA is a necessary condition for authorisation. On the other hand, the Directive's focus on procedural rather than substantive requirements as well as the emphasis placed on public participation reflect elements of the mediating ideal type.

With respect to the dimension of administrative structure, potential implications emerge primarily from the EIA Directive and the EMAS-Regulation. The EIA Directive is characterised by an integrated approach calling for the assessment of environmental impacts for any project that is likely to have such impact from a cross-media perspective. The integrated approach inherent to the EIA procedure points to the concentration or at least horizontal co-ordination of administrative control responsibilities. While the EIA Directive may imply changes in existing structures, the EMAS-Regulation requires new structures. Member states must create competent bodies for the accreditation of environmental verifiers and certification of companies successfully participating in the EMAS scheme. The structural implications of the other Directives, in contrast, are less obvious to be judged from the outset. The degree to which these measures imply pressures for structural adjustment cannot be assessed from the Directives' requirements, but has to be evaluated against the background of the particular constellation of domestic actors. The varying administrative implications of the five policies under study are summarised in table 6.1.

Having elaborated the varying contents and administrative implications of the five pieces of EU environmental policy selected, we will take a closer look at the implementation of these measures in Germany and Britain. Which patterns of administrative change and persistence can be observed in the two countries, given the varying adaptation requirements emanating from European legislation?

Table 6.1. *Administrative implications of the policies under study*

	Administrative style	Administrative structure
LCP	*Intervention Type:* hierarchical, uniform, substantive, low flexibility, deductive *Interest Intermediation:* formal, legalistic	structural impact depending on national conditions
Drinking Water	*Intervention Type:* hierarchical, substantive, low flexibility, deductive *Interest Intermediation:* formal, legalistic	structural impact depending on national conditions
Access to Information	*Intervention Type:* procedural *Interest Intermediation:* transparency, equal access	structural impact depending on national conditions
EIA	*Intervention Type:* procedural, high flexibility *Interest Intermediation:* (limited) public participation	integration, concentration and co-ordination of administrative competencies
EMAS	*Intervention Type:* self-regulation, procedural, high flexibility *Interest Intermediation:* (limited) public participation	building up new administrative structures

7   Germany: the constraints of a static core

The German implementation record of the five policies under study reveals that administrative transformation in the context of European policy demands can only be expected if two conditions are fulfilled. First, the adaptational pressures emerging from European policies must remain at a moderate level; European policies require substantive sectoral changes which, however, can still be achieved within the general core of national administrative traditions. In Germany, this condition was only fulfilled in two cases (EMAS and Drinking Water). The Directives on Access to Information and EIA required far-reaching adaptations in existing practices and structures which were in contradiction with German administrative traditions, while the LCP Directive fully confirmed domestic arrangements, hence implying no demand for change. Second, the actual occurrence of moderate transformations requires the support of domestic actor coalitions which, in view of their institutional opportunities and constraints, are able to successfully challenge existing arrangements. As we shall see, the specific actor constellation at the domestic level resulted in differing patterns of delayed adaptation in the case of Drinking Water and accepted adaptation in the case of EMAS.

The explanation of the German implementation story illustrates our theoretical considerations in two ways. First, it becomes apparent that a 'simple' institutionalist perspective based on the sectoral assessment of the compatibility of European and domestic arrangements provides no sufficient basis to grasp the institutional dimension of European adaptation pressure, i.e., the extent to which European policies demand changes that exceed or remain within the range of options defined by national administrative traditions. Second, the different domestic responses to the cases of Drinking Water and EMAS demonstrate that in constellations where EU legislation demands changes within the core of national administrative traditions, a merely institution-based approach is not sufficient to account for varying domestic responses. Actual patterns of administrative change can only be fully understood from an agency-based perspective, taking account of the preferences and strategies of relevant actors.

The varying domestic responses in the German cases can thus already be fully explained by relying on a less deterministic institution-based approach. There is no need for an additional modification of the institution-based argument to introduce a more dynamic perspective on institutional stability. Given the low capacity for far-reaching administrative reforms, this stability assumption with respect to the macro-institutional context bears high plausibility for the case of Germany. National administrative traditions provide a rather static core which determines the scope for sectoral adjustment to European policy demands.

7.1   Confirmation of the core: compliance without change

The LCP Directive is the only case where European requirements implied no or only negligible adaptation pressures on sectoral administrative arrangements. Germany could completely rely on existing practices and structures in order to comply with the Directive, as domestic arrangements were fully in line with and partly went even beyond the supranational provisions. The main reason explaining the high compatibility of national and supranational regulations lies in the highly influential role Germany played in supranational decision-making.

Both the LCP Directive as well as its 1984 Framework Directive to a large extent were modelled after German law. In 1982, Germany, in response to the forest dieback problem, had enforced a regulation on large combustion plants. After having acted at the national level, the Germans sought intensively to persuade the Commission that a similar measure should be adopted at the EU level. Apart from environmental objectives, the active German role may be explained most clearly by the competitive position of the national industry. At that point, German industry, confronted with strict standards, faced economic disadvantages in relation to its foreign competitors. Another motive for the Germans was their intention of opening up new markets for their highly developed environmental technology industry. In defining emission standards at the EU level in accordance with best available technological possibilities, the economic prospects of this industrial sector could be enhanced (Héritier, Knill and Mingers 1996).

Domestic arrangements and sectoral 'goodness of fit'

When analysing existing arrangements at the domestic level, it becomes apparent that European requirements basically confirmed sectoral administrative styles and structures with respect to the regulation of industrial plants in general as well as large combustion plants in particular. To begin with the administrative style, the existing regulation of pollution control in Germany comes quite close to the interventionist ideal type, and was hence well in line with the requirements implied by the LCP Directive and its 1984 Framework Directive. This holds true not only with respect to the characteristics of administrative instruments and practices (including aspects like regulatory mode, logic, density and content), but also with respect to the patterns of administrative interest intermediation (referring to the relationship between administrative and societal actors).

The interventionist approach underlying German air pollution control becomes first apparent in a hierarchical 'command and control' style. Regulatory requirements are legally prescribed from a 'top-down' perspective (Héritier, Knill and Mingers 1996; Weidner 1996). Inherent to this approach is a deductive logic of regulation with legal requirements being defined in abstract and general terms. Administrative activity to a lesser extent places its focus on specifying regulatory requirements in a particular case, but is more concerned with the question whether the legal conditions for applying the general rules to a particular case are given or not (Weale, O'Riordan and Kramme 1992: 209). As a consequence of the deductive regulatory logic, regulatory rules are highly specified and leave comparatively little flexibility and discretion for the administration to adapt control requirements in the light of particular circumstances, such as the economic situation of the industry or the state of the local environment. A final characteristic shaping administrative activity in industrial air pollution control refers to the regulatory content. Regulatory requirements are not confined to the prescription of detailed procedural rules (concerning, for instance, the authorisation process for industrial plants), but place their primary focus on substantive requirements, i.e., the definition of numerical and technological regulatory objectives, such as product, quality or emission standards.

The interventionist approach to regulate air pollution from industrial plants is based on the 1974 Federal Pollution Act (*Bundesimmissionsschutzgesetz – BImSchG*) which defines the basic principles for industrial pollution control. It specifies two essential requirements that have to be met by plant operators: compliance with emission, air quality and product standards as well as orientation on the principle of the Best Available Technology (BAT) to minimise pollution as far as possible even if there is scientific uncertainty on the potential damages caused by the emissions in question.

Although the use of rather general terms such as BAT leaves room for defining regulatory requirements in the light of individual circumstances, the scope for interpretation is actually restricted by the specification of technological requirements in regulations and administrative directives. The *BImSchG* enables the federal government to issue regulations (*Verordnungen*) and administrative directives (*Verwaltungsvorschriften*) in order to specify product standards, air quality standards, or emission limits. The *Technische Anleitung (TA) Luft* has been the most important administrative directive issued under the Federal Pollution Act. It defined what constitutes air pollutants, established licensing procedures and set emission standards for different types of installations.

Whereas the *TA Luft* specifies technological authorisation requirements for most types of industrial installations, technological requirements for large combustion plants are defined by a particular regulation, namely the 1983 LCP Regulation (*Großfeuerungsanlagenverordnung – GFAVo*).[1] The *GFAVo* confronts industry with nationally uniform emission limits as well as detailed monitoring rules. Emission limits are defined in a rather strict way for seven groups of pollutants, including SO_2, NO_X, dust, CO, halogens and carcinogens.

In view of the dominant practices of regulatory intervention and the legally highly specified definition of regulatory contents, patterns of administrative interest intermediation are generally characterised by formal and legalistic relationships between regulatory authorities and industry. Compared to the arrangements in Britain, there is limited room for the pragmatic specification of regulatory requirements by informal negotiations. When specifying the BAT concept, German regulators generally tend to 'go-by-the-book'.

To be sure, this does not completely preclude informal and consensual bargaining between regulatory authorities and industry. Given the implementation problems associated with the legalist and interventionist approach (Mayntz *et al.* 1978), existing patterns of regulation were questioned to some extent by alternative, less hierarchical and more informal forms, such as public law contracts and pre-application negotiations between industry and administration in order to make the authorisation process more effective (Bohne 1981; Benz 1990). Notwithstanding these tendencies, it has to be emphasised that – in sharp

---

[1] The Large Combustion Plant Regulation was the 13th Federal Regulation based on the 1974 Federal Pollution Control Act. A major factor stimulating the development of uniform emission standards by a specific LCP Regulation were the demands of the electricity industry which complained about the different interpretations of the BAT principle stated in the *TA Luft* by regional authorities (Boehmer-Christiansen and Skea 1991: 172).

contrast to the British case – bargaining and informal co-ordination take place under the 'shadow of the law'. The scope for pragmatic arrangements and agreements is constrained by the highly specific and rigid regulatory rules (Lenschow 1997; Jansen 1997).[2] The more legalistic approach becomes also apparent with respect to enforcement proceedings and prosecutions which are much more frequent in Germany than in Britain. Following the formal and legalistic patterns, public participation takes place in a legally specified setting, which allows for third-party access only in limited, legally specified cases (Winter 1996).

In view of the high compatibility of European requirements with sectoral patterns of administrative intervention and interest intermediation, the LCP Directive required no particular adjustments. The emission limits set in the LCP Directive were basically compatible with those established in the *GFAVo*. In particular, the regulatory requirements of the *GFAVo* go even beyond the standards and reduction targets defined in the Directive. Thus, in Germany every individual plant needs to fulfil certain reduction requirements (or be shut) whereas according to the Directive the requirements for old plants are linked to the status of national emission 'bubbles', i.e., individual plants may emit heavily as long as the national average remains below a certain ceiling (Boehmer-Christiansen and Skea 1991: 236–8).

The relative 'fit' of the requirements of the LCP Directive with existing arrangements in Germany becomes apparent not only with respect to the dimension of the administrative style, but also with respect to administrative structures. In particular, this can be traced to the high degree of legal centralisation concerning the allocation of competencies in German air pollution control, which allowed for effective practical compliance with the Directive. Although the *Länder* have a rather autonomous position when deciding on structural and organisational arrangements to implement federal legislation (implying high variance in regional administrative structures and organisation[3]), the

---

[2] Given the large number and complex structure of regulatory rules, the focus of bargaining between administration and industry is often less related to the question of how certain rules are specified than which rules apply in a particular case (Lenschow 1997: 3).

[3] Varying regional arrangements can in particular be observed with respect to the question of whether regulatory responsibilities are allocated to the general administration of the local districts or cities or to special agencies which are no integral part of the general administration. In Baden-Württemberg and Bavaria, for instance, the main pollution control responsibilities at the local level lie with the districts and cities, with the special agencies, the factory inspectorates (*Gewerbeaufsichtsämter*), participating in the decision-making process with respect to advice on technical matters of the regulatory process. In North Rhine-Westphalia, by contrast, local responsibilities in air pollution control are allocated to special agencies (*Staatliche Umweltämter*) (Lübbe-Wolff 1996: 93). In the other regions, the allocation of responsibilities to the general administration or to special

implementation of European legislation therefore required no shifting of regional administrative competencies to the federal level or the establishment of a federal pollution control inspectorate.

The high degree of legal centralisation emerges from two factors. First, based on constitutional amendments in 1974, most policy areas in the environmental field, including that of clean air policy, are subject to competing legislatory competencies (*konkurrierende Gesetzgebung*) of *Bund* and *Länder*. Since in the environmental field the federal level has made extensive use of its legislative powers, most areas are covered by federal legislation, hence significantly reducing the scope for corresponding activities at the regional level. In the case of air pollution, for instance, not only the primary legislation, the Federal Pollution Act, but also subsequent regulations (including the Regulation on Large Combustion Plants) and technical guidance notes (the *TA Luft*) specifying the regulatory content of the primary legislation were enacted at the federal level (Lenschow 1997). Second, in the LCP case, the specification of federal law occurred in the form of a particular regulation rather than administrative circulars (the *TA Luft*). German arrangements were fully in line with European transposition requirements. Following several judgements of the ECJ, it would not have been sufficient to formally transpose European Directives by relying on administrative directives, such as the *TA Luft*, since these norms establish no reliable and legally binding basis for the practical implementation of European legislation (Schwarze 1996: 177).[4]

Pattern of administrative adaptation: compliance without change

Given the complete compatibility of administrative styles and structures in German clean air policy with the administrative implications embodied in the LCP Directive as well as its 1984 Framework Directive, Germany was able to comply with European requirements without any notable administrative changes.

On the other hand, the high level of institutional embeddedness of sectoral administrative arrangements suggests that we would have ob-

agencies is less pronounced. Basically, we find mixed forms with the general administration being in charge of the issuing of authorisations and the special agencies being responsible for monitoring and periodical revision of authorisations (cf. Mayntz and Hucke 1978; Eisen 1993).

[4] While the transposition of the LCP Directive thus fulfilled the requirements of the ECJ, Germany had to change its arrangements with respect to several other Directives in the field of air and water pollution control. These cases refer to the Directives concerning air quality standards for sulphur dioxides and particulates (80/779/EEC) and lead (82/884/EEC) as well as the Directives on ground water (80/68/EEC) and the Framework Directive on water pollution (76/464/EEC).

served considerable administrative resistance to change, if European legislation had not been fully in line with domestic styles and structures. The interventionist sectoral administrative style reflects institutionally well-entrenched core patterns of national administrative arrangements which can be traced to the German tradition of legalism and hierarchical intervention. Institutional stability of sectoral patterns emerges not only from their linkage to the macro-institutional context, but also from the regulatory tradition within the field of clean air policy. Pollution control activities date back to the late nineteenth century and were, since that time, based on a hierarchical approach reflecting the tradition of the 'police law' (*Polizeirecht*) empowering the bureaucracy to restrict the operation of industrial plants in the public interest (Boehmer-Christiansen and Skea 1991: 160). The hierarchical approach was reinforced during the 1970s, when a variety of governmental programmes and a comprehensive body of laws laid down the foundation for a modern environmental policy. The technology-based approach selected to resolve problems of environmental policies is well in line with and even reinforced the interventionist administrative style (Müller 1986; Weidner 1997).

7.2   Contradiction of the core: resistance to change

In Germany, two of the five cases under investigation implied challenges to well-established core patterns of national administrative traditions, namely the cases of Access to Information and EIA. Given the high pressure for institutional adaptation in each of these cases, we observe considerable resistance to adapt domestic arrangements to European requirements, hence leading to ineffective implementation of supranational legislation.

Domestic arrangements and sectoral 'goodness of fit'

A comparison of sectoral arrangements with corresponding requirements implied by the Directives on Access to Information and EIA already reveals a considerable degree of incompatibility. In the Information case, sectoral 'misfit' refers to the dimension of administrative style, while the impact of the EIA Directive is particularly related to the dimension of administrative structure.

The Information Directive

To begin with the Information case, the Directive's requirement in favour of unconditional public access to environmental information was in sharp contrast with sectoral arrangements at the domestic level. The open and transparent forms of administrative interest intermediation implied by the Directive were hardly compatible with the more closed practice to be found in Germany where access to environmental information is generally restricted to parties directly affected by and involved in administrative activities and procedures (Wegener 1993: 17).

In Germany, the regulation of public access to environmental information follows from general principles guiding the access of third parties to administrative data. The basic concept relevant in this context is the 'principle of restricted access to records' (*Grundsatz der beschränkten Aktenöffentlichkeit*), which is laid down in the Administrative Procedures Act. Following this principle, administrative authorities are only obliged to provide access to official documents if requesters can claim that access to 'their records' is necessary to defend their legal interests in the context of administrative procedures (Erichsen 1992: 414; Eifert 1994: 544; Burmeister and Winter 1990). The intention behind this restriction of access rights was to strike a balance between administrative secrecy and the complete openness of administrative data (Reinhardt 1997: 167).

While the Administrative Procedures Act defines the general rule for access to administrative information, there exist specific procedures in some areas with a more open regulation of access rights. In cases considered to be of particular societal relevance and interest, access to information may be given to anybody regardless of interest. These exemptions of the general rule refer to comprehensive authorisation procedures of industrial and nuclear plants or regional planning procedures. Furthermore, some regions provide public access to public water registers containing data about industrial discharges into the water. In addition to the more open access rules, the administration is obliged to actively provide legally specified information in the context of more comprehensive licensing procedures (Schwanenflügel 1993: 97).[5]

Notwithstanding these wider access opportunities in some areas of environmental policy, it has to be emphasised that also in these cases the provision of access is contingent upon a corresponding decision of the authority in question. The only difference to the general rule defined in the Administrative Procedures Act lies in the fact that authorities are not

---

[5] The German rules on access to data distinguish three types of inspection: first, the duty of the administration to furnish information, which requires notice to be given and the information to be laid open to public inspection (*Auslegung*); second the duty to inform, where only the disclosure (*Offenlegung*) of information is required, and finally the duty of registration, where processing and laying open to inspection is required but no notice of its availability (*Bekanntmachung*) (Burmeister and Winter 1990: 93).

bound by detailed legal rules, but have discretionary powers in handling individual information requests (Reinhardt 1997: 167). Moreover, the detailed investigation of the implementation of the administration's active information obligations has revealed that interested parties have considerable obstacles to overcome even when the documents are open to public inspection during permitted proceedings, with data on expected emissions or technical data often missing as well (Führ 1990: 154–8).

In view of these legal and practical constraints to access of environmental information, the European Directive required a considerable departure from existing sectoral arrangements (Erichsen 1992: 419). In providing individuals with a subjective right of access to environmental information, the Directive implies significant changes in the status of the public with respect to the administration. Rather than serving the protection of individual rights in the context of administrative procedures (the conception underlying the German principle of restricted access), the Directive aims at making administrative activities accountable to the public, hence instrumentalising public access as a means of administrative control (Schwarze 1996: 172).

The EIA Directive

In the EIA case, a similar picture of sectoral 'misfit' can be observed which becomes obvious in particular with respect to structural and organisational arrangements. The sectoral incompatibility of European and domestic arrangements emerges mainly from the integrated cross-media approach to environmental protection which is in sharp contrast to corresponding procedures in Germany (Erbguth 1991). The EIA Directive implies the concentration or at least intensified co-ordination of different consent procedures and structures with respect to different environmental media, such as air, water and soil. Moreover, in prescribing the designation of a 'lead agency' responsible for the overall control and co-ordination of the EIA procedures, the Directive points to a certain centralisation of administrative competencies (CEC 1993: 101). However, neither of these implications corresponded with existing arrangements in Germany where administrative processing of a project is medium-specific both vertically and horizontally, and consequently not co-ordinated in either legal terms or practical performance.

To be precise, German environmental law is not characterised by a single body of consistent and co-ordinated rules, but consists of a maze of different laws, regulations and directives at the federal and regional levels with sometimes contradicting legal implications and terminology (Kloepfer and Durner 1997: 1082). Consequently, the legal and procedural requirements with respect to the protection of different environmental media reveal significant variance.

The fragmented nature of German environmental regulation becomes evident not only in legal and procedural complexity, but also in the far-reaching segmentation of administrative 'control chains' for different environmental media. Although the administrative autonomy of the regions implies certain variation in the structure and organisation of the environmental administration, there exist separate hierarchical chains from the local to the ministerial level with respect to different environmental media. Administrative segmentation can be observed at all administrative levels, with co-ordination efforts between different units at the same level being confined to 'negative co-ordination'.

Horizontal fragmentation is particularly evident at the local and the ministerial level. At the lower level, where most of the practical implementation tasks are fulfilled,[6] administrative responsibilities are not only organisationally divided between different administrative units of the general administration, but also institutionally between general administration and special agencies, such as the factory inspectorates or the health authorities. The same holds true for the ministerial level, where depending on the issue, different ministries are involved (agriculture, economics, environment, health). Segmentation emerges not only from organisational fragmentation within the ministries, but also from the fact that there is variance with respect to the ministries in overall charge of the issue (e.g., the health ministries in drinking water control, the environment ministry with respect to discharges into the water) (Eisen 1993; Lübbe-Wolff 1996).[7]

In sum, the Directives on Access to Information and EIA have in common that their administrative implications considerably differed from existing sectoral arrangements in Germany. While the Information Directive required a significant widening of the fairly restricted right of access to environmental information, the EIA Directive pointed to the need for more integrated and concentrated administrative structures and procedures. As will be shown in the following, neither in the

---

[6] In the five East German regions, however, the main focus of practical implementation of environmental regulations lies with the county level. This can be traced to the comparatively small size of these regions and the therefore more limited administrative capacity of the local districts (Lübbe-Wolff 1996: 93).

[7] This overall picture of fragmented administrative structures holds true, although many regions have established specific regional environment agencies (*Landesumweltämter*). This can be traced to the fact that, as their federal counterpart, these agencies have merely advisory functions with respect to technical and scientific matters rather than being in charge of concrete enforcement and implementation tasks (Lübbe-Wolff 1996: 92).

Information nor in the EIA case have corresponding adaptations of domestic arrangements occurred.

Pattern of administrative adaptation: resistance to change

The Information Directive

Resistance to adaptation to the Information Directive becomes evident not only in the belated formal transposition, but also in obvious failure to comply practically with the provisions of the Directive. Although implementation of the Directive in national law was to have been achieved by the end of December 1992, it was only in 1994 that the *Bundestag* passed the Environment Information Act (*Umweltinformationsgesetz – UIG*) by which the Directive was transposed into German law (Scherzberg 1994: 733). It is, however, questionable whether the belatedly adopted Act meets all the requirements of the European legislation, as the formal transposition of the Directive has been characterised as unsatisfactory by both the scientific experts, lawyers and environmental associations for several reasons.

First, it was pointed out that the circle of authorities required to furnish information has been restricted to a few special bodies with primary responsibilities in the environmental field. This implies that many authorities which are 'relevant authorities' in the sense of the Directive remain outside the coverage of the law. In a related matter, authorities involved in legislation and the judiciary are exempt from the information provision.[8] The question arises whether the implementation of regulations (including the drafting of relevant administrative regulations) is covered under 'legislation' as the German information law now assumes. Such exclusion of the norm-setting processes in environmental legislation from the provision of access to information effectively biases such access in favour of those actors already involved in that process (SRU 1996; Scherzberg 1994: 735; Winter 1996: 88–90).

Second, the practical regulation of the way access to information shall be granted is not specified in the German transposition law. Somewhat contrary to German transposition practice in general, parts of the Directive were literally taken and copied into federal law. While lack of specificity is not necessarily a breach of the EU Directive, it may result in substandard practical implementation of the law, as civil servants directly involved in the implementation may not know how to interpret

---

[8] In the practical application of the law, both the Ministry for Transport and the Ministry for Finance felt no initial obligation to provide environmental information. While tax data remain exempt from the information law, the Ministry for Transport had to give in after a lengthy battle within the cabinet (Interview *BMU*, April 1997).

certain aspects of the law. The necessary interpretation of the open texture required on the ground presents particular problems in the German system with its 'rule of law' tradition (where civil servants are not used to much discretion but expect clear operational guidance from the law) and its federal structure which requires unambiguous federal law in order to ensure uniform implementation in the *Länder* (Interview *BMU*, March 1997; Lenschow 1997: 36).

Third, the exemption circumstances justifying a refusal to disclose data are so vaguely defined that they far exceed in extent the residual access rights. Firm secrets, for instance, are determined on the basis of the firm's own evaluation; a negative list, specifying information that principally should not be protected, to limit the abuse of this exemption clause, is lacking (SRU 1996; Engel 1992: 112). Moreover, judicial and preliminary investigation proceedings are excluded from free access to information. In Germany the notion of 'preliminary proceedings' has been broadly defined to potentially include all administrative proceedings, ignoring the functionally more narrow intention of the EU Directive. With respect to ongoing legislative and authorisation proceedings another ambiguity arises, since often it is unclear when such a proceeding is actually closed and hence may become the object of information requests. Also internal communications in and among public authorities are excluded, hence leaving room for abuse in the practical implementation of the Directive, especially when several authorities are involved in a process with potential environmental relevance.

Finally, while the Directive allows member states to 'make a charge for supplying the information' whereby such 'charge may not exceed a reasonable cost', the German phrasing is broader and permits information seekers to be charged even for a denial of their request. The mere refusal of a request for information may be charged with up to DM 2,000 which contradicts the intention of Community law (Scherzberg 1994: 744).

The Environmental Information Act is thus an inadequate implementation of the Directive. It is not designed to optimise the conditions for the public monitoring of implementation in the environmental field, but to maintain the *status quo* of restricted administrative openness to the greatest possible degree (Scherzberg 1994: 745). However, not only the public is affected by the reticence of the authorities. The Federal Environment Office is frequently refused information by factory inspectorates and local authorities are refused emission data on firms in their region which they need to set local quality standards (Héritier, Knill and Mingers 1996: 240).

The EIA Directive

Turning to the EIA Directive, we observe a similar picture of administrative resistance to change. As with the Information case, implementation was neither on time nor did it do justice to the central objectives of EIA in the sense of assuming an integrated and open outlook on environmental issues. Instead, the process was characterised by efforts to minimise the effects of the Directive on national permitting practice. Only two years after expiry of the deadline set by the Directive were steps taken in Germany to transpose it. In 1990 the Environmental Impact Assessment Act (*Umweltverträglichkeitsprüfungsgesetz – UVPG*) was adopted. However, this did not mean that industrial plants subject to authorisation needed to carry out an EIA. A further legislative modification was necessary, which came only in 1992 with the amendment of the Regulation on the implementation of authorisation procedure under the Federal Pollution Control Act. Since this amendment, EIA has been an integral part of authorisation procedure under the law relating to pollution control (Spindler 1992: 53).

However, by integrating the EIA into existing structures and procedures (Lambrechts 1996: 77; Schwarze 1996: 169), Germany continues to be single-media rather than cross-media oriented and fragmented in its legal and administrative structures, notwithstanding the fact that a certain intensification of co-ordination between different sectoral agencies can be observed (Interview *STUA*, March 1997). Given the mere integration of the Directive into existing proceedings, the EIA is watered down to the fulfilment of technical standards defined in regulations and administrative directives, such as the *TA Luft*, in the context of different licensing proceedings. The inadequate account taken of the cross-media perspective implies a dilution of EIA requirements at the implementation level. Thus, the EIA generally does not make much difference for the German authorisation practice which is still based on a single-media approach (Lenschow 1997; Erbguth 1991).

The described pattern of administrative resistance holds true, although it is currently discussed to provide a more integrated regulatory framework for environmental legislation in Germany. The 1997 draft proposal for a comprehensive Environmental Code (*Umweltgesetzbuch*) suggests the integration of the media-specific procedures in the context of one single authorisation, implying the balancing of different environmental impacts in the context of a cross-media approach (Kloepfer and Durner 1997).[9] However, while there is considerable uncertainty as to whether the proposal will be politically accepted, the proposals are

---

[9] The basic need to integrate different authorisation procedures emerges from the 1996 Directive on Integrated Prevention and Pollution Control (IPPC) (96/61/EEC).

restricted to legal structures, hence excluding the problem of administrative fragmentation in the context of practical application.

The institutional limits for successful support

Following our theoretical considerations, the sectoral incompatibility of domestic and European requirements does not automatically imply that European adaptation requirements are resisted at the national level. Especially when taking into account that effective adaptation to the provisions of both the EIA and Information Directive was strongly supported by domestic actor coalitions, one could have expected more substantial changes in existing administrative arrangements. In contrast to other European countries, Germany is characterised by a high level of environmental awareness and the existence of numerous, politically rather influential environmental organisations. Political influence is facilitated by the electoral law and the multiplicity of political arenas in the federal system, both providing the basis for the emergence of the Green Party during the 1980s (Hey and Brendle 1992; Héritier, Knill and Mingers 1996).

The Information Directive

This general characteristic of a strong environmental movement is of particular relevance in the Information case, given that the Directive is explicitly directed towards the strengthening of such actors, i.e., is explicitly intended to make use of support by domestic actors (Knill and Lenschow 2000b). Notwithstanding the strong support of environmental associations which became evident in the initiation of numerous legal proceedings in administrative courts (*Süddeutsche Zeitung*, 9 January 1995; Environment Watch: Western Europe, 18 July 1997), however, existing administrative arrangements remained more or less unchanged.

The surprising patterns of non-adaptation despite considerable domestic support can only be explained when investigating the institutional scope of European adaptation requirements in closer detail. As European requirements implied challenges to administrative core principles rather than changes within the range of options defined by the macro-institutional background, even strong domestic support in favour of adaptation was not sufficient to overcome vested interests benefiting from the *status quo*.

The 'principle of restricted access to records', which defined existing sectoral arrangements in the context of the Information Directive, is deeply rooted in the macro-institutional context of the German state and legal tradition. Within the German tradition of the state, the civil service is accountable to the state and to the law rather than to society, hence implying no particular necessity for administrative transparency (König 1996). Moreover, the *Rechtsstaat* principle places its emphasis on the protection of subjective individual rights rather than the participation of the public in administrative decision-making. In contrast to the United States, the German principle of the *Rechtsstaat* implies that justice emerges not from procedural fairness and equal access opportunities to the administrative process, but from the substantively correct content of administrative decisions (Scharpf 1970: 38; Burmeister and Winter 1990: 91). Following the German conception of administrative activity, substantive content-related norms are more important than mere procedural rules allowing for a fair contest between different parties. Access to administrative decision-making therefore is limited to those cases, which are – given the legalistic approach – exactly specified by administrative law (Winter 1996), namely cases where the content of administrative decisions may affect subjective individual rights and access to official files is necessary in order to defend these rights.

This is in sharp contrast to the approach of the Information Directive which provides a subjective access right *per se*, i.e., the claim for administrative information has not necessarily to be linked to the other subjective individual rights (Reinhardt 1997). Considering these strongly entrenched principles, it comes as no surprise that the German response to European legislation within the scope of national administrative traditions was not sufficient to meet the European requirements.

The EIA Directive

In the EIA case, the resistance to change the horizontally fragmented administrative structures and procedures in favour of an integrated cross-media approach can be understood in the light of the wide institutional breadth of regional administrative arrangements, hence implying a rigid administrative backbone. As illustrated in chapter 5, structural stability emerges from different sources. First, the principle of administrative federalism gives the regions considerable autonomy and discretion when deciding upon administrative structures and organisation. Second, given the highly formalistic and legalistic political decision-making process, structural changes face severe institutional constraints emerging from various institutional veto points. Finally, the structural and procedural stability is the result of complex and comprehensive arrangements to be found at both the federal and regional levels (Benz and Goetz 1996).

In this context, it is of particular importance that horizontally fragmented arrangements gain institutional stability from their embeddedness into vertically integrated, hierarchical structures. Given these tight institutional linkages, punctual changes at one level would automatically require corresponding adaptations at other levels, hence increasing the costs of adaptation. From this constellation follows a high institutional stability of these arrangements. Compliance with European legislation therefore required changes in well-established core patterns of German administrative structures. As adaptation was not possible within these basic principles, the observed resistance to change is hardly surprising. In this light, it is also highly questionable to what extent the Environmental Code currently under discussion will actually contribute to reducing significantly structural and procedural fragmentation.

7.3   Change within the core: mixed patterns of adaptation

In contrast to the Directives on Information and EIA, European adaptation requirements remained at a modest level in the two remaining cases of Drinking Water and EMAS. European policies did not challenge the core of national administrative traditions but could be implemented within the core. As an institution-based perspective in such constellations is not sufficient to explain administrative change or persistence, the observed patterns of delayed adaptation in the case of Drinking Water and accepted adaptation in the EMAS case can only be fully understood when supplementing the institution-based argument by an agency-based perspective. This way, both cases illustrate the 'deterministic limits' of an unspecified institutional perspective based on the sectoral compatibility of European and domestic arrangements, which would have suggested resistance to EMAS requirements and 'easy' adaptation to the Drinking Water Directive.

Drinking water: long resistance despite sectoral compatibility

Although the Drinking Water Directive implied no challenges to well-established core principles of German administrative traditions, its implementation was characterised by significant resistance to adjusting domestic arrangements to the only moderate European requirements. The long delay to enact these – only incremental – changes can only be understood from a less abstract agency-based perspective taking account of the strategic interaction of relevant actors in the light of given institutional opportunity structures.

Domestic arrangements and sectoral 'goodness of fit'

Administrative structures in German water policy in general and drinking water policy in particular are characterised by a considerable degree of complexity and fragmentation (Rüdig and Kraemer 1994). Concerning the division of legislatory competencies between the *Bund* and the *Länder*, the body of water law is shaped by a mix of two constitutional principles. As a general rule, the federal level has merely the framework competence as far as the quality of waters is concerned. It has established the overall legal structure (*Wasserhaushaltsgesetz* – *WHG*), but the primary competence for setting specific standards rests with the regions. On the other hand, as far as the presence of dangerous substances in water and the emission of such substances as well as matters of health policy are concerned, *Bund* and *Länder* have competing powers. Hence, once the federal level has assumed responsibility, federal law overrules (previous) *Länder* practices. The *Länder* are therefore responsible for the practical implementation of the law. The latter separation of competencies (i.e., competing powers) applies to the legislation for drinking water which traditionally belongs to the field of health policy.

Structural complexity also becomes obvious in the far-reaching fragmentation at both the federal and regional levels. The Federal Health Ministry has the portfolio for the control of dangerous substances *within* the medium of water (since they represent a threat to human health), whereas the Environment Ministry is in charge of establishing the framework for water quality and the control of emissions *into* the water. As a consequence, the Health Ministry is responsible for the regulation of drinking water quality, but has no competencies with respect to the regulation of industrial discharges into the water which might affect the quality of drinking water.

This horizontal fragmentation of competencies is reflected in two separate hierarchical chains with respect to the practical application of drinking water legislation. On the one hand, the operations of local water providers (*Wasserversorgungsunternehmen* – *WVU*) are controlled by specialised agencies, namely the local health authorities (*Gesundheitsämter*). They operate under the supervision of the regional health authorities which are typically linked to the regional health ministries. On the other hand, the control of industrial discharges into the water as well as the authorisation for the operation of water providers lies with the lower water authorities (*Untere Wasserbehörden*) which are part of the general administration. The water authorities are subject to hierarchical control of the county administrations which in turn are under the supervision of the regional environment ministries, as far as water pollution control is concerned.

As the main responsibility for the cleanliness of water lies with the water providers, this structure results in an 'end-of-the pipe' approach to ensuring drinking water quality. Since neither water providers nor the health authorities have authority over the emitters of polluting substances into water (typically industry and agriculture), water providers have to apply the necessary cleaning technologies in order to meet regulatory requirements (Rüdig and Kraemer 1994: 61–2).[10]

Similar to the clean air field, the dominant administrative style in German drinking water regulation is characterised by an interventionist approach. On the basis of the German Water Framework Legislation, the 1976 Drinking Water Regulation defines uniform and legally binding standards concerning the permissible concentration of substances in drinking water, the substances that can be used for water treatment and the procedures and technologies for controlling drinking water quality.

Water providers are legally obliged to ensure the achievement of these standards. Depending on the type of pollution and the means available, water providers may apply the necessary cleaning measures following the best available technology as prescribed in the Drinking Water Regulation, mix contaminated water with clean water, and in an extreme case close down water provision. Moreover, water providers are obliged to regularly measure the quality of the water and report to the health authorities. The health authorities themselves regularly inspect water reservoirs and the operation of water providers (especially the measuring procedures); they are also charged with the control of drinking water quality at the place of consumption (to limit contamination beyond the control of water providers, e.g., through the local pipe system). In view of the detailed substantive requirements, there exists little flexibility and discretion for the health authorities when regulating and supervising the operations of water providers, implying a formal and legalistic approach (Lenschow 1997; Interviews *BGH*, March 1997; *BGW*, April 1997).

The comparison of existing administrative arrangements in German drinking water policy and corresponding implications of the European

---

[10] Besides administrative fragmentation, a further problem for co-ordinating the regulation of drinking water quality and industrial discharges emerges from the decentralised and diversified structure of water provision. There exist about 7,000 *WVU* in Germany operating about 20,000 water extraction plants. They differ in their organisational structure, legal status, size and range of responsibilities. It is the responsibility of the local government to make available drinking water to households, business and industry; they may fulfil this responsibility themselves (*Eigenbetrieb*), in conjunction with other localities (*Regiebetrieb*), head a functional association (*Zweckverband*) or rely on private law associations or enterprises who operate on the basis of a concessional agreement with the locality (*BGW* 1995).

Directive reveals a picture of high compatibility. With reference to sectoral structures, this can be traced to the rather limited implication of the Directive in this respect. In prescribing substantive standards for drinking water quality, the Directive is well compatible with the fragmented structures in Germany and the end-of-the-pipe approach following from these arrangements. Furthermore, the fact that the definition of drinking water standards occurs in the form of a federal regulation (as opposed to administrative circulars), meant that German arrangements were well in line with the European requirements for nationally uniform transposition.

Concerning the dimension of administrative style, the Directive's interventionist approach based on substantive and legally binding standards as well as the specification of monitoring procedures and technologies seemed to fully correspond with sectoral arrangements at the domestic level. Similar to the LCP case, there was only limited variation with respect to the number and the concrete setting of standards. With regard to a number of parameters, German law was actually going beyond the provisions of the EU Directive. On the other hand, the limits for nitrates and pesticides in particular were to some extent stricter than corresponding German standards. Although the Directive therefore required a certain upgrading of domestic requirements, the scope of these changes did not seem to imply a decisive departure from sectoral intervention. Hence, the EU Directive implied only incremental adaptations of existing administrative arrangements in German drinking water regulation.

Pattern of administrative adaptation: resistance to change

In view of the high level of sectoral compatibility of domestic arrangements and European requirements, one would have expected 'easy' adaptation to the limited pressures exerted by supranational legislation. Surprisingly, however, even these minor adaptations were resisted by the German administration. Administrative resistance becomes apparent in significant deficiencies with respect to both the formal transposition and practical application of the Drinking Water Directive.

Germany formally transposed the Directive with four years' delay in 1986, with the pesticide parameters being included only in 1989 and then incompletely.[11] The final transposition of the Directive took place

---

[11] In 1990, the Commission had taken Germany to the ECJ over this issue. In its 1992 judgement, the Court upheld the Commission's complaint about the shortcomings of the 1986 Regulation. However, the Commission had already conceded that the 1990 amendments of the Regulation fully met the formal requirements of the Directive, but claimed that German authorities were not implementing the Directive in practice.

in 1990 by subsequent amendments of the Drinking Water Regulation[12] (Bodiguel 1996). With respect to practical application, Germany had been charged with ignoring some of the pesticide parameters in the Directive and for allowing the *Länder* to authorise suspensions of certain requirements (for long terms if they proved to imply no health risk).[13] Although the water providers are generally rather effective in ensuring drinking water quality, their technological and financial capabilities were not sufficient to comply with some pesticide and nitrate parameters in the context of an 'end-of-the-pipe' approach (Interview *BGW*, March 1997; Lenschow 1997).

The institutional constraints for pragmatic compliance

How can we explain the observed patterns of administrative resistance to change in the light of the high sectoral compatibility of domestic and European arrangements? While the institution-based perspective only indicates that domestic adaptation is possible but not 'determined', we need to have a closer look at the specific domestic context, including institutional opportunity structures as well as the interests and strategies of relevant actors in order to explain the long delay in domestic compliance.

As will be shown, the particular aspects shaping the domestic context during the implementation of the Directive provided significant obstacles for effective compliance. In this context the main reason for the German adaptation problems has to be seen in the existing institutional opportunity structures which significantly reduced the scope of available options for compliance. The institutional context excluded options that found the broad support of most actors involved, while favouring options which provoked the particular resistance of influential actors.

The institutional context restricted the scope of available options for compliance in basically two ways. First, it excluded a 'pragmatic approach' to reduce adaptational requirements by making use of regulatory inconsistencies of the Directive. Given the long preparation phase preceding the adoption of the Directive, the measurement procedures imposed to test for the presence of the regulated parameters were found incapable of performing the fine measurement required to detect the small values called for in the Directive (Interview *BGM*, March 1997; McGillivray 1997). This inconsistency created the opportunity for

---

12 Verordnung über Trinkwasser und über Wasser für Lebensmittelbetriebe (BGBL I., p. 227, 1986); Neufassung der Verordnung über Trinkwasser und über Wasser für Lebensmittelbetriebe (BGBL I., No. 66: 2613–29); with correction of 23.1.1991 (BGBL I: 227).
13 These acts of non-compliance resulted in Court case C 237/90.

'easy' compliance with the Directive by simply following the detailed but inconsistent provisions with respect to measurement and monitoring. This way, the Directive would have had only *formal* consequences (higher standards), but its *practical* impact in terms of improved cleaning technologies would have been limited. This opportunity of reducing the costs of compliance would have reflected no particularly tricky or exceptional strategy, but was commonly 'applied' in many other member states, especially where administrative capacities to monitor water pollution were at a low standard anyhow[14] (Knill 1998).

However, while 'feasible' for other countries, the option of 'easy' compliance was institutionally excluded in Germany, as it was in sharp contradiction with administrative core principles of interventionism and legalism. As shown in chapter 4, the combination of hierarchical intervention 'from above' and legalism is deeply rooted in the German state and legal tradition, which presupposes a superior role of the state *vis-à-vis* society; with the binding of the administration to the law (following the principle of the *Rechtsstaat*) traditionally serving as a substitute for democratic representation. The binding of the administration to the law implies that, as a general rule, the scope and mode of administrative activity is specified by law. Public administration serves the application of the law rather than policy-making, hence possesses comparatively little flexibility and discretion when implementing legal provisions (Ellwein and Hesse 1989: 392; Peters 1995: 137). Obvious legal inconsistencies as contained in the Drinking Water Directive therefore would have significantly weakened and delegitimised the German regulatory logic of intervention.

In the case of drinking water, these legalistic and interventionist patterns become apparent in the comparatively strict requirements with respect to monitoring techniques and procedures. Water providers are obliged to conduct regular and frequent testing of water quality making use of modern measuring tools. Breaches of the imposed quality standards must be immediately reported to the health authorities who, in turn, will notify the public in the case of potential danger. According to the German water providers, this regulatory thoroughness has con-

---

[14] It is difficult to judge whether the inconsistencies in the Directive were intentionally included during Council negotiations in order facilitate domestic compliance. Analyses of the decision-making process do not seem to confirm this assumption. Gehring (1996) emphasises, for instance, that the scientific part of the Directive, i.e., standards and measurement procedures, was basically defined by scientific expert committees and was not subject to politicisation during the Council negotiations. Bargaining was mainly centred around the general part of the Directive, including aspects such as exemption rules and compliance deadlines.

tributed to the instant discovery of cases of non-compliance with the Drinking Water Directive, in contrast to countries where measuring is done less frequently, not in the same geographic density and with less sensitive measuring equipment (Interviews *BMU*, March 1997; *BGW*, March 1997; *NRW-MURL*, April 1997).

The second institutional restriction for appropriate compliance emerged from the strong administrative segmentation of competencies with respect to the control of industrial discharges into the water and the regulation of drinking water quality, implying that neither the water providers nor the health authorities have regulatory competencies with respect to the control of water pollution. Consequently, the regulation of drinking water follows an 'end-of-the-pipe' approach based on the principle of 'consumer pays' rather than 'polluter pays'. This approach emerging from administrative segmentation is institutionally entrenched in different hierarchical chains which are based on a comprehensive multi-tier structure, a pattern that we have observed as a general characteristic of German administrative structures. Given this high degree of institutional stability of existing arrangements, the scope for the development of alternative, more integrated concepts to regulate drinking water quality was quite restricted.

In view of these institutional rigidities, the underlying constellation of interests and actors created particular difficulties to effectively adapt to European requirements. As alternative, either innovative or pragmatic, concepts were excluded by existing institutional constraints, compliance was only possible by improving existing cleaning technologies. Given the high economic costs required for such improvements, the development of corresponding solutions was delayed by fundamental distributional conflicts.

Both water providers and environmental organisations pushed for stricter regulation to limit the industrial pollution of ground water used for the provision of drinking water. But any such attempt had to contend with the interests of the farmers who were forcefully represented not only by their own associations, but also by the federal and regional agriculture ministries, who opposed any compulsory limits on the use of fertilisers (Rüdig and Kraemer 1994: 69). Additional opposition emerged from the chemical industry as a producer of pesticides (Interview *BGW*, March 1997; Lenschow 1997).

The farmers were only willing to limit their use of fertilisers if they were compensated financially for their loss. Notwithstanding the strong opposition of water providers and environmentalists that this solution would violate the 'polluter pays' principle, it was clear that no government was prepared to engage in a major conflict with agricultural interests. Consequently, the fifth amendment of the *WHG* in 1986 allowed the payment of compensation to farmers (Conrad 1990).

While at the federal level therefore only a framework for a potential solution was established, the details of the scheme had to be worked out by the *Länder*. Given that attempts to find a uniform solution at the level of the *Länder* Working Group Water turned out to be fraught with difficulties as agricultural and environmental concerns clashed, the initiative was thus firmly in the court of individual regional governments (Rüdig and Kraemer 1994: 69).

As a consequence, the concrete arrangements differ across regions, following, however, two basic models (Baldock and Bennett 1991; Kraemer and Warnke 1992): legally-binding compensation concepts like the water penny (*Wasserpfennig*) in Baden-Württemberg or the reliance on corporatist agreements between the regional administration, the federation of water providers and agricultural associations in North-Rhine Westphalia and Bavaria (*BGW/DVGW* 1993: 15; Interview *BGW*, March 1997). It becomes obvious that none of these strategies provides a departure from the well-established 'consumer pays' principle, albeit to some extent modifying the 'end-of-the-pipe' approach by trying to tackle problems of drinking water quality already at the stage of pollution.

In conclusion, the implementation of the Drinking Water Directive in Germany illustrates that in cases of moderate European adaptation requirements within the core of national administrative traditions, an institutional perspective provides no sufficient explanation for actual patterns of administrative change. To explain the concrete pattern of delayed adaptation, we have to take account of the particular interests of relevant actors and their strategic interaction in the light of given institutional opportunity structures. As the institutional context provided a rather restrictive framework for compliance within existing administrative core principles, it took considerable time to develop domestic compromise solutions which were accepted by the actors involved.

EMAS: accepted adaptation within the core

The implementation of the EMAS-Regulation is the only case out of the five pieces of legislation under study where European adaptation requirements instantly resulted in corresponding administrative changes in Germany. This can be explained by two factors: the institutional scope of adaptation pressure remained within the core of administrative traditions and adaptation to European requirements was successfully supported by domestic actor coalitions.

Domestic arrangements and sectoral 'goodness of fit'

Viewed from a mere sectoral perspective, the administrative implications of the EMAS-Regulation were in clear contradiction to corresponding administrative arrangements in German environmental policy. This statement holds true with respect to both analytical dimensions under investigation, i.e., administrative styles as well as administrative structures.

On the one hand, the Regulation's emphasis on self-regulation, procedural rules as well as voluntary participation stood in sharp contrast to the administrative style dominant in German environmental policy, with its patterns of hierarchical 'top-down' regulation, substantive technological requirements as well as uniform and compulsory rules. Regardless of the concrete environmental medium concerned, German environmental regulation is 'police law', i.e., reflects an interventionist administrative style. There is a widespread belief among administrative actors that only hierarchical and substantive regulations are capable of efficiently ensuring environmental protection. But also the industry prefers this kind of approach, given its high degree of legal predictability and clarity (Héritier, Knill and Mingers 1996: 69–70). From the late 1970s the interventionist approach has been criticised as being an economically inefficient regulatory tool and leading to deficient implementation results (Mayntz *et al.* 1978; SRU 1987). Despite these criticism, however, practical environmental policy continued to place little emphasis on alternative solutions, such as economic instruments or self-regulation (Weidner 1996).[15]

The requirements of the EMAS-Regulation were not only in contradiction with the interventionist administrative style, but also with present administrative structures. The Regulation requires member states to create competent accreditation and certification bodies in order to set up the necessary regulatory framework for the domestic environmental management system to be applied by industry. This way, Germany was required to set up new administrative authorities at either the federal or regional levels, i.e. to create new structures, or to allocate

---

[15] To be sure, environmental policy-making in Germany is characterised by certain forms of corporatist arrangements. It is important to emphasise, however, that these arrangements cannot be considered as exceptions from the dominant interventionist approach. Rather, they exist *within* this approach, as regulatory authorities have delegated certain tasks to corporatist bodies acting on their behalf. Corporatist bodies involved in the environmental field are institutions (generally private registered associations) that are responsible for defining indeterminate categories of reference (Association of German Engineers), plant inspection (Technical Control Association) or standardisation (German Institute for Standardisation) (Boehmer-Christiansen and Skea 1991: 158).

new responsibilities to already existing units, hence implying considerable organisational changes.

Pattern of administrative adaptation: accepted adaptation
In view of the sectoral incompatibility of domestic arrangements with
the requirements of the Regulation, which had also become evident in
the strong German opposition during the supranational policy formulation process, the German implementation record concerning the
Regulation is rather surprising. The 1995 Environmental Audit Law
(*Umewltauditgesetz*) lays down the basic regulatory structure for a national EMAS which is fully in line with the requirements spelled out in
the Regulation.[16] As prescribed by European legislation, the law sets up
a specific institution responsible for the accreditation and control of the
so-called verifiers which are in charge of the external evaluation of the
company internal auditing process, namely the *Deutsche Akkreditierungs-
und Zulassungsgesellschaft für Umweltgutachter (DAU)*. Following the
principle of industrial self-regulation, the *DAU* is financed and organised by the industry and trade associations. The professional criteria to
be met by the verifiers and the guidelines for their control to be followed
by the *DAU* are established by the Environmental Verifier Committee
(*Umweltgutachterausschuß – UGA*) which is a multi-partite expert committee consisting of representatives of industry, the environmental
administration from the federal and the *Länder* level, environmental
verifiers, the economic administration from the federal and the *Länder*
level, trade unions, and environmental associations. The *UGA* is under
legal control of the Ministry of the Environment (Lübbe-Wolff 1994;
Héritier, Knill and Mingers 1996).

The fact the *UGA* is enabled to develop administrative directives
governing the work of the *DAU* constitutes an innovation in German
law which does not usually entrust legislative functions to quasi-inde-
pendent expert committees. The German government perceives this as
an illustration of its wish to co-operate with the private sector in the
implementation of environmental policy (Interview *BMU*, May 1997).
Besides the far-reaching participation of the industry in the regulatory
scheme, the federal government has provided financial and operational
assistance especially for small and medium-sized enterprises (cheap
credits, advisory services) in order to facilitate a large participation in

---

[16] Given its character as a Regulation, the European EMAS legislation is directly
applicable in the member states; hence requiring no additional national legislation for
formal transposition. In view of its structural requirements as well as the partly rather
openly formulated procedural rules, Germany decided to specify the requirements of
the Regulation in the form of a national law.

EMAS (Lenschow 1997). Following the considerable administrative adaptations to European requirements in favour of industrial self-regulation and regulatory participation, Germany emerged as the 'European champion' in implementating the EMAS-Regulation, with 894 industrial sites registered by March 1998, compared to 48 in Britain and 16 in France (Bouma 2000).[17]

Domestic support for change within the core

How can we explain the fact that domestic administrative arrangements have been adapted to European requirements despite their considerable sectoral incompatibility? Why was there no administrative resistance to establish new concepts which imply rather innovative elements to existing sectoral styles and structures? As we will see, effective adaptation emerges from the combination of two factors: the requirements of the Regulation still remained within the general core of national administrative traditions and change within the core was successfully supported by domestic actors.

The moderate institutional scope of European implications lies first in the fact that EMAS provides an additional regulatory instrument *supplementing* the tools already in place rather than *replacing* existing core arrangements, i.e., the interventionist approach in Germany (Knill 1998). In addition, the supplementary requirements implied by the Regulation correspond with another important element of the German state tradition, namely, the tradition of corporatist arrangements which are reflected in a whole range of intermediary organisations that partly assume public functions and partly represent private interests (Lehmbruch 1997; Benz and Goetz 1996). Hence, albeit in contradiction with the dominant regulatory patterns in the environmental field, the idea of societal self-regulation as advanced by EMAS is not in contradiction to the general core of German administrative traditions. The basic elements of the regulatory system set up in the context of EMAS, i.e., limited corporatist self-administration as well as a legal representational monopoly guaranteed by the state which oversees the functioning of the system, have a strong affinity to the arrangements found in the domains of social policy, health policy, education and labour relations.

---

[17] There is some concern that the high success rate of the EMAS-Regulation may be the consequence of a too industry-friendly regime (SRU 1996: 100). Since the establishment and operation of the *DAU* preceded the establishment of the *UGA*, a regulatory vacuum emerged which allowed the *DAU* to build the foundation for the EMAS scheme and possibly constrain the future input of the non-industry actors who are now also represented in the *UGA*. Thus, there is some concern that the first group of accredited verifiers are coming from a too-heavy 'industry background'. This bias may be countered by the transparency component in the Regulation, however.

Interestingly, the present corporatist approach emerged as a compromise solution between two competing models implying either a pure 'state approach' or a pure 'industry approach'. The Environment Ministry tried to deal with the institutional adjustments required by falling back on classical forms of sectoral regulation. The preferred model was to entrust ascertainment of the reliability and impartiality of verifiers to the Federal Environment Office. Only the technical assessment of verifiers was to be assigned to the *DAU*. The counterproposal of the industry, which also found the support of the Economics Ministry, aimed to establish a self-administrative, decentralised accreditation system by chambers of industry and commerce and chambers of handcrafts (Sellner and Schnutenhaus 1993; Schneider 1995: 368).

As outlined in the analytical framework, however, the fact of only moderate adaptation requirements does not automatically imply that administrative change actually takes place. This now depends on the underlying interest constellation, beliefs, and institutional opportunity structures characterising strategic interaction of domestic actors. These conditions actually favoured administrative adjustments.

Thus, notwithstanding certain discussions on the concrete implementation, the political arena was characterised by broad support for the Regulation from both industrial and environmental organisations, which in part could be traced to the fact that implementation happened to resonate with concurrent national debates on deregulation and administrative reforms. An important aspect explaining the strong support from industry in this context refers to the expectation that authorisation and inspection procedures might be 'slimmed' for EMAS participants. Although this issue is still discussed at the federal and regional levels, so far no concrete steps have been taken. Bavaria has gone furthest in trying to operationalise the linkage between different instruments and reduce the procedural requirements placed upon industry. Also, together with Baden Württemberg, Bavaria plans an initiative in the Federal Council to simplify authorisation procedures regulated under the BImSchG for EMAS registered sites (Lenschow 1997).

In sum, the implementation of the EMAS-Regulation in the overall context of the German deregulation debate favoured the emergence of a broad support coalition for proper compliance at the domestic level. The fact that this support actually was successful, however, can only be understood against the background of the macro-institutional context which allowed for the administrative adaptation within the general core of national administrative traditions.

7.4   Conclusion: a static scope for administrative adaptation

The implementation of the five pieces of European legislation in Germany reveals a rather unsystematic pattern of administrative transformation. Apart from the LCP Directive which confirmed domestic requirements, moderate adaptations within the core of national administrative traditions have only occurred in the cases of EMAS and, after a considerable delay, the Drinking Water Directive. In the cases of Information Access and EIA, by contrast, required adaptations were resisted as a result of the core challenges to administrative core patterns implied by these measures.

The different patterns of administrative adjustment can be explained on the basis of a modified, less deterministic institution-based approach. We have seen that in cases where the institutional scope of European adaptation pressure is either too low or too high, the outcome of administrative persistence can already be inferred from a mere institutionalist perspective. It is only in cases of moderate adaptation pressure (where adjustment to European requirements can be achieved within the range of options defined by national administrative traditions) that the institutionalist argument needs to be supplemented by an actor-based perspective in order to explain administrative change or persistence.

In the case of Germany, the institutional scope of European adaptation pressure varies basically with the design of European legislation rather than changes in the domestic institutional context. In view of the low capacity for administrative reform, there is a comparatively low potential that the level of European adaptation pressure might be reduced as a result of endogenous reform developments. As a consequence, national administrative traditions reflect a rather static framework which imposes considerable constraints when adjusting to European policy demands.

This limited scope for far-reaching changes is reflected in the general development of German environmental policy. The basic principles of German environmental policy remain effective to the present day, notwithstanding the widely acknowledged problems associated with them, namely inflexibility, ineffective implementation and bureaucratic inefficiency. Alternative conceptions play so far only a limited role in German environmental policy. This holds true not only for the introduction of new instruments relying on economic incentives, voluntary agreements and industrial self-regulation (Weidner 1997), but also with respect to the scientific demands for a 'co-operative state' (Ritter 1990; Wolf 1990) and the development of informal mediation procedures between different societal actors (Beuermann and Burdick 1997; Jansen

1997; Ladeur 1990). Corresponding attempts to alter the existing logic of administrative intervention take place under the shadow of the legalist and interventionist approach; they are considered as supplementary or subsidiary elements rather than alternative options.

In this light, it comes as no surprise that political commitments from the early 1990s onwards to promote the economic competitiveness of the '*Standort Deutschland*' by reducing the regulatory burden on industry as well as the 'opportunity window' provided by the process of German reunification, had an only limited impact on German environmental policy. 'Innovations' were primarily related to marginal changes in order to accelerate authorisation and planning procedures (Troja 1997). Moreover, notwithstanding the fact that German reunification created opportunities for the new Eastern regions to develop more integrated regulatory structures in the environmental field, the fragmented arrangements to be found in the 'old' regions were almost completely exported to the Eastern regions, implying only minor adaptations (Eisen 1993). This static scope for administrative adaptation given in German environmental policy clearly contrasts with the case of Britain, to which we will turn in the following chapter.

The implementation record of Britain with respect to the five policies under study is in sharp contrast with its general reputation as environmental laggard, at least with respect to the adjustment of administrative styles and structures to the requirements spelled out in European legislation. Considerable administrative changes took place in order to comply with the Directives on LCP, Drinking Water and Access to Information. Domestic resistance to change can only be observed in the EIA case, whereas the EMAS Regulation confirmed existing arrangements, hence requiring only negligible adjustments.

In contrast with Germany, where patterns of administrative transformation could be understood by conceiving of national administrative traditions as a static phenomenon, the explanation of the British cases illustrates the need for a dynamic conception of European adaptation pressure. This perspective takes account of the fact that adaptation pressure may not only vary with the design of European policies, but also as a result of endogenous national reform developments affecting the core of administrative traditions. The British cases demonstrate that the stability and continuity assumption underlying institution-based explanations cannot be taken for granted in countries which are characterised by a high capacity for administrative reforms, given the institutional features of the political and administrative system. Although implying no complete overhaul of national administrative traditions, far-reaching reforms led to substantial changes in administrative core patterns, hence altering the scope for sectoral adaptation. In other words, administrative reforms occurring independently of European influence reduced the institutional incompatibility of European and domestic arrangements, hence opening up new opportunities for sectoral adjustment.

Moreover, and similar to the German case study, the British cases underline that the level of European adaptation pressure has to be assessed from the general institutional context of national administrative traditions rather than from a mere sectoral perspective. The far-reaching administrative reforms that contributed to changes in the level of European adaptation pressure were not specifically linked to the environmental field, but occurred at a general level. Nevertheless, these general rather than sector-specific developments played a crucial role in influencing patterns of sectoral adjustment.

Finally, the British cases show the limits of a deterministic institution-based explanation in 'institutionally more open' constellations of changes within the core. In such cases, the institutional explanation has to be supplemented by an agency-based perspective taking account of the institutional context and the interest constellations of the actors involved. As we will see, this context favoured domestic adjustment in the cases of LCP, Drinking Water and Access to Information, while in the EIA case administrative adaptations were neglected as a result of missing domestic support and mobilisation.

8.1 Confirmation of the core: compliance without change

The EMAS Regulation is the only case of the five pieces of European legislation under study which confirmed existing sectoral arrangements in Britain, hence allowing for compliance without administrative change. This can be traced to the fact that the British development of a national environmental management standard occurred just as the EU was seeking to establish its own version of these regulatory mechanisms. In this context, the British players successfully set the agenda by pushing their own proposals at the European level (Zito and Egan 1997).

Domestic arrangements and sectoral 'goodness of fit'

Given the British 'first mover advantage' in shaping the regulatory content of the European Regulation, it comes as no surprise that the administrative implications of the Regulation were well in line with existing sectoral arrangements, namely the 1992 domestic environmental management standard developed by the British Standards Institution (BSI) which came to be known as BS 7750.

Similar to the implications of the Regulation, the British standard emphasised an administrative style based on procedural rules, self-regulation and voluntary participation; i.e., the concrete regulatory requirements for registration under BS 7750 were fairly compatible with EMAS. This holds especially true with respect to the requirements on company internal audits, continuous environmental improvements and external verification. If a company wishes to be registered under BS 7750, it must set up a documented system to ensure that it meets its environmental objectives and policies. In this context, the standard requires an ongoing commitment to continuous improvement which is defined as a year-on-year enhancement of overall performance, resulting from the constant effort to improve in line with the company's environmental policy (BSI 1993). To demonstrate compliance with BS 7750, companies require certification by external verifiers or auditors who need official accreditation (Tromans 1996: 6).

Nevertheless there exist slight differences between both concepts which implied, however, only minor adaptational requirements. EMAS is based on a site-specific approach, while BS 7750 follows a company-based approach, including different sites of the same company. In addition, successful participation under EMAS requires the publication of an independently verified environmental statement and the certification by a 'competent body' to be appointed at the national level. Under BS 7750, by contrast, companies are not obliged to publish environmental statements and certification lies not with an official body, but with accredited verifiers (Interviews DoE, February 1997; Environment Agency, February 1997).

The picture of high sectoral compatibility also becomes evident when considering the dimension of administrative structure. In this context, the Regulation requires member states to set up specific bodies responsible for the accreditation and control of the verifiers who are in charge of the external evaluation of the company internal auditing process and for the certification and registration of participating companies. This requirement implied only negligible changes in Britain, as a corresponding body responsible for the accreditation of external auditors had already been set up under the national environmental management system, namely the National Accreditation Council for Certification Bodies (NACCB), a multi-partite body linked to the Department of Trade and Industry (DTI), composed of experts from industry, accreditation organisations, scientific organisations, the Department of the Environment (DoE)[1] and the DTI. This way, the only additional requirement implied by the regulation was to appoint a competent certification body; an implication which caused no particular problems, as the Regulation gives member states broad discretion with respect to their organisational decision (Interview DoE, February 1997).[2]

[1] After its takeover in May 1997, the Labour Party changed the organisational structure at the departmental level. In this context, the DoE was merged with the Department of Transport, now forming the Department of the Environment, Transport and the Regions (DETR). Since this analysis is basically related to developments that took place before this organisational change, throughout the text reference is made to the previous organisational structure, unless indicated explicitly.

[2] The establishment of the multi-partite NACCB was a compromise solution emerging

Pattern of administrative adaptation: compliance without change

In the light of the high sectoral compatibility of European requirements and domestic arrangements, the EMAS Regulation, which is – in contrast to Directives – directly applicable at the national level, was adopted without introducing any additional legal and administrative changes. Apart from several Guidance Notes issued by the DoE in order to specify the provisions of the Regulation, Britain made use of arrangements already in place in order to fulfil the requirements of EU legislation (Interview DoE, February 1997).

Administrative responsibility for the accreditation of verifiers was allocated to the NACCB which in 1996 became the UK Accreditation Service (UKAS) (Knill 1997b).[3] The functions of the 'competent body' responsible for certification and registration are fulfilled by the DoE. The main reason for leaving these functions with the DoE was the fact that Eco-Audit is still perceived as a developing area and therefore potential adaptations are easier to achieve when the DoE remains involved. Moreover, other options had been considered as less appropriate. On the one hand, the option to allocate the functions of the 'competent body' to the national Environment Agency was rejected in order to keep regulatory and self-regulatory functions separated. On the other hand, the appointment of UKAS as a competent body was not considered as feasible. In view of the dominant role of industry within UKAS, this option would have questioned the independent role of external verifiers (Interview: DoE, February 1997).

Despite the fact that European requirements could be easily complied with by slightly modifying already existing administrative arrangements at the domestic level, the registration process developed rather slowly (Bouma 2000), hence indicating low industrial support for EMAS. Lacking industrial support can first be understood against the backdrop of some confusion concerning the differences between varying environmental management systems offered for industrial application, namely BS 7750, EMAS, as well as ISO 14001, the standard developed by the

out of a political struggle between the scientific environmental policy community (including the DoE, environmental organisations and environmental consultancies) and the economic policy community (including the BSI, the DTI and industrial associations) whose expertise is found more in sound management priorities rather than environmental criteria and auditing (Zito and Egan 1997).

[3] In the context of this organisational change, which was not related to European implications but followed from the national context, two formerly separated accreditation bodies for management standards (the responsibility of the NACCB) and laboratories were merged. Moreover, UKAS is no longer part of the DTI (as was the case with the NACCB), but was established as an independent body (Interview: DoE, February 1997).

International Standardisation Organisation as a response to European activities (cf. Tromans 1996: 6; Zito and Egan 1997). In view of the lack of clarity on the compatibility and peculiarities of the different concepts, British industry preferred to register under BS 7750 (Interviews: DoE, February 1997; Environment Agency, February 1997). To facilitate the switch from BS 7750 to EMAS, the DoE issued Guidance Notes, specifying the additional requirements of EMAS. Moreover, small and medium-sized enterprises are offered financial incentives to promote participation under the EMAS scheme (Knill 1997b).

Second, low industrial support may be linked to the fact that a formal linkage between EMAS and environmental regulation is still lacking, e.g., in a sense that registered companies are granted regulatory relief with respect to plant authorisation. Due to the missing integration of both procedures there exists no particular incentive for industry to register under EMAS. The absence of an integration of voluntary and regulatory approaches, which seems at first glance surprising, given the traditional British preference for industrial self-regulation, has to be understood in the light of transitory problems emerging from the establishment of the Environment Agency in 1996. Since the Agency integrates the formerly separated regulatory regimes of air and water pollution control, the integration of EMAS into existing regulatory procedures was complicated. EMAS fits better with the process-oriented approach followed in air pollution control which has its focus on the performance of individual plants. With respect to water pollution, on the other hand, the focus was more on environmental effects; that is, the process and operation of the plant (where EMAS comes in) is less important than the overall water quality (Interviews DoE, February 1997; Environment Agency, February 1997).

In sum, the EMAS Regulation confirmed existing arrangements at the domestic level, hence implying no particular pressures for administrative adaptation. However, despite the fulfilment of the administrative preconditions as they are defined in the European legislation, industrial interest in EMAS developed slowly. This aspect can be traced to transitory problems, rather than to domestic resistance to comply with European requirements.

8.2   Change within the core: neglected adaptation

As with the German cases of Drinking Water and EMAS, the British EIA case illustrates that an exclusive focus on institutional factors may render only insufficient results in 'institutionally more open situations' of moderate adaptation pressure, i.e., where European requirements can be complied with by changes within the core of national administrative traditions. Satisfactory explanation of adaptation performance requires a lower level of abstraction, i.e., the analysis of actor coalitions within a given institutional context. The fact that adaptations to European requirements were neglected in the British EIA case in the absence of administrative core challenges can only be understood when considering the low domestic support in favour of effective compliance.

Domestic arrangements and sectoral 'goodness of fit'

Viewed from a mere sectoral perspective, we observe a picture of high compatibility of European and domestic arrangements. The administrative implications of the EIA Directive seemed to fit quite well with existing sectoral styles and structures in British environmental policy. Sectoral compatibility emerged from two factors, namely the open texture of the Directive and the fact that its 'spirit' corresponded with domestic arrangements.

The EIA Directive can be seen as a framework law rather than a detailed regulatory approach. It leaves the member states considerable discretion on the detailed transposition into national legislation, provided the basic principles and procedural requirements were satisfied (Lee 1995: 78; Alder 1993: 205). As pointed out in chapter 6, the Commission had markedly broadened margins for action in implementation at the national level. In this context, Britain had played a rather active and influential role in order to secure the compatibility of European requirements and domestic arrangements. As a result, the list of projects subject to EIA was significantly cut. Member states were also given the right to exempt certain projects without explicit Commission approval. The type and extent of information to be supplied by the applicant was now to be determined by the member state concerned and no longer at the Community level (Coenen and Jörissen 1988: 138–40).

The thus-amended Directive accorded very closely with existing sectoral arrangements. The implications of the Directive concerning an administrative style based on procedural regulation, high flexibility and discretion came quite close to British development control procedures laid down in the Town and Country Planning Act, where a version of an EIA existed already since the 1970s, albeit on a legally non-binding and unsystematic basis (Turnbull 1988: 25; Haigh 1996).

In this context, British planning authorities enjoyed wide discretion in deciding if and how the environmental impacts of a project have to be taken into consideration. They could take into account any information they considered as being relevant, i.e., both economic, political and environmental factors (Alder 1993: 211). Moreover, there were only limited possibilities for formal participation and judicial review of planning decisions (Cupei 1994: 50). Contrary to this practice, the EIA Directive called for more formalised and transparent procedures in order to secure a systematic and comprehensible application. However, given the open character of the Directive, these requirements would have implied only minor changes in existing domestic arrangements.

The same holds true with respect to the dimension of administrative structures. The main responsibility for implementing the Town and Country Planning Act lies with the local authorities. Depending on the scope and nature of a certain project, either the County or District Councils are in charge of issuing land-use authorisations (Interviews: Environment Agency, April 1997; AMA, March 1997). Given the overall planning responsibility of the local authorities, which are statutorily obliged to consult other public bodies with environmental responsibilities (e.g., the Environment Agency), the integrated regulatory structures were well in line with the conception of an integrated approach, as implied by the Directive.

Additional co-ordination requirements emerged, however, from the fact that in general the authorisation of industrial processes in Britain is based on a two-stage process, implying the planning permission for land-use and the operation authorisation under the corresponding pollution control legislation. Both authorisation procedures serve different purposes and therefore have different information requirements: the planning authority needs to decide whether, in principle, the proposed development should be permitted to take place at a certain location. For this, a comprehensive assessment of likely effects is necessary, but it remains at a rather general level focusing on aspects of landscape and nature conservation. At the pollution control stage, by contrast, much more detailed technical information about emissions is taken into account, whereas landscape impacts play a minor role (Cupei 1994: 49). Hence, both authorisation procedures consider different aspects of environmental impacts, which, for the purpose of an integrated perspective, should be considered in a co-ordinated way. The Directive's implication with respect to administrative co-ordination between land-use planning and pollution control becomes particularly apparent in cases where different administrative levels are involved, i.e., where pollution control is under the responsibility of the central authorities (Interview Environment Agency, February 1997).

Apart from this structural requirement to improve co-ordination between local planning and central pollution control authorities and the need for a certain formalisation and systematisation of existing planning procedures, the EIA Directive fully corresponded with existing sectoral arrangements at the national level. In view of this sectoral 'fit', one could have expected effective compliance with the remaining adaptational implications. This expectation, however, is in contradiction with empirical findings, suggesting that as a consequence of Britain's minimalist approach to implementation, even these minor adaptation requirements were neglected.

Pattern of administrative adaptation: neglected adaptation

Following this minimalist approach to implementation, Britain sought only formal compliance with the minimum requirements of the Directive while at the same time avoiding any changes in existing administrative practices. To reduce potential impacts during practical implications, Britain transposed the Directive by integrating EIA requirements into already existing procedures. No new primary legislation was enacted to transpose the Directive. Rather, the Directive was formally implemented by a whole series of Regulations which were based on existing national laws. Besides these statutory instruments, a number of Circulars and advisory booklets have been issued (Haigh 1996: 11.2–6). The main statutory instrument is the Regulations[4] based on the Town and Country Planning Act which applies only for projects requiring planning permission (Lambrechts 1996: 69).[5]

Given these efforts to minimise legal and institutional adjustments, many complaints were made to the Commission on the incomplete transposition of the Directive (Kunzlik 1995). Problems occurred especially with respect to the projects listed in Annex II of the Directive, where an EIA is only required if these projects have significant effects on the environment. Initially, the government held the view that it had complete discretion whether or not to require EIAs for Annex II projects. Following representation from the Commission, however, Britain accepted that the member states' discretion only lies in deciding whether a project potentially has significant effects on the environment,

---

[4] Most important in this respect are the Town and Country Planning (Assessment of Environmental Effects) Regulations 1988.

[5] Some developments listed in the Directive fall outside Britain's normal land-use planning procedure. For major infrastructure projects such as trunk roads, motorways, power stations, power lines, ports and harbours, authority to give consent rests with the appropriate Secretary of State. Moreover, some projects may be approved by a private Act of Parliament, while others, such as Crown developments, afforestation, and some agricultural drainage schemes are subject to no form of planning permission at all (Lambrechts 1996: 72). The responsibility for carrying out an EIA in these cases mainly lies with the relevant government departments (Haigh 1996).

rather than excluding Annex II projects from *ex ante* (Haigh 1996: 11.2–14).[6] A subsequent DoE Circular 15/88 gave guidance as to when an Annex II project requires an EIA. Three main categories are suggested: projects with more than local importance; projects in particularly sensitive locations; and projects with unusually complex and adverse environmental effects (Haigh 1996: 11.2–11). The Circular, however, is not legally binding for the planning authorities who decide in the light of 'unfettered discretion' (Cupei 1994: 48).

In view of the integration of EIA requirements into existing planning procedures, the EIA Directive implied no departures from the highly flexible British planning practice in favour of a more comprehensive approach (Interview Environment Agency, February 1997). The wide discretion and flexibility become apparent with respect to several factors. Firstly, planning authorities have great leeway for deciding whether a project falling under Annex II of the Directive has significant effects on the environment or not. The opportunities to legally challenge these decisions are highly restricted to cases where authorities have acted in a 'completely irrational' way (Alder 1993: 214). Secondly, the planning authority has considerable discretion for determining the content of the EIA and its adequacy (Lambrechts 1996: 77). Thirdly, the planning authorities have wide discretion with respect to balancing the results of the EIA against other information to be considered in the authorisation process, such as financial and economic interests. Again, the balancing of competing considerations is only to a limited extent subject to court review. The courts only review the procedural aspects, e.g., if all interests have been taken into account, but leave the concrete decision to the discretion of the local authorities (Alder 1993: 212; Interview: Environment Agency, February 1997).

The practical application of the EIA Directive in Britain therefore lacks certainty and transparency for both the project developer and interested third parties such as environmental organisations. In this context, the position of the project developer is still more comfortable than that of third parties. There are generally close and informal discussions between the planning authorities and the project developer in order to specify the scope and content of the EIA. These consultations normally take place without public participation. Moreover, only the decision requiring an EIA has to contain a statement of reasons. A

---

6   Moreover, there was discussion between the British government and the Commission as to whether projects which had already been in the 'pipeline' before the Directive came into force but not yet authorised, fall under the Directive or not. This dispute was finally resolved by a clarifying statement of the Commission in 1995, accepting Britain's restrictive approach to apply the Directive only where the procedure for consent started after the Directive came into force (Haigh 1996: 11.2–19).

negative decision need not be justified and so cannot be challenged by third parties (Lambrechts 1996: 73). Similar restrictions exist with respect to challenging planning permissions. A right of appeal to the Secretary of State exists only when a planning permission is refused but not where permission is granted. Third parties who wish to challenge a planning permission on environmental grounds must therefore resort to the ordinary courts thus facing procedural and financial barriers (Alder 1993: 216).

Patterns of resistance to change can also be observed with respect to the structural implications of the Directive, namely the need for improved co-ordination between local planning and central pollution control authorities. In the absence of co-ordination procedures, local authorities have to carry out an EIA without knowing the technical details of the industrial process since these are subject to the process authorisation issued by the Environment Agency. The Agency has rejected giving local authorities these details in advance, since this would imply an anticipation of the process authorisation. Local authorities are therefore confronted with significant uncertainty as to how to assess the environmental impacts of industrial projects. In order to overcome this situation, local authorities often grant planning permissions only in connection with certain technological conditions the applicant has to fulfil. These specifications, on the other hand, often run into conflict with the technological considerations made by the Environment Agency when issuing the process authorisation (Interview Environment Agency, February 1997).

As a consequence of the neglected adaptation to European requirements, the quality of environmental statements in general is not very satisfactory. Many provide only little more information than a standard planning application, and few provide information on the alternatives considered, or the mutual interaction of the effects on different environmental media (Alder 1993; Cupei 1994; Haigh 1996: 11.2–18).

Lacking support for changes within the core

How can we explain the observed pattern of administrative resistance to only minor sectoral changes? In view of the only moderate adaptational requirements of EU legislation, lacking administrative adjustment cannot be explained from a mere institution-based perspective. To understand whether changes within the core take place or not, we have to supplement the institutional perspective by a less abstract explanation taking account of the extent to which effective compliance with European requirements was supported or resisted by national actor coalitions.

On the one hand, the Directive's implications in favour of more systematic and comprehensive planning procedures were not in contradiction with the British tradition of a mediating rather than interventionist administrative style as outlined in chapter 4. The Directive required no departure from the basic aspects characterising this style, namely procedural regulation, self-regulation, administrative flexibility as well as informal, pragmatic and consensual patterns of administrative interest intermediation, but implied that planning authorities played their mediating role in a more consistent way, i.e., by making use of clear and transparent principles underlying their decision. On the other hand, the Directive's requirement of improved co-ordination of central pollution control and local planning could be achieved by changes within rather than of the core of national administrative traditions. This holds true, although central–local relations in Britain are traditionally characterised by the absence of hierarchical control structures; i.e., local authorities carry out their functions without being subject to legal and administrative control by central government. However, the development of more effective co-ordination mechanisms to promote the exchange of EIA-relevant information would not have violated this traditional principle of separation of local and central spheres of government, since co-ordination would not necessarily have implied the establishment of hierarchical control relationships between central and local authorities.

In view of the only moderate adaptational requirements implied by European legislation, a mere institution-based perspective, albeit indicating that adaptation is generally possible, does not allow for the explanation of actually observed patterns of change and persistence, but has to be supplemented by examining the particular domestic context which was not supportive in Britain during the mid-1980s, that is, during the time of the EIA implementation. While both industry and the administration resisted any changes that would have increased the regulatory burden on project developers or complicated existing planning procedures (Haigh 1996: 11.2–3), the activities of environmental organisations in favour of effective compliance with the Directive remained rather modest. The primary focus of environmental awareness during the 1980s was on the debate about SO_2 – a context where Britain had been proclaimed to be the 'dirty man of Europe'. With respect to the rather 'dull' EIA, which could not easily be linked to environmental disasters, there was no public pressure keeping the political level 'honest' in implementing the Directive (Knill 1998). In the light of this constellation, Britain neglected adaptational requirements implied by the EIA Directive, although the required changes implied no challenges to national administrative traditions.

8.3   Change within a changing core: accepted adaptation

The implementation of the Directives on LCP, Drinking Water, and Access to Information in Britain illustrates the need for a dynamic approach when analysing the Europeanisation of domestic administrations. The actual domestic changes which occurred in the light of European requirements can be sufficiently explained neither from a sectoral nor from a more differentiated, less deterministic institutional perspective. The observed pattern of accepted adaptation does not correspond with our expectation of administrative resistance to change, as indicated not only by the sectoral 'misfit' of European and domestic arrangements, but also by the fact that supranational requirements were in contradiction with existing core patterns of national administrative traditions.

This surprising finding can only be understood when taking into account that these core patterns were 'moving' rather than 'static', given the impact of national administrative reforms. National reforms altered the scope for sectoral adaptation; allowing for compliance by changes within rather than of the core of national administrative traditions. In contrast to the EIA case, where appropriate adaptation was neglected as a result of lacking domestic support, the implementation of the three 'dynamic cases' was characterised by a favourable context implying that the required changes within a changing core actually took place. As will be shown, the favourable context was in turn a consequence of the national reforms which affected the interests, strategies and resources of public and private actors involved.

Domestic arrangements and sectoral 'goodness of fit'

For all of the three Directives considered in this context one would have expected patterns of administrative resistance, given the high degree of sectoral incompatibility of domestic arrangements and European implications.

The LCP Directive

Jurisdiction over the control of stationary sources of air pollution in Britain is shared by central and local authorities. Processes requiring higher technical expertise for control such as power generation in large combustion plants had been subject to central control. The local authorities were competent with respect to all other processes.[7] The

---

[7] In particular local authorities monitored smoke and particulate emissions by private households and industrial plants that did not fall within the purview of central control (Héritier, Knill and Mingers 1996: 92).

responsible regulatory body at the central level was the Industrial Air Pollution Inspectorate (IAPI) which was the successor body of the Alkali Inspectorate established in 1863 (Weale 1996a: 110).[8] The most important statutory basis for IAPI's activities was the Alkali etc. Works Regulation Act 1906 which later was incorporated into the Health and Safety at Work Act (HSWA) 1974. There was a schedule to the Act listing all plants required to register with IAPI before beginning operation ('registered works'). The schedule covered plants with operational processes that were technically difficult to monitor or which emitted particularly noxious and hazardous substances. A schedule of the emissions subject to monitoring was also appended to the Act (Knill 1995).

The basic regulatory instrument applied in this context was the concept of best practicable means (bpm). Although bpm has never been clearly defined, in effect its definition amounted to weighing local conditions against modern technology and the cost to the factory of control measures. Great importance was placed on economic components. Its concrete application in practice was characterised by high flexibility and discretion for inspectors, as well as by its procedural rather than substantive orientation. There were no statutory emission limits or quality standards in order to specify the concrete content of bpm. This was justified on grounds of greater flexibility, which permitted individual reaction to given technological, operational and local situations (Vogel 1986: 76). Neither legislation nor the courts provided substantive specification of the bpm principle and its application, leaving the inspectors wide discretionary powers. The Inspectorate itself was considered the sole judge as to whether the plants under its jurisdiction are applying the bpm for controlling their emissions. The only reference point for the definition of bpm has been the 'notes on bpm' issued by the Chief Inspector in close co-operation with industry. The notes contained so-called 'presumptive limits' which provided the basis for negotiations between the inspectors and industry with respect to pollution abatement activities (McLoughlin 1982: 81–3).

The general relationship between inspectors and industry could be characterised as very consensual and co-operative. Inspectors relied more on persuasion and voluntary agreements and less on coercion (Vogel 1983: 89). Furthermore, the style of interaction was very pragmatic rather than legalistic. This was encouraged by the Inspectorate's wide discretion in interpreting bpm. Accordingly, prosecutions and legal

---

[8] In 1987 the Industrial Air Pollution Inspectorate, the Radiochemicals Inspectorate, the Hazardous Waste Inspectorate, and the Water Quality Inspectorate were integrated into one single Inspectorate: Her Majesty's Inspectorate of Pollution (HMIP) (Weale 1996a: 110). For further details on this reorganisation see below.

action have been extremely rare events (McLoughlin 1982: 87). The close co-operation between industry and inspectors left little room for effective participation by other actors, such as environmental organisations. Implementation of British clean air policy took place in 'family-like . . . close-knit groups of experts proud of their traditions and the trust placed in them by the public' (O'Riordan 1979: 239). This general informality and opaqueness of the regulatory system in place became particularly apparent in the extremely restrictive information policy of IAPI. This policy, which was given statutory status by the HSWA in 1974, forbade the Inspectorate from releasing emission data on registered works to the public without authorisation from the works concerned (Frankel 1978: 67). The informal and pragmatic patterns of interest intermediation served the interests of both the Inspectorate and industry. Due to its rather weak legal position, IAPI was dependent on the voluntary co-operation of industry in order to achieve pollution reduction successfully. A co-operative relationship, on the other hand, had the advantage for industry of influencing the implementation process in the light of the specific economic situation of the individual company. Furthermore, co-operation provided the opportunity for a pragmatic and time-saving procedure (Knill 1995: 105).

In the light of the above patterns characterising the administrative style in British air pollution control, the LCP Directive implied significant adjustment pressures. The interventionist orientation of the Directive, which emphasises uniform, substantive and legally binding criteria for regulatory decision-making stood in sharp contrast to the procedural bpm concept which allowed for high discretion and flexibility in its individual application on a case-by-case basis (Boehmer-Christiansen and Skea 1991).

Furthermore, the changes in the regulatory instruments were calling into doubt the established patterns of administrative interest intermediation. First, legally binding emission limits significantly reduced the leeway for pragmatic relationships. Secondly, the EU Directives implied a more formal and transparent conception and left less room for secretive and 'cosy' interaction styles. With respect to the second aspect, the 1984 Framework Directive played an important role. Although the basic principle with respect to the authorisation of industrial plants, BATNEEC, was more or less in line with the British bpm, the Directive implied a certain formalisation of the authorisation process. Thus, the existing registration system had to be replaced by a system of written consents. Moreover, the Directive required that both the application and authorisation of industrial processes had to be made available to the public concerned (Knill 1995: 187).

However, the impact of European legislation was not confined to the dimension of administrative style, but also affected structural and organisational aspects of the British system of pollution control. To be precise, the 1984 Framework Directive required both a significant widening of the local authorities' regulatory competencies and the establishment of hierarchical procedures for the control of local activities by the central level, given the overall implementation responsibility of central government towards Brussels. This can be traced to the fact that the authorisation conditions, as defined in the Framework Directive, applied to only a portion of the installations in Britain. These were the so-called 'registered works' which were under the supervision of the IAPI. All other processes were supervised by local authorities, which possessed no preventative controlling powers. They could intervene only if demonstrable damage and environmental degradation were caused by operation of the plant (public nuisance procedure). The licensing requirements of these locally controlled processes thus failed to meet the conditions defined by the Directive (Haigh 1990: 226). As a consequence, local authority powers had to be expanded and hierarchical control procedures had to be established in order to fulfil the Directive's reporting requirements (Knill 1995: 224).[9]

The Drinking Water Directive

In contrast to Germany, the regulation of water pollution and drinking water supply was carried out within a more integrated administrative structure. The biggest amount of drinking water was supplied by ten Regional Water Authorities (RWAs) which had been established by the Water Act 1973. The RWAs were designed as multi-purpose public-sector bodies. Their functions combined those of water supplier and regulator. In particular, they had regulatory responsibility not only for managing and controlling their own discharges (stemming from sewage treatment), but also for issuing consents to industrial operators (Weale 1996a: 120; Richardson, Maloney and Rüdig 1992: 159).[10]

The RWAs were responsible to the DoE which set broad objectives within which they had significant leeway in their day-to-day management. Control of the RWAs was mainly restricted to financial aspects, i.e., ceilings for borrowing and water charges. The relationship can be

---

[9] The factual need to enlarge local authority powers rather than transferring local responsibilities to the IAPI is attributable to the fact that IAPI resources would not have permitted it to implement this reorganisation, whereas only comparatively small changes were needed at the local level (Knill 1995).

[10] The RWAs provided drinking water to about 80 per cent of the population. The remaining 20 per cent was provided by 21 private companies dealing with water supply only (Interview: OFWAT, February 1997; WSA 1996: 6).

described as one where the RWAs determined their own objectives within the strict financial framework laid down by government (Maloney and Richardson 1994: 116).

The principles applied in the regulation of water pollution and drinking water were rather similar to those dominant in clean air policy. With respect to water pollution control, the essence of the regulatory system was to avoid national uniform emission standards and to set discharge consent levels in the light of the quality and use of the receiving medium as well as sound science on the harmful effects of the discharges (Weale 1996a: 120). The regulation of drinking water quality was based on the flexible principle of wholesomeness. Wholesomeness was never defined in quantitative terms, such as quality standards. The only point of reference was a broadly defined understanding that water was to be 'clear, palatable and safe' (Interview: DWI, February 1997). Water suppliers were statutorily obliged to provide wholesome water. Local authorities had to ascertain the wholesomeness of public and private supplies within their area. Any dispute between local authorities and water suppliers had to be referred to the Secretary of State for the Environment (Haigh 1996: 4.4–5).

Besides the regulatory functions of local authorities and the financial control exerted by the DoE, the core of the old regulatory system in drinking water policy was therefore self-regulation (Maloney and Richardson 1995: 104). The RWAs were allowed significant discretion and flexibility with respect to their obligation on drinking water supply, since the term 'wholesome' had never been clearly defined. In this context, the growing financial restrictions placed on the RWAs during the 1980s implied that the RWAs regulated themselves with a rather light hand and that investment into improvements of water quality remained far behind the levels in other European countries (Weale 1996a: 121; Maloney and Richardson 1995: 145).

The patterns of interaction between the RWAs and societal actors were characterised by the same characteristics as could be observed in the case of clean air policy. Contacts with the polluting industry could be described as informal, closed, pragmatic and consensual (Richardson 1983; Hawkins 1984; Vogel 1986). Consumer and environmental interests, on the other hand, were granted only limited access. Although at the level of each RWA there were established Consumer Consultative Committees representing a broad range of different interests (including consumer and environmental groups), the influence of these committees was rather symbolic. This is demonstrated by the fact that the polluting industry showed no interest in the committees and continued to lobby as core insiders by traditional routes. This holds true especially for the

Confederation of British Industry (CBI) and the National Farmers Union (NFU) (Maloney and Richardson 1994: 117).

In view of existing domestic arrangements, the Drinking Water Directive implied fundamental changes to the dominant administrative style based on procedural rules, high flexibility and informal and pragmatic patterns of administrative interest intermediation. In calling for uniform, legally binding quality standards as well as standardised sampling procedures, the Directive significantly reduced the wide discretion of the RWAs in defining wholesome water (Ward, Buller and Lowe 1995; Jordan 1997; Matthews and Pickering 1997). In doing so, the Directive implied not only changes in the mode, but also with respect to the level of regulation. Although the Directive established a certain flexibility for derogation and an extended period for compliance, it was clear that fundamental investment would be necessary in order to comply with several standards defined in the Directive, given the existing system of 'light-handed self-regulation' (Haigh 1996: 4.4–3).

The Information Directive

As in Germany, the Information Directive's requirement in favour of unconditioned public access to environmental information was in sharp contrast with sectoral patterns of administrative interest intermediation which were characterised by a high degree of informality and secrecy. Both in air and water pollution control, secretive and informal relationships between public authorities and industry had been a typical characteristic of the dominant administrative style. In the case of air pollution, for instance, this policy which was by no means a legal imposition, was even given statutory status by the HSWA 1974 (see above).

Although the existing practice was increasingly challenged during the 1980s, corresponding changes remained at an incremental level. In particular the Royal Commission for Environmental Pollution (RCEP)[11] had touched on information and confidentiality in some of its reports (RCEP 1976; 1984), and recommended 'a presumption in favour of unrestricted access' (Haigh 1996: 11.5–3). The suggestions of the RCEP were supported by persistent activities of environmental organisations and the Campaign for the Freedom of Information (CFI). The result of these activities, however, was confined to the introduction

---

[11] The RCEP is an independent standing body advising Queen, Parliament and the public on environmental protection matters. Traditionally, Royal Commissions and Parliamentary Committees enjoy an influential role in British policy-making. They constitute important filters and channels for policy ideas (Knill 1995: 300).

of public registers in the sector of water pollution in 1985. The legal provisions for these registers, which contain information about discharges from sewage and trade effluents, had already been enacted by the Control of Pollution Act 1974, but had never been implemented since that time. However, access opportunities to water registers were fairly limited in practical terms, thus discouraging the public from accessing environmental data. Besides the limited number of registers (which were available only at the headquarters of the RWAs), data were provided in a rather incomprehensible way. It was hardly possible for information requesters to compare the performance of a discharger with the conditions specified in the consent. Moreover, in view of the long timespan between legal introduction and practical implementation, the general awareness with respect to the availability of the registers was low. Notwithstanding these limited tendencies towards more transparent patterns in environmental regulation, the Information Directive therefore required a significant departure from existing sectoral arrangements.

In sum, the three pieces of European legislation involved significant adjustments of sectoral administrative arrangements in Britain. In view of this high level of sectoral incompatibility, one would have expected resistance rather than adaptation to European requirements. However, in all cases domestic arrangements were significantly adjusted, hence allowing for effective compliance with supranational legislation.

Pattern of administrative adaptation: accepted adaptation

The LCP Directive

The adaptational requirements implied by the LCP Directive as well as its 1984 Framework Directive were fully complied with by the 1990 Environmental Protection Act (EPA) by which Britain thoroughly changed existing administrative styles and structures in the environmental field.

To begin with the dimension of administrative style, legal and practical changes took place which are fully in line with the implications of the Directives in favour of a more interventionist approach. With respect to administrative instruments, regulation is now based on legally binding emission and air quality standards which are prescribed in a hierarchical and uniform way. The shift in regulatory activities towards a more interventionist approach is reflected in more formal and transparent patterns of administrative interest intermediation because the set substantive objectives now leave less room for 'cosy' and pragmatic bargaining between regulatory authorities and industry (Jordan 1993; Knill 1995).

Large combustion plants are regulated within the concept of Integrated Pollution Control (IPC) which is defined in Part I of the EPA. The introduction of IPC is a fundamental innovation for the British control system. Instead of separate control for each environmental medium, all technically complex processes are now supervised within the framework of an integrated approach which intends to ensure optimum load allocation among the various environmental media. The industrial processes and substances subject to IPC are listed in the Environmental Protection (Prescribed Processes and Substances) Regulations. Every process listed needs prior authorisation before beginning operation.

The authorisation can only be granted if several conditions are met. Firstly, the applicant has to apply BATNEEC in order to avoid and reduce pollutant emissions. If a plant discharges emissions into several environmental media, the operator must meet not only the BATNEEC condition, which is monitored separately for each medium, but must also ensure that pollution of the environment is minimised as a whole. This requirement finds expression in the Best Practicable Environmental Option (BPEO). Secondly, it must in all cases be ensured that all the relevant international and national limits are respected, regardless of whether they are quality or emission standards (DoE 1991: 6). Thirdly, it has to be ensured that emissions from prescribed processes are in conformity with any national plan. The Environment Secretary is empowered to issue a legally binding national plan in subordinate legislation laying down the progressive annual reduction of emissions by the industrial sector.

To implement the LCP Directive, the DoE issued a national plan which has to be taken into account by the Environment Agency when granting authorisations under the IPC regime (DoE 1996: 6). The national plan lays down progressive annual reductions for SO_2 and NO_x emissions. While initially the plan allocated quotas to different industry sectors and regions, this distinction was abandoned in 1997 in favour of overall national figures. Emission allocation is now the task of the Environment Agency which, within the IPC authorisation scheme, is required to ensure that the overall national emission bubbles are achieved (Interviews: Environment Agency, February 1997; DoE, February 1997).

In view of these changes in administrative instruments, patterns of administrative interest intermediation are characterised by more formal and transparent arrangements. Most important in this respect is the introduction of so-called public registers which contain all the data relevant to licensing and operation that are in the controlling authority's possession. They include not only application, authorisation, any legal proceedings and public authority objections, but also the results of emission measurements made by the authorities or the undertakings. Whereas previously bargaining between inspectors and industry took place in a rather secretive atmosphere, third parties such as environmental organisations now have many more possibilities for effective participation. Thus, representations made by third parties to applications have to be considered by the Agency when issuing authorisations (Interview: Environment Agency, February 1997). This greater openness and transparency has at the same time brought about more formal relationships between industry and inspectors, although this does not mean that informal discussions no longer take place. They are essential in order to facilitate the processing of the far-reaching exchange of information between inspectors and industry which is necessary in the light of the scope and complexity of authorisations. However, in the interests of transparency and openness no informal discussions on the substantive content of applications take place as long as the application has yet to be published in the register (Interviews: Environment Agency, February 1997; PowerGen, February 1997).

Far-reaching changes even exceeding European requirements also occurred with respect to administrative structures. Authorisations under IPC are under the jurisdiction of the Environment Agency which was established in 1996. In order to implement an integrated approach to environmental protection, in 1987 the IAPI, the Radiochemicals Inspectorate, the Hazardous Waste Inspectorate, and the Water Quality Inspectorate had already been integrated into Her Majesty's Inspectorate of Pollution (HMIP) (Weale 1996a: 110). The creation of the Agency brings together HMIP, the National Rivers Authority (NRA) which had responsibility for the control of discharges into the water, and 83 waste disposal authorities which until then were part of the local authorities. The new body established has the status of a so-called executive agency, which is still responsible to the DoE but is relatively independent with respect to its day-to-day management.

Moreover, to implement the requirements of the 1984 Framework Directive, local authority controlling powers for those processes not subject to IPC were considerably expanded. For the first time they now have the possibility of intervening preventively and not only when nuisances and damage have already occurred. At the same time, however, more detailed mechanisms of hierarchical guidance of local activities by central government were established. Hence, local flexibility is considerably reduced by concrete regulatory specifications contained in legal and administrative guidance notes issued by the Environment Agency (Knill 1997b).

The Drinking Water Directive

In contrast to the LCP case, administrative adaptation to the changes called for in the Drinking Water Directive only took place after a considerable delay. Initially, Britain sought to avoid the adaptation pressure emerging from legally binding European standards by transposing the Directive in the form of administrative circulars which are not binding for the regulatory authorities. The circulars placed responsibility for administering the Directive on the water suppliers and local authorities (Haigh 1996: 4.4–5). The EU Commission, however, considered the implementation by administrative circulars as being insufficient to bring into force binding provisions ensuring complete implementation. Against this background, and the fact that many water suppliers failed to meet the quality standards defined in the Directive, the Commission started infringement proceedings against Britain under Article 169 of the Treaty. Subsequently, the ECJ ruled in 1992 that Britain had failed adequately to incorporate the Directive into national legislation and supported the Commission's claim that water supplied in Britain had exceeded the limit values for nitrates in 28 supply zones in England (Matthews and Pickering 1997; Interview: DoE, February 1997).

The initial pattern of administrative resistance changed towards the late 1980s, however, when fundamental reforms in British water policy allowed for effective adaptation to European requirements. A completely new regulatory and administrative structure was established by the Water Act 1989 and subsequent legislation in 1991.[12] In the context of these reforms, two basic regulatory changes occurred. First, regulatory functions were separated from the operational activities of the RWAs. The regulatory functions were transferred to different newly established regulatory bodies, while the RWAs and their remaining functions were sold off to the private sector. The new legal and administrative structure is based on three core regulators: the Drinking Water Inspectorate (DWI) which is in control of drinking water quality, the Environment Agency responsible for environmental regulation of industrial discharges, and the Office of Water Services (OFWAT) which is in charge

---

[12] The Water Industry Act 1991, the Water Resources Act 1991, the Land Drainage Act 1991, the Statutory Water Companies Act 1991, and the Water Consolidation Act 1991. Before these Acts were passed water legislation was spread over twenty Acts dating back to the 1930s. Consolidation has not led to any substantial amendments to the 1989 legislation (Bowman 1992: 565).

of economic regulation of the water industry. Central to the powers of the Environment Agency is the issuing of discharge consents to polluters and the associated conditions to ensure that the discharge will not have a significant detrimental effect on the receiving waters. Before the creation of the Agency, these tasks were fulfilled by the National Rivers Authority (NRA) which was established in 1989. The task of OFWAT is to ensure that water companies are financially able to carry out their activities without overcharging the customers (Bowman 1992: 566). The judgements of OFWAT with respect to increases in charges are based on the company's performance and investment plans (Interview: OFWAT, February 1997).

Second, the separation of regulatory and operational functions co-incided with adaptations in the administrative style underlying the regulation of drinking water supply. The former system of self-regulation on the basis of procedural rules was abandoned in favour of a more interventionist approach relying on legally binding quality standards. The DWI, which is part of the DoE, has responsibility for enforcing and controlling water suppliers' compliance with their statutory duties. The main statutory duty of the water suppliers still is to provide wholesome water. Wholesomeness, however, is now quantified by legally binding quality values, most of them stemming from the EU Drinking Water Directive (DWI 1996: 2). The main instruments available to the DWI to enable it to fulfil its functions are technical auditing of the water companies and enforcement action. Technical auditing relates to the assessment of the samples companies are required to take, and to checking the operation, monitoring and sampling techniques applied by the company. Enforcement action relates to cases where companies are in breach of their legal obligations. In such cases companies generally give an undertaking to take appropriate steps in order to secure compliance within a reasonable time. It is also possible that the DWI specifies the content of the undertakings (Interview: DWI, February 1997; DWI 1996: 3).

Turning to patterns of administrative interest intermediation, there is a general shift towards more formal and transparent relationships. Compared to the former system, the possibilities for environmental and consumer associations to get access to the regulatory process have significantly improved. Water companies have to provide a public record of their sampling data. Customers and associations have access to these data and can require copies. The Environment Agency has to make available on public registers details of discharge consents and of water quality monitoring (Bowman 1992: 566). Furthermore, the DWI each year publishes a detailed report providing a massive database regarding water quality, water pollution and degrees of compliance (Maloney and Richardson 1995: 110; Interview: WSA, February 1997; Interview: DWI, February 1997).[13] Monitoring of the companies is thereby carried out by way of self-regulation. The analytical methods, as well as the technical and operational standards of the monitoring equipment, are checked by UKAS, an independent certification body. Furthermore, the DWI on a regular basis inspects the companies' monitoring equipment (Interviews: DWI, February 1997; WSA, February 1997). An additional factor strengthening the openness of the new system emerges from regulatory fragmentation and the fact that different regulatory bodies involved have, from time to time, carried out their conflicts in public and thereby have mobilised support from their own 'constituencies', i.e., consumer interests with respect to OFWAT and environmental interests with respect to the Environment Agency (Maloney and Richardson 1994: 128).

The Information Directive

In order to comply with the administrative implications of the Information Directive, adaptations took place that partly went even beyond supranational requirements. The EPA of 1990 requires regulatory authorities to establish so-called public registers which contain all relevant permitting and operational data as well as the results of emission monitoring for all processes falling under the Act. These arrangements exceed the requirements of the EU Directive which provides only a passive right of information on request, whereas the British rule grants an active right of access to information. Since the public registers contain only certain data pertinent to the authorisation procedures in environmental pollution control at the central and local levels, the 1992 Information Regulations provided the basis for additional administrative adaptation in those areas not covered by the EPA.

In the light of these administrative changes, we observe a general tendency towards more open and transparent patterns of administrative interest intermediation, implying improved opportunities for the access and participation of third parties in regulatory decision-making. As revealed by the examples of clean air and water policy, former patterns of secretive and closed relationships between regulatory authorities and industry have largely been abandoned in favour of a more open approach.

The striving to effectively adjust to European requirements is furthermore indicated by the interpretation of the vague wording of the

---

[13] British water companies are required to take 3.5 million samples each year (Interview: WSA, February 1997).

Directive in favour of a more open regime, as opposed to the German case where European provisions were interpreted in a highly restrictive manner. This statement holds true in particular for the administrative practice of the Environment Agency under the EPA 1990. In order to avoid ambiguous interpretations of the Directive with respect to exemptions from disclosure, the EPA requires that potential harm has to be demonstrated where exemption from disclosure is claimed rather than relying on mandatory grounds for exemptions from disclosure (House of Lords 1996: para. 17). To avoid inconsistencies with respect to different regimes of access to information, the Environment Agency handles aspects of confidentiality along the same – more rigorous – lines defined in the EPA for all information requested, i.e., from public registers or for other information requested on the basis of the Directive (Interview: Environment Agency, February 1997).[14]

Moreover, to increase public awareness, the Agency pursues an active policy in order to make the public aware of the significance of the Directive and the range of information available (Rowan-Robinson *et al.* 1996; House of Lords 1996: para. 25). The Agency has published a guide which explains to the public the nature and scope of environmental information available (Environment Agency 1996) and strives to develop a corporate policy on public access to information and thus to harmonise the information policies of its formerly separate units. The policy of the Agency in this respect is based on four complementary elements: information held in public registers; information based on the EU Directive; the Open Government Code of Practice which establishes standards with respect to accountability and the performance of public bodies; and information provided by general inquiries (i.e., by responding to letters and telephone calls asking for general information) (Interview: Environment Agency, February 1997).

In sum, empirical evidence reveals a common pattern of administrative adaptation to European requirements, notwithstanding the considerable degree of sectoral 'misfit' between existing domestic arrangements and the administrative implications of the Directives on LCP, Drinking Water and Access to Information. In all cases, domestic changes occurred that were not only fully in line with, but even exceeded, the requirements defined in European legislation.

---

[14] These arrangements had been enacted against the resistance of the industry which claimed that the decision whether information is commercially confidential or not is subject to the company's own assertion: 'It is actually quite difficult to question that information is not commercially confidential if the provider has said it is' (DTI quoted in House of Lords 1996: para. 21).

Adaptation within a changing core

In contrast to the former German and British cases, the adaptation patterns to be observed with respect to the remaining three Directives cannot be resolved by refining a deterministic institutional perspective by the distinction of varying levels of adaptation pressure and the supplementary application of an agency-based argumentation in constellations of changes within the core. The application of a modified, more differentiated institutional perspective even increases rather than reduces our empirical puzzle. As European requirements were in contradiction with well-established core principles of British administrative traditions, the theoretically derived prediction would have been resistance rather than adaptation, even from a refined, less deterministic perspective.

This statement can be illustrated with respect to all three pieces of European legislation considered. The adaptational pressures implied by the Directives on LCP, Drinking Water and Access to Information were not only in contrast with existing sectoral arrangements, but also with core patterns of British administrative traditions; hence exceeding the scope for sectoral adjustment.

First, the interventionist character underlying the Directives on LCP and Drinking Water interfered with the traditional conception of administration as mediation between competing societal interests. As described in chapter 4, the emphasis on procedural rather than substantive rules, industrial self-regulation, administrative flexibility as well as pragmatic, informal and consensual patterns of administrative interest intermediation is to be understood in the light of the macro-institutional peculiarities of the British state, legal and civil service tradition. It is in this context, that the initial resistance to adapt domestic arrangements for the regulation of drinking water have to be understood. Second, the structural adaptations implied by the 1984 Framework Directive with respect to the establishment of hierarchical structures for the control of local authorities' regulatory performance by central government reflected a clear departure from the traditional separation of 'high' and 'low' politics, i.e., the absence of central government agents to influence and co-ordinate the operations of local government (Rhodes 1991; Weale 1996a). Third, the implications of the Information Directive with respect to regulatory transparency and openness were in sharp contrast with the traditional and almost legendary secrecy generally associated with administrative practice in Britain (Tant 1990; Knill 1995).

The 'moving core'

The fact that administrative arrangements were adjusted to European requirements despite their incompatibility with institutional core arrangements can only be understood when taking into account that this core was itself subject to dynamic developments. Fundamental administrative reforms from the early 1980s onwards partly modified the general institutional background of administrative activity in Britain. Although these 'core movements' implied no complete overhaul of national administrative traditions, they significantly altered the scope for sectoral adjustment within a changing core. Thus, the mediating administrative style still plays an important role, but was 'enriched' by new concepts, such as regulatory transparency and more substantive, performance-oriented administrative activities.

As pointed out in chapter 5, Britain, as opposed to Germany, is characterised by a high structural capacity for initiating and implementing far-reaching administrative reforms. The strength of executive leadership, the low institutional entrenchment of administrative structures as well as the conditional rather than absolute influence of the bureaucracy in policy-making provide rather favourable institutional conditions for administrative innovations. This became particularly apparent in the reform policies of the Thatcher government, which had profound implications for British public administration. To improve the efficiency and effectiveness of the public sector, policies were directed at administrative reorganisation, management reforms and privatisation, with all of these elements potentially challenging existing administrative traditions.

Important structural changes were introduced with the Next Steps initiative. It implied the creation of semi-autonomous agencies responsible for operational management, separating these management functions from policy-making functions which remained the responsibility of the relevant departments. Structural changes also took place at the local level, with the abolition of the metropolitan councils and continuous government intervention in local authorities' spending and operation. Private-sector management and performance regimes introduced noteworthy operational reforms. The performance drive, but also the need to compensate for the lack of democratic control of the independent agencies, led to a tendency to make the agencies' activities more transparent and accountable to the public. A further feature of national reforms was the privatisation of public utilities, including the nationalised energy and water-supply industries. Regulatory regimes were created to control the market activities of these privatised utilities (Hood 1991; Rhodes 1996).

With respect to the implementation of the Directives on LCP, Drinking Water and Access to Information, these domestic reforms favoured administrative adjustments to European requirements in three ways. First, domestic core changes altered the scope for sectoral adaptation, implying that European requirements could be achieved by changes within rather than changes of the core of national administrative traditions. Second, in changing the institutional opportunity structures at the sectoral level, national reforms created new resources and strategic options for domestic actor coalitions supporting effective implementation of European legislation. Finally, national reforms created new opportunities for administrative adaptation to European requirements, facilitating the persistence of administrative core patterns which were not affected by national reform dynamics, but were initially challenged by European legislation.

The reduction of adaptation pressure

In modifying administrative core arrangements, national administrative reforms reduced the institutional scope of European adaptation requirements, which prior to national reforms had implied adaptations which exceeded the scope of sectoral changes within the core. First, European implications in favour of a more interventionist administrative style in the regulation of large combustion plants and drinking water no longer reflected a core challenge to national administrative traditions, given the similar impact of domestic reforms. As a result of the establishment of performance-oriented regimes, privatisation and the creation of independent regulatory bodies, we saw a shift towards more formal and open patterns of administrative interest intermediation. Moreover, the establishment of independent agencies implies a formalisation of administrative co-ordination, which, in turn, reduces the leeway for informal interaction between administrative and private actors, at least in cases where the latter are regulated by different (e.g., economic and environmental) agencies (Rhodes 1996).

Privatisation and the establishment of regulatory agencies significantly affected existing arrangements in air and water pollution control. The Central Electricity Generating Board (CEGB), the publicly owned industry responsible for the whole energy supply for England and Wales, was split up and sold off to the private sector in the early 1990s (Collier 1995: 10), while the RWAs were privatised in 1989. Privatisation went along with the establishment of regulatory agencies controlling the economic performance of the privatised industries, OFWAT and the Office for Electricity Regulation (OFFER).

In the light of the previous system of environmental self-regulation, water privatisation furthermore required the establishment of regulatory bodies dealing with the regulation of water pollution and drinking water. Contrary to the government's initial plans to leave the RWAs' regulatory functions with the privatised industry, EU water legislation (including the Drinking Water Directive) required the establishment of a competent national authority responsible for the implementation of EU provisions. While the government initially had intended to privatise the RWAs as a whole, i.e., without separating regulatory and operational functions, the Commission clearly stated its doubts as to whether private companies could be accepted as competent authorities in the sense of EU legislation. Moreover, there was strong opposition from national actors such as the CBI who rejected the principle that one privatised company should exercise control over the affairs of another private company (Maloney and Richardson 1994: 123). As a consequence, we saw the establishment of two additional regulatory bodies, namely the DWI and the NRA, responsible for environmental regulation and drinking water provision.[15]

Second, in the light of the Conservative policies to restructure local government, the European requirements in favour of centrally formulated standards to be implemented at the local level no longer implied a core challenge to the traditional separation of central and local politics. It was the basic objective of Conservative reforms to restrict the discretion of local authorities in their day-to-day decision-making. Local authorities were seen as agents of central government rather than autonomous bodies having overall responsibility for centrally specified areas (Rhodes 1991: 81; Knill 1995). This way, the structural implications of the 1984 Framework Directive were fully in line with the overall direction of national administrative reforms. Although the Directive actually implied the strengthening of local regulatory powers, and hence seemed to be in contradiction with the Conservative striving for centralisation, the increase in local competencies coincided with enhanced mechanisms for the hierarchical control of local activities (Weale 1996a: 128).

Third, in the context of domestic reforms directed at opening up government and increasing administrative transparency and accountability, the provision of access to environmental information, as required

---

[15] Government decided to separate the regulatory functions of the DWI and the NRA in the light of their differing objectives. While the DWI is concerned with health protection, the functions of the NRA are related to environmental protection. Since the standards for protecting health and environment do not necessarily have to be identical, an institutional separation of the two functions was seen as being more appropriate (Interviews: DoE, February 1997; DWI, February 1997).

by the Information Directive, was no longer perceived as a core challenge to the traditional patterns of secretive and closed patterns of
interest intermediation (Knill 1998, Knill and Lenschow 1988).

Promoting support for compliance

In view of these domestic core changes, administrative adjustment to
European requirements was possible in the context of changes within a
modified institutional core. However, as pointed out in the theoretical
framework, in such a constellation of moderate adaptation pressure, the
specific sectoral actor constellation plays a crucial role in defining
whether appropriate changes actually take place or not. In this context,
domestic reforms not only reduced the institutional scope of European
adaptation pressure, but also provided an opportunity structure which
facilitated the emergence of successful support for effective compliance.

In the cases of LCP and Drinking Water, privatisation played a crucial
role in providing a more favourable domestic context for effective
compliance. This can be traced to the fact that the economic costs of
compliance with European standards (which were considerable given
the underinvestment into control technologies up to that point) no
longer interfered with the Conservative government's objective of reducing public spending, as the costs for retrofitting existing plants now
had to be borne by the private sector. This way, administrative actors to
a lesser extent resisted international pressures, long-standing demands
of environmental organisations, as well as reform concepts advanced by
the RCEP. In the light of the more favourable domestic context,
administrative changes in air pollution control even went beyond European requirements, in particular with respect to the establishment of
public registers and an integrated approach to pollution control. This
can be traced to the fact that the government was able to rely on already
existing proposals which were promoted by the RCEP since the mid-
1970s (Knill 1995).

In the case of drinking water, the abolition of self-regulation in favour
of a fragmented system of environmental and economic regulation
additionally strengthened the voice and influence of environmental and
consumer groups, hence providing a new institutional context which
favoured the compliance with European objectives. The Environment
Agency is generally quite responsive to environmental interests, whereas
OFWAT, the economic regulator, fulfils the basic task of consumer
protection. In recent years, the relation between both agencies has been
rather conflictual, especially with respect to the balance between quality
improvements on the one hand and the extent to which these improvements may result in increasing water charges to be paid by consumers.

These conflicts, however, contributed to increased regulatory transparency, hence favouring the perception of and adaptation to European requirements (Maloney and Richardson 1995; McGillivray 1997).

Strong support from domestic actor coalitions in favour of public access to environmental information provided a favourable basis for effective compliance with the administrative requirements of the Information Directive. The institutional opportunities for the domestic actors to successfully influence administrative change had significantly increased in the context of national reforms. The impact of the changed institutional environment can be inferred from previous domestic occurrences. The RCEP as well as environmental organisations and the Campaign for the Freedom of Information had urged the adoption of more transparent environmental information and reporting practices in Britain since the mid-1970s but they were ignored in a national context still characterised by a secretive regulatory style. Similar resistance we would have expected had an EU Directive required more open practices at that time. Administrative change became possible as the regulatory core in Britain moved towards accountability and opening up government. These general dynamics created a more favourable institutional framework for domestic environmental policy entrepreneurs to voice their demands and gradually modified the government's receptiveness for action (Knill 1997b).

New options for persistence

National reforms allowed for administrative adaptation to European requirements not only by reducing the institutional scope of adaptation pressure and by providing a more favourable opportunity structure for domestic actors in favour of effective compliance. They also facilitated compliance by creating new opportunities for the persistence of certain core patterns which were initially challenged by European requirements.

With respect to the Directives on LCP and Drinking Water this becomes apparent in the considerable degree of administrative flexibility and pragmatism to specify control requirements in the light of the particular context. Notwithstanding the uniform and legally binding European standards, these patterns have 'survived' without leading to non-compliance with European legislation.

In the LCP case, the implementation of the national plan leaves great flexibility in order to achieve the emission reductions. This flexibility stems from two factors characterising the system. First of all, IPC authorisations for large combustion plants are based on a company-approach instead of a plant-approach. This implies that every energy-generating company is allocated a 'company bubble', i.e. a total of yearly maximum emissions. This way, operators are allowed to allocate emissions with respect to different plants of their company as long as the total of all plant emissions remains below the 'company bubble' (Interviews: DoE, February 1997; PowerGen, February 1997; National Power, February 1997). Besides the opportunity for company internal emission-trading, the changes introduced in 1997 provide a second possibility which allows for flexible implementation of the LCP Directive. By abolishing the allocation of emission quotas to different industrial sectors, it is possible to transfer 'company bubbles' between plants in different ownership and different industrial sectors (DoE 1996: 19). There is higher flexibility for the Environment Agency 'to allocate limits to different sectors of industry as market circumstances change' (Interview: PowerGen, February 1997).

In view of the considerable flexibility and discretion of inspectors, we still observe pragmatic elements with respect to the interaction between regulatory authorities and plant operators which find their expression in negotiations on 'company bubbles' and the periodic review of plant authorisations by the Environment Agency (Interviews: DoE, February 1997; Environment Agency, February 1997; PowerGen, February 1997; National Power, February 1997). It is important to note, however, that the position of the inspectors in these negotiations has been strengthened by the fact that – in contrast to the former arrangements – they can now rely on legally binding plans for overall emission reductions.

The persistence of flexible and pragmatic arrangements was facilitated by the new structure of the British energy sector. Whereas formerly the British energy sector was dominated by a public monopolist, the CEGB, privatisation led to a highly competitive situation, with twenty private suppliers operating in the market. To reduce market risks operators no longer rely on one single type of fuel but have based their business on a fuel portfolio. In contrast to the CEGB which had to rely primarily on British coal, the private companies operate a whole range of plants using different types of fuels, such as coal, gas, oil, as well as combined-cycle gas turbines which can burn different types of fuels. This portfolio allows the companies to adapt flexibly to price variations on the fuel market (Interviews: PowerGen, February 1997; National Power, February 1997).

In view of this constellation the role of uniform emission standards in driving the retrofitting of existing plants with improved abatement technology becomes less important. Since the competitive market no longer allows the operators to pass on the costs of new abatement technology to the customers, the incentive structure for retrofitting existing plants has changed. Under these circumstances it is often cheaper to pursue other strategies, such as fuel switching, burning low sulphur coal, or replacing old plants by new less emission-intensive sites (Interviews: PowerGen, February 1997; National Power, February 1997; Environment Agency, February 1997).

In the case of drinking water, administrative discretion was necessary to facilitate the privatisation process. In particular, it was required to reduce economic uncertainties for private investors which emerged from potential infringement proceedings initiated by the European Commission seeking compliance with EU water legislation (Haigh 1996: 4.4–9; Knill 1998). Flexible handling within the context of the new, binding quality standards is achieved through the concept of legal undertakings which water suppliers can submit to the DWI in the case of a breach of standards. The undertakings establish the kind of improvements operators need to accomplish within a given period of time in order to achieve the binding standards. This occurs in the light of the local situation, such as the quality of the water source, and practicability, in terms of available technology and needed water supply (Interviews: DoE, February 1997; DWI, February 1997). Flexible regulation in turn allows for consensual and pragmatic interaction between the DWI and the water industry. DWI co-operates with industry 'in order to enable water suppliers to satisfy the standards' (Interview: DWI, February 1997). However, concerning the room left for pragmatic and consensual interaction, it must be remembered that the standards prescribed in the EU Directive define a clear framework within which co-operation takes place (Haigh 1996: 4.4–9).

Turning to the Information Directive, national administrative reforms facilitated the partial persistence of the former secretive practice in basically two ways. On the one hand, the scope of the Directive is restricted by the privatisation policy. According to the Directive both public authorities and any other bodies with public responsibilities for the environment and under control of public authorities are obliged to provide public access to the environmental information they hold. For reasons of administrative practicability the DoE, when drafting the Information Regulations, rejected its initial intention to establish a comprehensive list of 'relevant persons' to which the Regulations apply and decided to leave it to the bodies themselves to judge whether they are subject to the obligations of the Regulations (Haigh 1996: 11.5–3). Based on these provisions both the privatised water companies and electricity generators have classified themselves as not falling within the scope of the Directive, although they would have had this status as former publicly owned utilities (House of Lords 1996: para. 57).

The scope of the Directive is not only reduced by the government's privatisation policy, but also by the increasing fragmentation and separation of regulatory functions by establishing executive agencies (Rhodes 1996). This situation means that demand for co-ordination between different bodies significantly increased. As we have seen in the case of water policy, for instance, the DWI, responsible for the regulation of drinking water quality, has to co-ordinate its activities with the Environment Agency and OFWAT. In many cases, communications between different regulatory bodies have been declared as internal and therefore falling under the exemptions of disclosure (FoE 1996; Knill 1997b; House of Lords 1996: para. 63).

8.4   Conclusion: a dynamic scope for administrative adaptation

The British implementation record with respect to the five pieces of European legislation under study is characterised by significant administrative changes. Apart from the EMAS-Regulation, which confirmed domestic arrangements, and the resistance to adjust to the requirements implied by the EIA Directive, far-reaching administrative changes can be observed in order to implement the Directives on LCP, Drinking Water and Access to Information.

The British implementation performance, which is rather surprising in view of the core challenges called for by the last three Directives, reveals a high potential for adapting to European policies in the context of more dynamic administrative traditions. The high capacity for administrative reform increases the opportunities for sectoral adjustment by reducing the institutional gap between European requirements and existing national arrangements. As opposed to Germany, where sectoral arrangements are strongly entrenched in a static institutional core, this core is potentially more flexible in Britain.

As demonstrated by the cases of LCP, Drinking Water and Access to Information, national reform dynamics may facilitate administrative adjustment to European requirements not only by reducing the institutional scope of adaptation pressure, but also by altering the sectoral context in favour of effective compliance. In changing the institutional opportunity structure for strategically interacting actors, domestic changes might alter the distribution of costs, benefits and resources between national actors in favour of those coalitions supporting administrative adjustment.

Paradoxically, national reforms created not only new opportunities for sectoral adjustment within a changing core, but at the same time provided new options for the persistence of other core patterns which were not affected by national dynamics, but nevertheless challenged by European requirements. Administrative flexibility enhances the opportunities for administrative persistence in compliance with supranational implications.

Having elaborated on the impact of EU environmental policy on administrative styles and structures in Germany and Britain, it is the objective of the following part to assess and illustrate our theoretical and empirical findings from a comparative perspective. In this context, particular emphasis is placed on the analysis of whether and to what extent the findings derived from the case studies can be generalised.

IV

The Europeanisation of national administrations: comparative assessment and general conclusions

The starting point of this study was to investigate the impact of European policies on national administrations. To what extent can we expect administrative change at the national level in order to comply with European policy demands and to what extent does domestic change lead to administrative convergence across member states? How can the observed patterns of administrative transformation be explained? In addressing these questions, the purpose of this concluding part is twofold, namely, to illustrate our theoretical and analytical considerations from a comparative perspective and to assess the extent to which these considerations can be generalised.

9 Comparative assessment: the explanatory value of institutions

The previous chapters analysed the administrative impact of EU environmental policy from a country-based perspective; they were based on the separate investigation of distinctive European policies for each country. It is the intention of this chapter to assess the validity of our modified institutionalist framework from a comparative perspective. It is on the basis of this assessment, that we are able to understand the extent to which Europeanisation has implied administrative convergence or divergence with respect to administrative styles and structures in German and British environmental policy.

9.1 European adaptation pressure and patterns of domestic change

The cross-country and cross-policy assessment of administrative transformation underlines the need for a more differentiated institutional approach which explicitly seeks to reduce the deterministic and conservatist bias inherent to 'simple' institution-based explanations, expecting administrative adaptation in cases of sectoral 'fit' and non-adaptation in cases of sectoral 'misfit'.

To avoid the problem of explanatory determinism, we have to rely on a more differentiated conception of European adaptation pressure which distinguishes different levels of institutional incompatibility, namely, whether European policy demands are in contradiction with institutionally strongly embedded core patterns of national administrations or whether administrative adjustment is still possible within the range of options defined by this macro-institutional context. Defining the institutional scope of European adaptation pressure in such a way, we are able to specify the explanatory relevance of institutions as independent variables, i.e., how much institutions matter in order to account for patterns of administrative change. In the cases of institutional 'misfits' on the level of core contradictions they matter very much; we are able to predict the expected result of administrative resistance to European requirements already from a mere institution-based perspective. If European demands remain 'within the core', by contrast, we are in the 'undetermined' realm of the institution-based model. To account for actual patterns of administrative change, the institution-based model has to be supplemented by an agency-based perspective, taking account of prevailing actor constellations within a given institutional context. Institutions are no longer conceived as independent, but intervening variables structuring the strategic inter-action of domestic actors.

In addition, the British cases demonstrated the need for a dynamic conception of European adaptation pressure, suggesting a further modi-fication of the institution-based framework. Although a static institu-tional core of national administrative traditions should be considered the 'normal case', given the general stability associated with macro-level institutions, the British cases indicate that we cannot completely pre-clude the possibility of core changes. We have seen that the potential for such core dynamics is linked to the level of administrative reform capacity which is itself an institutionalised feature of a country's poli-tical-administrative system. In this context, it has to be emphasised that the analytical admittance of institutional 'core movements' does not contradict the previous institution-based argumentation. The scope of European adaptation requirements continues to be assessed in relation to domestic institutional structures, though now from a dynamic per-spective.

The inadequacy of a sectoral perspective

In order to analyse the empirical cases, we started with the most intuitive explanation based on the sectoral compatibility of European and do-mestic arrangements. Approaching the concept of adaptation pressure from this 'simple' institutional perspective, two broad categories of 'fit' and 'misfit' can be distinguished. Sectoral 'fit' implies that European requirements are broadly in line with domestic arrangements. In view of only minor or incremental adaptations required by European legislation, this explanatory approach expects 'easy' adaptation at the domestic level under such constellations. Resistance to change is likely, by contrast, in constellations of sectoral 'misfit', where European policy implications are in contradiction with existing sectoral arrangements at the domestic level.

Assuming that constellations of administrative adaptation or, in the extreme case, compliance without change are most likely in cases of high sectoral compatibility, we should have observed these patterns in the

Table 9.1. *The explanatory value of a 'simple' institutional perspective of sectoral 'fit' and 'misfit'*

Policy/Country	Germany		Britain	
	Sectoral Fit/Misfit	Adaptation Pattern	Sectoral Fit/Misfit	Adaptation Pattern
LCP	Fit	Confirmation	Misfit	Change accepted
Drinking Water	Fit	Change delayed	Misfit	Change accepted
Information	Misfit	Change resisted	Misfit	Change accepted
EIA	Misfit	Change resisted	Fit	Change resisted
EMAS	Misfit	Change accepted	Fit	Confirmation

░░░ Cases not sufficiently explained

German LCP and Drinking Water cases as well as in the British EMAS and EIA cases. On the other hand, resistance to administrative adaptation is expected to be the dominant pattern with respect to the sectoral 'misfits', i.e., the cases of EMAS, Information, and EIA in Germany, and the cases of LCP, Drinking Water and Information in Britain. As illustrated in table 9.1, however, the actual patterns of domestic adjustment only partly confirm these expectations. To be specific, the simple theory 'fits' only in four cases (EMAS in Britain as well as LCP, Information and EIA in Germany), leaving six cases unresolved (indicated by grey hatching).

The institutionally less specified perspective on European adaptation pressure therefore leaves us with rather puzzling results, which can be illustrated by comparing the implementation of European policies within as well as across the two countries under investigation. On the one hand, we find examples in both countries where required adaptations were resisted or delayed despite high sectoral compatibility (EIA in Britain and Drinking Water in Germany) or corresponding requirements for administrative change were accepted, notwithstanding a considerable degree of sectoral 'misfit' (LCP, Drinking Water and Information in Britain; EMAS in Germany). On the other hand, the Information Directive provides a case where we find different adaptation patterns across countries (German resistance and British adjustment), although the Directive's requirements were similarly incompatible with existing arrangements in both countries.

Even when supplementing the sectoral perspective by explanations derived from implementation research, we are not able to resolve the remaining puzzles. As pointed out in chapter 1, implementation theory expects that the likelihood of domestic adaptation increases with the degree of domestic support for effective adjustment to European legislation, i.e., with the extent to which the domestic implementation of European policies is supported by 'favourable' national context conditions. As German environmental organisations are generally considered as politically more influential than their British counterparts, the 'support hypothesis' would suggest a generally higher 'adaptation rate' in the German rather than British 'misfit' cases. This expectation, however, is in contradiction with the empirical findings. We find administrative compliance in all British 'misfit' cases, while in Germany strong domestic support in favour of effective compliance with the requirements of the EIA and Information Directives was not sufficient to trigger corresponding administrative changes.

The obvious limits of these simple and intuitive explanatory concepts with respect to our empirical cases underline the need for alternative, more differentiated and sophisticated approaches. As demonstrated in the country studies, the explanatory results can be significantly improved when analysing European adaptation requirements from a modified, less deterministic and less static institutional perspective, taking account of the varying explanatory impact of institutions on political outcomes.

Modification 1: different levels of institutional change

A first improvement of the explanatory results can be achieved by applying a more differentiated perspective on the institutional scope of European adaptation pressure. In contrast to the simple institution-based predictions based on sectoral 'fit' or 'misfit', the distinction of constellations where institutions matter and thus explain 'very much' (changes of the core) and where institutions have to be conceived as intervening rather than independent factor (changes within the core) provides a more reliable factor for hypothesising on domestic administrative change. This distinction of institutionally 'more determining' and 'more open' constellations avoids the problem of explanatory determinism inherent to institution-based approaches without completely giving away the analytical advantages of more abstract and parsimonious concepts.

I have argued that the institutional scope and therefore the degree of adaptation pressure increases with the extent to which challenged administrative arrangements are embedded in the macro-institutional core of national administrative traditions. Given the high stability of these core arrangements, domestic adjustments can be expected only as long as the institutional scope of European requirements remains at a moderate level, implying changes *within* rather than changes *of* the core of national administrative traditions.

While this more differentiated institutional perspective allows for the clear identification of constellations of domestic resistance to change, the abstract institution-based approach has to be supplemented by an agency-based analysis of the sectoral policy context in cases of moderate adaptation pressure, requiring the independent analysis of sectoral actors' coalitions within the given institutional context. Analysing European adaptation pressure from a less determinist institutional perspective, we are not only able to provide further theoretical insights with respect to the explanation of the four cases sufficiently explained by a sectoral perspective, but also to resolve three remaining empirical puzzles, namely the cases of Drinking Water and EMAS in Germany as well as the case of EIA in Britain.

To begin with the 'puzzle cases', the application of the more differentiated perspective indicates a moderate level of European adaptation pressure. In other words, European policies required certain changes in domestic arrangements, without, however, challenging well-established core patterns of national administrative traditions. The Drinking Water Directive required the upgrading of certain standards and monitoring procedures in Germany, but was well in line with the existing legalist and interventionist tradition. In a similar way, industrial self-regulation favoured by the EMAS Regulation challenged existing patterns of sectoral regulation, but is well in line with the corporatist regulatory tradition in Germany. This way, adaptation was possible within the core of national administrative traditions. The same holds true for the British EIA case, where certain changes in existing procedures were required which remained within the range of options defined by national administrative traditions.

The three cases therefore reflect constellations where an abstract institution-based perspective is not sufficient to account for the actual patterns of domestic transformation, but has to be supplied by an agency-based explanation. Domestic institutions matter 'not enough' to allow for the prediction of political outcomes. Thus, the fact that domestic adaptation within the core actually took place in the German EMAS case can only be fully understood when taking account of the sectoral policy context which was rather favourable, given the high support from industry and environmental organisations in favour of domestic adjustments to European requirements. Lacking support from domestic actors, by contrast, characterised the implementation of the EIA Directive in Britain. Although the institutional scope of European

Table 9.2. *The explanatory value of a differentiated institutional perspective*

Policy/Country	Germany		Britain	
	Institutional Fit/Misfit	Adaptation Pattern	Institutional Fit/Misfit	Adaptation Pattern
LCP	Within the Core	Confirmation	Core Challenge	Change accepted
Drinking Water	Core Challenge	Change delayed	Core Challenge	Change accepted
Information	Core Challenge	Change resisted	Core Challenge	Change accepted
EIA	Core Challenge	Change resisted	Within the Core	Change resisted
EMAS	Within the Core	Change accepted	Within the Core	Confirmation

▨ Cases not sufficiently explained

requirements remained within the core of national administrative traditions, corresponding changes were neglected. Referring to the German case of Drinking Water, we saw that the particular constellation of interests and actors as well as the institutional restrictions of available options for compliance implied that domestic adaptations were initially neglected, being accepted only after a long delay.

The assessment of European adaptation pressure from a differentiated institutional perspective furthermore explains patterns of administrative resistance observed in the cases of Access to Information and EIA in Germany, notwithstanding the high level of sectoral support for effective compliance given in both cases (see table 9.2). As opposed to the EMAS-Regulation, the two Directives implied institutional core challenges to strongly entrenched administrative traditions; hence the emergence of strong domestic support coalitions was not sufficient to trigger administrative change in the light of high institutional adaptation costs associated with institutional core changes and the existence of vested interests favouring the *status quo*.

Modification 2: a dynamic perspective on institutional change

Notwithstanding the explanatory improvements emerging from a less deterministic and differentiated conception of European adaptation pressure, this perspective was not sufficient to resolve all puzzles left from the sectoral perspective, namely the cases of LCP, Drinking Water and Access to Information in Britain. In these cases, the observed patterns of accepted adaptation were in sharp contrast with the expectations derived from both a sectoral and an institutional perspective. How can we understand the occurrence of domestic adjustments in spite of the core challenges to national administrative traditions implied by European requirements in all of the three cases?

The above problem can only be resolved, when further refining the institutional conception of European adaptation pressure by a dynamic perspective. A dynamic perspective takes into account that the institutional scope of European requirements varies not only with European policy implications, but may also be affected by national reform developments altering administrative core patterns.

To be sure, the dynamic perspective does not imply the rejection of the institution-based argumentation, as the range of sectoral options for adjustment is still constrained by the macro-institutional context of national administrative traditions. Rather it indicates, that, in exceptional cases, even this context might be subject to change in the context of far-reaching administrative reforms. Given the particularly high structural potential for such reforms in Britain, a dynamic conception of adaptation pressure can be generally considered as more important than in Germany, where the high number of institutional veto points implies a rather low capacity for administrative reform, and hence a highly stable macro-institutional background.

One could certainly argue that administrative adjustment in the British cases of LCP, Drinking Water and Information is simply the result of changing preferences, strategies and resources of domestic actors; i.e., the emergence of strong domestic support for effective compliance, including, for instance, the growing influence of environmental organisations from the mid-1980s onwards or the higher environmental awareness of the general public. However, such a perspective would overlook two aspects. First, the analysis of the British cases has shown that the changes in strategic opportunities and constraints of domestic actors were basically the result of preceding institutional changes. National reforms therefore not only reduced the scope for institutional adaptation, but also provided environmental actors with new strategic opportunities to effectively influence political and administrative decisions. Second, if the sectoral policy context alone had been sufficient to trigger core changes when implementing supranational policies, we should not have seen such a high level of administrative resistance in Germany, where environmental actors are generally in a more influential position than their British counterparts.

9.2   Convergence versus divergence

One of the crucial questions underlying this study refers to the extent to which the Europeanisation of domestic administrations leads to converging administrative styles and structures across member states. The evaluation of our findings with respect to this question indicates an ambiguous picture, including not only the convergence, but also the divergence and persistence of administrative differences across member states.

The most obvious case illustrating sectoral convergence refers to the EMAS Regulation. Convergence emerges from the fact that the implementation of the Regulation led to considerable administrative adaptations in Germany, while basically confirming existing structures and practices in Britain. This way, we find rather similar administrative arrangements in both countries with respect to the regulation of environmental management systems. This becomes apparent in the equal emphasis on industrial self-regulation as well as similar administrative structures concerning the accreditation of environmental auditors and the verification of environmental management systems. While in Britain these arrangements are well in line with the tradition of mediation, the Regulation fits well with the German tradition of corporatism.

The picture of administrative convergence, as it is indicated by the EMAS Regulation, is significantly modified, however, when considering the other policies under investigation. This becomes particularly evident with respect to the Directive on Access to Information which reflects a clear case of administrative divergence. The Directive's requirements in favour of a more transparent and open regulatory practice implied almost identical adaptation requirements for the two countries, since both in Germany and Britain access to environmental information was strongly restricted. While the British practice was characterised by high informality and secrecy, access to official information was confined to a low number of legally specified cases in Germany. As we have seen, however, corresponding adjustments to European requirements took place only in the British case, while in Germany the existing practice basically persisted. Given the different patterns of change and persistence in spite of a similar starting position, Europeanisation favoured the divergence of German and British administrative arrangements.

In contrast to the cases of Access to Information and EMAS, the implementation of the EIA Directive implied neither converging nor diverging administrative arrangements in British and German environmental policy. Rather, existing differences between both countries remained unchanged. Persistence of administrative differences can be traced to the fact that corresponding adjustments to European requirements were resisted in both countries; the Directive was implemented by relying on existing structures and practices. In Germany, resistance was the result of the incompatibility of the Directive with core aspects of administrative structure and organisation. In Britain, by contrast, adaptation was neglected in the light of lack of support from domestic actor coalitions, notwithstanding the only moderate level of European adaptation pressure.

While the three policies analysed so far are characterised by a clear pattern of either convergence, divergence or persistence of differences, the picture is more ambiguous for the remaining cases of LCP and Drinking Water. With respect to these measures, the empirical evidence indicates mixed signals, including all of the three conceivable options. Since both Directives had only a minor impact on administrative arrangements in Germany, modifications in the differences between British and German arrangements were basically the result of British adjustments.

A first glance at the administrative adjustments that took place in Britain reveals indeed converging tendencies. In terms of the administrative style, state intervention moved towards a more substantive orientation with numerical objectives to be achieved. In the LCP case, this becomes basically evident by the establishment of a so-called national plan, which defines annual reduction targets required by the Directive. In issuing authorisations for large combustion plants, regulatory authorities make sure that these targets are fulfilled. With respect to the Drinking Water Directive, the vague principle of wholesomeness was specified by legally binding quality standards. The shift in regulatory activities towards a more interventionist approach, as it is applied in Germany, is reflected in more formal and legalistic patterns of administrative interest intermediation because the set substantive objectives leave less room for 'cosy' and pragmatic bargaining between regulatory authorities and industry.

These developments, however, reflect only one part of the administrative adjustments occurring in the context of these Directives. At the same time, we observe a considerable degree of administrative continuity; hence indicating the persistence of administrative differences between both countries. Continuity refers primarily to the traditional elements of flexibility, informality and pragmatism which, albeit less important, are still of relevance for administrative intervention and interest intermediation in Britain. Within the concept of a more interventionist orientation, there is still some room for flexible procedures. In the LCP case, flexibility is achieved by the concept of so-called 'company bubbles', i.e., a total of yearly maximum emissions. Companies are allowed to allocate emissions with respect to their different plants as long as emissions for each plant remain within a certain margin that is defined by the Environment Agency in the light of local environmental conditions. With respect to drinking water, flexible handling emerges from the concept of legal undertakings which water suppliers can submit to the regulatory authority in the case of a breach of standards. The undertakings offer the opportunity for a more flexible approach within the general framework of quality objectives by establishing the necessary improvements the operator has to achieve within a given period of time, in the light of the local situation and available technologies.

In addition to the picture of administrative convergence and the persistence of administrative differences, we find that British compliance with European legislation is partly achieved in a context of new administrative arrangements which – compared to the former constellation – depart even further from corresponding arrangements in Germany; hence indicating administrative divergence. This becomes evident in particular in the field of clean air policy. In this area, increasing emphasis is placed on market-based approaches, implying an even higher difference from the interventionist approach underlying German pollution control, as was the case with respect to the former British regulation based on the flexible bpm principle. These new concepts characterising administrative arrangements in British clean-air policy are not only reflected in the recent introduction of 'regulated emission trading' between plants in different ownership and different industrial sectors under the supervision of the Environment Agency. An, albeit less pronounced, emphasis on market-based regulation is also evident in the field of water policy, especially by the concept of 'competition by comparison' which implies that the economic and environmental performance of the privatised water companies is assessed in a comparative way by the different regulatory bodies involved (Interviews: Environment Agency, April 1997; DWI, February 1997; OFWAT, February 1997). As summarised in table 9.3, we therefore find a rather mixed picture with respect to the converging or diverging impact of European policies on national administrative arrangements.

The comparative assessment of our empirical findings suggests three basic conclusions with respect to the cross-national impact of Europeanisation. First, there is no clear tendency in favour of either convergence, divergence or the persistence of administrative differences across member states. As revealed in table 9.3, all options are equally distributed across and within different policies. This mixed picture can be traced to the high variety of both European policy implications and domestic institutional conditions. We find considerable variation in the institutional scope of European adaptation pressures across countries and policies, and hence no consistent pattern of domestic transformations in the light of supranational requirements. Taken together, the

Table 9.3. *Administrative convergence/divergence under the impact of European legislation*

Policy	Adaptation Pattern		Differences Across Countries
	Germany	Britain	
LCP and Drinking Water	No change	Change	Convergence Divergence Persistence
Information	No change	Change	Divergence
EIA	No Change	No Change	Persistence
EMAS	Change	No Change	Convergence

combination of differing European implications and varying domestic adaptation paths favours no dominant tendency of administrative convergence, divergence or persistence.

Second, there are different constellations of domestic adaptation paths in which either convergence, divergence or persistence of administrative differences is more likely. Convergence, to begin with, is to be expected in cases where either both countries undertake administrative adaptations in order to comply with European requirements (adaptation/adaptation) or adjustment takes place in one country with existing arrangements being confirmed in the other (adaptation/confirmation). The latter scenario refers to the cases of EMAS and LCP. Divergence, on the other hand, emerges in cases where administrative adaptations are required in both countries, but are accepted only in one country while being resisted in the other (adaptation/resistance). As illustrated above, this constellation was underlying the implementation of the Information Directive. Persistence of administrative differences, by con-7trast, is given when European policies confirm administrative arrangements (confirmation/confirmation) or are resisted (resistance/resistance) in both countries, as became apparent in the EIA case.

Third, it has to be emphasised that the identification of these general constellations may serve only as a rough indicator for hypothesising on administrative convergence, divergence and persistence. This is especially illustrated by the cases of LCP and Drinking Water, where we observe all of these options at the same time, although the underlying adaptation constellation basically suggests administrative convergence. As indicated by the British case-study, the changes in administrative core patterns implied by national reforms not only favoured convergence by adaptation to European policy requirements, but at the same time created new opportunities for compliance with European implications in a way that partly diverges from corresponding arrangements in Germany or favoured the persistence of administrative differences between both countries. The fact that administrative adaptation to European requirements takes place does not exclude the fact that compliance in different member states implies divergence or the persistence of administrative differences.

10   Towards generalisation: different mechanisms of Europeanisation

To what extent can the findings derived from the implementation of EU environmental policy in Germany and Britain be generalised with respect to other European policies? To assess the general validity of these findings, an analytical distinction between different mechanisms of Europeanisation is introduced, identifying three basic patterns of how European policies might impact upon domestic administrative styles and structures. European policies might be very demanding and prescribe a concrete institutional model for domestic compliance; they might be confined to changing domestic opportunity structures; or, in their 'weakest' form, have no institutional impact at all, while being primarily directed at changing domestic beliefs and expectations (Knill and Lehmkuhl 1999).

I argue that it is this specific Europeanisation mechanism rather than the nominal category of the policy area that is the most important factor to be considered when investigating the domestic impact of varying European policies. In this context, it must be emphasised that this distinction is analytical rather than empirical, as many European policies might be characterised by a mixture of different mechanisms of Europeanisation. The existence of such 'Europeanisation hybrids' does not call the general argument into question, but indicates the need for careful analysis of the underlying Europeanisation mechanism in order to understand the domestic impact of a certain policy.

As will be shown, the existence of distinctive mechanisms of Europeanisation underlying different policies does not call into question the general validity of the analytical framework. However, the relative explanatory value of institution-based and agency-based approaches within this model varies significantly in view of different Europeanisation mechanisms. To illustrate this argument, I will rely on empirical evidence from European policies on road haulage and railways.[1]

---

[1] The empirical data with respect to these policy areas are based on a comparative research project on 'European Transport Policy and the Transformation of the State',

10.1   Europeanisation by institutional compliance

In their most explicit form European policies may trigger domestic change by prescribing concrete institutional requirements with which member states must comply. EU policy explicitly prescribes an *institutional model* to which domestic arrangements have to be adjusted. Accordingly, member states have only limited institutional discretion when deciding the concrete arrangements for compliance with European requirements.

The mechanism of Europeanisation by institutional compliance is particularly, albeit not exclusively, pronounced in policies of positive integration (Taylor 1983), including environmental protection, health and safety at work, consumer protection, and sections of social policy. These policies are directed at reducing negative externalities emerging from market activities; they are therefore 'market-shaping' rather than 'market-making', since they define distinctive regulatory requirements concerning the production, consumption and exchange of goods and services.

As shown in chapter 3, these requirements generally have concrete institutional implications. There is a tight linkage between the content of European policies and their impact on national administrative styles and structures. In other words, policies of positive integration in general imply and prescribe specific institutional requirements for domestic compliance. They affect domestic styles and structures not only by altering the institutional opportunity structure or the beliefs and expectations of domestic actors, but also, and predominantly, by prescribing the institutional outcome of domestic change, i.e., the equilibrium solution which has to be achieved. Policies of positive integration are therefore institutionally more demanding than other European policies; they imply explicit pressures for institutional adaptation at the domestic level. It is this most obvious impact of European policies on domestic arrangements that led us to select the environmental field as one area of positive integration as an empirical case for the underlying study.

We have seen that different patterns of administrative transformation at the domestic level can be explained on the basis of a modified institution-based perspective. In this context, institutions serve as an independent explanatory factor to identify the level of European adaptation pressure, and hence the cases where adaptation will be resisted (changes of the core), where adaptation is possible (changes within the core), and where no adaptations are required.

which was financed by the *Deutsche Forschungsgemeinschaft* under the Leibniz Fund Programme and directed by Adrienne Héritier (see Héritier *et al.* 2001).

In this context, we have identified two limitations characterising the independent explanatory relevance of institutions. First, the level of adaptation pressure might not only vary with European policy demands, but also with domestic core changes, i.e., fundamental administrative reforms affecting basic patterns of national administrative traditions. Second, in constellations of moderate adaptation pressure (changes within the core), the institution-based perspective needs to be supplemented by an agency-based approach in order to account for patterns of administrative adjustment. At this level, institutions are conceived as intervening rather than independent explanatory factors. The primary focus is on the preferences, beliefs and strategic interaction of domestic actors which interact in the context of given institutional opportunities and constraints. In the following, I will investigate to what extent this 'division of labour' between institution-based and agency-based approaches also provides a fruitful analytical starting point for policies characterised by a different logic of Europeanisation.

10.2   Europeanisation by changing domestic opportunity structures

Rather than positively prescribing an explicit model for domestic compliance, the domestic impact of European policies might be confined to altering domestic opportunity structures, and hence the distribution of power and resources between domestic actors. Such changes in domestic opportunity structures may in turn imply a successful challenge to existing institutional equilibria. Whilst European policies contribute to these potential challenges, they do not prescribe any distinctive institutional model of how the new equilibrium should actually look. This is not to say that European policies are not directed towards achieving certain regulatory objectives at the national level. However, they are intended to achieve these objectives in a less direct way, by altering domestic opportunities structures rather than prescribing institutional outcomes.

The mechanism of Europeanisation by changing domestic opportunity structures can be found in many market-making policies of the EU (negative integration). These policies basically exclude certain options from the range of national policy choices, rather than positively prescribing distinctive institutional models to be enacted at the national level. Their impact is generally restricted to the abolition of domestic administrative arrangements which distort the functioning of the Common Market, such as national regulations protecting domestic industrial sectors against foreign competition. Apart from these requirements, there is no direct institutional impact of European legislation on national administrations. Member states are not directly forced to replace their regulatory arrangements in favour of an institutional model prescribed by European legislation. Rather the requirement is much less demanding, namely to make national regulations compatible with European market regulation or *gemeinschaftverträglich* (Scharpf 1994) by abolishing those arrangements that are in conflict with the functioning of the internal market. To be sure, the important role of this mechanism with respect to EU market-making policies, however, does not exclude the existence of other Europeanisation mechanisms. Policies of negative integration vary a great deal in the extent to which they additionally prescribe institutional models for domestic compliance, such as, for instance, the EU policies on liberalising the energy sector.

The Europeanisation mechanism of changing domestic opportunity structures can be illustrated by the European policy to liberalise road transport. The project to establish a liberal transport market throughout the Community has made significant progress since the mid-1980s with the most crucial issue concerning the establishment of a single European transport market being the introduction of cabotage – the operation of non-resident hauliers in foreign domestic markets – in 1993[2] (Kerwer and Teutsch 2001).

A key characteristic of European road-haulage policy is that its domestic impact emerges from a restricted positive definition of requirements for domestic market-policy regulation, and the provision of new strategic opportunities and constraints for domestic actors. Thus, the liberalisation of cabotage removed the protection of national transport markets, so that states were no longer able to restrict the access of non-resident operators to their domestic markets. Apart from these restrictions, however, European legislation allowed for the maintenance of quantitative restrictions and price controls, that is, the co-existence of highly regulated domestic markets alongside a deregulated international market which includes the right to provide domestic transport for non-residents. In this way, European policies required only limited instrumental and institutional changes in the domestic regulation of road haulage.

On the other hand, the liberalisation of cabotage opened domestic markets up to international competition, hence affecting the strategic opportunities and constraints of domestic actors and challenging well-established regulatory arrangements. The introduction of cabotage, which limited the opportunity for member states to protect their

---

[2] Council Directive 93/3118 laying down the conditions under which non-resident carriers may operate national haulage services within a member state.

markets from foreign competition, created new strategic options for certain groups of actors, such as users of transport services (e.g., companies can decide whether they have their goods transported by foreign or domestic hauliers), while reducing the number of feasible options for others (e.g., in the light of European competition domestic tariff regimes for road transport are no longer sufficient to promote the market position of national hauliers). In other words, the European liberalisation of cabotage operates through the mechanism of 'regulatory competition', putting pressure on the member states to redesign domestic market regulations in order to avoid regulatory burdens restricting the competitiveness of their domestic industries.

How can we explain varying domestic responses to European policies which are basically directed at changing the institutional opportunities and constraints for domestic actors? To what extent can we rely on the explanatory framework developed to analyse the domestic impact of policies prescribing an institutional model for domestic compliance? Since policies directed towards changing domestic opportunity structures only redistribute powers and resources between domestic actors, and hence challenge existing equilibria rather than prescribing the concrete shape of the new equilibrium, domestic change or persistence is not primarily a matter of European adaptation pressure (which can generally be considered as low, given the considerable degree of institutional discretion for domestic compliance), but must be explained by analysing the extent to which European policies have altered the strategic position of domestic actors. These peculiarities emerging from the distinctive mechanism of Europeanisation have several implications with reference to our explanatory model.

First, and similar to policies relying on the mechanism of Europeanisation by institutional compliance, a merely sectoral assessment of the compatibility of European and national arrangements provides no sufficient basis to account for varying domestic responses. In the absence of European pressure for adaptation, it is hardly possible to assess any 'goodness of fit' of national arrangements with European policy demands. If, and to what extent, such adaptational pressures might emerge, cannot be judged from the comparison of European and domestic arrangements, but depends on the specific way European policies impact upon the domestic political process.

This point is illustrated by the different responses to EU haulage liberalisation in Britain, France, Germany and Italy. Britain and France had liberalised their national transport markets already before corresponding developments at the European level took place and hence were in a rather similar starting position when being confronted with European policy impacts. Nevertheless, we observe different responses in the two countries. While existing administrative arrangements remained basically unchanged in Britain, EU liberalisation policy triggered a counter-development towards increased intervention and social reregulation in France. A similar pattern can be observed for Germany and Italy, where the highly interventionist pattern of market regulation differed crucially from the liberal approach pursued at the European level. In response to the European liberalisation, Germany completely liberalised its national haulage market, while Italy even increased the level of state intervention (Héritier and Knill 2001).

Second, given the lack of institutional pressures for adjustment, then the more differentiated institution-based assumption, namely that domestic change can only be expected as long as European adaptation requirements remain within the range of options determined by the core of national administrative traditions, is of limited explanatory relevance. Since policies relying on this mechanism of Europeanisation prescribe no concrete equilibrium solution to be achieved at the national level, but only challenge existing equilibria, we are not able to hypothesise *ex ante* on patterns of administrative transformation on the basis of institutional adaptation pressure.

To be sure, the limited explanatory value of the institution-based argument does not question its general validity. This can be traced to the fact that policies directed at affecting domestic opportunity structures in general refer to changes within the (changing) core of national administrative traditions. In view of the lacking demand for institutional compliance, these policies generally fulfil the institution-based condition for change, namely that the required adjustments can be achieved within the range of options defined by the institutional core of administrative traditions.[3]

The fact that there is sufficient leeway to adjust to European pressures within the core can be illustrated by the rather different patterns of haulage liberalisation to be observed in Britain, France, Germany and Italy. Thus, the absence of any accompanying activities to curb negative externalities of a completely liberalised market is well in line with the British tradition of liberalism (Knill 2001), while the German activities

---

[3] There are, however, exceptions with reference to this general statement. This holds true in particular for cases in which the abolition of trade barriers in a certain sector constitutes a challenge to domestic core arrangements. For instance, Finland and Sweden faced demands for removing the state monopoly on the import of alcohol as a result of EU requirements. Since the monopoly in these countries was tightly linked to health and social concerns, hence reflecting an important part of the conception of the Nordic welfare state, European policies implied challenges to national administrative traditions.

to promote the competitiveness of their haulage industry as well as the French attempts towards social reregulation can be understood in terms of still persisting, albeit strongly modified traditions of sectoral corporatism and interventionism (Douillet and Lehmkuhl 2001; Teutsch 2001). Moreover, the ongoing pattern of interventionist regulation is well in line with core patterns of administrative traditions in Italy (Kerwer 2001).

Third, since the institution-based perspective only indicates that domestic change is not excluded by the macro-institutional context, the actual pattern of adaptation or non-adaptation within the core can only be explained on the basis of an agency-based perspective. In other words, the agency-based perspective constitutes the most important explanation in order to account for the domestic impact of European policies relying on the mechanism of changing domestic opportunity structures. Whether and how domestic regulatory arrangements are changed cannot be inferred from European policies, but depends on national politics. We have to ask whether European liberalisation has sufficiently altered domestic opportunity structures to enable national actors to successfully challenge existing regulatory arrangements.

In Britain and Italy, to begin with, European liberalisation policy did not modify the domestic opportunity structures to such an extent that it posed a successful challenge to the dominant policy coalition. Britain had liberalised its transport markets as early as 1968 in a way that resembled what has since emerged as the European approach to international transport. This way, European liberalisation implied no significant changes in domestic opportunity structures. Domestic hauliers were already confronted with unrestricted competition, hence having limited opportunities to protect their market position by restricting market access or prescribing minimum tariffs, as was the case in other countries. Domestic users of transport services, by contrast, already benefited from competition in the transport market. European policies therefore basically confirmed existing administrative arrangements. As domestic opportunity structures were not affected, no challenge to national equilibrium solutions can be observed (Knill 2001).

In a similar vein – although in terms of policy content, it is the other way round – the domestic constellation in Italy was characterised by a dominance of those actors opposing any liberalisation of the transport sector. The European impact was not strong enough to alter the domestic opportunity structures to such an extent that they posed a successful challenge to the strong position of domestic hauliers and the many institutional vetoes with which they could block reform attempts. In this context, it was in particular the factual veto position of the small hauliers which inhibited corresponding reforms. This group of actors often resorts to contortionist practices and calls strikes, in order to press the Ministry of Transport for new tax subsidies and to prevent deregulation, and their attempts are usually successful. Given these institutional constraints, industrial transport users, who are basically in favour of a more liberal regime, were not able to successfully challenge the existing regulatory arrangements, not even with the support and new opportunities provided by the European liberalisation policy. As a consequence, European policies did not increase the capacity of public actors for formulating policy goals autonomously and for implementing these against societal interests. Rather, the government and administration gave way to the aggressive policy of the smaller hauliers, which in turn led to a perpetuation of the domestic market regulation to protect Italian hauliers in the light of international competition (Kerwer 2001).

In Germany, by contrast, the European impact on domestic opportunity structures triggered fundamental regulatory changes. Initially, the German market regulation was characterised by a highly interventionist approach. Market access was restricted in quantitative terms and concerning market operations, tariffs were determined by the definition of minimum and maximum levels. The strong regulation of the transport market thus protected the position of those hauliers operating in the market, while at the same time restricting the opportunities of transport users to benefit from lower transport tariffs emerging within a competitive market. However, although the existing arrangements were biased in favour of domestic hauliers, they provided a much weaker veto position against liberal reforms than the position enjoyed by the small hauliers in Italy. Given the well-established patterns of corporatist relationships with the transport administration, contortionist practices and strikes were not a feasible option for German hauliers wanting to push through their interests. Hence, in contrast to Italy, in the political contest between pro-liberalisers and anti-liberalisers, the European reform policies played a decisive role. They helped to overcome the *de facto* veto points by strengthening the position of the liberaliser coalition, that is, the opposition of the road hauliers with their vested interests in maintaining market regulation, tipping the scales in favour of the pro-liberalisation coalition. European liberalisation had crucially challenged the strategic options for domestic actors, as the effectiveness of domestic protectionism was undermined by international competition. In view of the modified opportunities and constraints for the strategic interaction of domestic actors, European influence implied a move away from quantitative restrictions for market access in favour of qualitative access criteria. Moreover, the system of bracket tariffs was abolished in 1994.

At the same time, market liberalisation is accompanied by domestic attempts to strengthen the competitive position of domestic hauliers in the European market, in particular by promoting the harmonisation of regulatory and fiscal conditions at the European level (Teutsch 2001).

In sharp contrast with Germany, European policies in France shifted the balance in favour of a reregulation coalition. The subsequent regulatory changes included not only the strengthening of professional requirements and working time limitations for hauliers, but also the regulation of minimum prices for transport services so as to protect small haulage companies and sub-contractors from cut-throat competition. Since the liberalisation process in the late 1980s, the French road haulage market has been much more market-oriented than it was in the 1970s. However, in the aftermath of domestic liberalisation and the advent of liberalised European transport markets, actors in favour of reregulation progressively gained ground. Hauliers' associations increasingly co-ordinated their activities and trade unions emerged as a new and vigorous actor in the field, channelling the demand for protection of the national industry and their workforce. In this context, European liberalisation policy constituted a strategic resource for the reregulation coalition in order to increase their political influence. By emphasising the fact that European liberalisation may aggravate the social and political problems emerging in the newly liberalised domestic market, European legislation provided an important opportunity for these actors to promote their social reregulation proposals. In other words, the domestic actors opposing European developments became politically more influential than those actor coalitions supporting European liberalisation policy (Douillet and Lehmkuhl 2001).

10.3   Europeanisation by framing domestic beliefs and expectations

In their 'weakest' form European policies neither prescribe concrete institutional requirements nor modify the institutional context for strategic interaction, but seek to trigger domestic adjustments to EU regulatory objectives even more indirectly, namely by altering the beliefs and expectations of domestic actors. Changes in domestic beliefs may in turn affect strategies and preferences of domestic actors, potentially leading to corresponding institutional adaptations. Hence, the domestic impact of European policies is primarily based on a cognitive logic.

The dominance of this mechanism can be particularly observed in European policies whose aim is basically to prepare the ground for subsequent, institutionally more demanding policies of positive or negative integration. Rather than prescribing concrete outcomes or substantially altering institutional opportunity structures, these policies are designed to change the domestic political climate by stimulating and strengthening the overall support for broader European reform objectives (Ingram and Schneider 1990; Knill and Lehmkuhl 2000). The emergence of such policies of framing integration is particularly likely when the European decision-making context allows for the adoption of policies which are only vague and more or less symbolic, given the underlying conflicts of interests between the member states.

A good example of such activities for framing domestic beliefs and expectations is the European railways policy. While the underlying direction of European activities is clear, namely to arrive at a liberalised European 'railways market' concerning the transport of persons and goods, corresponding measures so far remained at a rather symbolic level, neither significantly altering the institutional context in which domestic actors operate nor prescribing concrete institutional outcomes to be achieved.

Although proposals to liberalise the European railways had been on the agenda of the Commission since the mid-1970s, attempts at appropriate legislation never got past the initial stage. The reasons for this deadlock were twofold. On the one hand the heterogeneity of the member states implied significant agreement problems. In the larger member states in particular, the railways were not seen as purely economic actors, but as the providers of a public service with obligations that had to be maintained for political reasons. Hence, there was marked resistance to any Community attempt to intervene in domestic railways policy. On the other hand the Commission only had limited legal and institutional powers to overcome the resistance of the member states.[4]

It was not before the early 1990s that supranational reform efforts were accepted by the member states (Erdmenger 1997). This sudden take-off in European railways policy can be understood in terms of a changing approach to integration. While the Commission initially based its reform proposals on a legally demanding compliance approach, the 1991 Directive on the development of the Community's railways emphasises the building of domestic support for railway liberalisation

---

[4] As a result of their strong dependence on national subsidies, unlike the energy and telecommunications sectors, the railways could not easily be subjected to European competition law which formally empowers the Commission to break up national monopolies without the agreement of the Council. However, even if the Commission was able to rely on these formal legal powers, the practice of European policy-making in telecommunications and energy reveals that the *de facto* application of these powers is dependent on the consent of the member states (see Schmidt 1997a).

rather than legally forcing member states to reform their railways. Its basic intention is to alter the national policy-making context by increasing the support for its reform programme.

If the Directive was to be a success, it wasn't so much a success with what it did directly, but what it did indirectly. And that is to create a new thought process to be applied to the railways, to think again about what railways were supposed to be doing, and how they were supposed to be run. (Commission official, quoted in Kerwer and Teutsch 2001)

The 1991 Directive thus contains hardly any serious challenges to the well-established railway policies at the domestic level.[5] The Directive is designed in a non-compulsory style and a sufficiently ambiguous texture in order to give domestic implementers far-reaching flexibility and discretion to comply with its modest requirements. Thus, the most demanding requirement of the Directive is that member states shall take the necessary measures to ensure that the accounts for business relating to the provision of infrastructure and those for business relating to the provision of transport activities are kept separate. In other words, the Directive requires only a change in national accounting systems rather than organisational or institutional adaptations (Knill and Lehmkuhl 2000).

The lack of explicit institutional pressure for domestic adaptation, and hence the limited explanatory value of a perspective which considers the institutional compatibility of European and domestic arrangements, applies similarly to the third mechanism, Europeanisation by framing domestic beliefs and expectations. Like European policies directed at changing domestic opportunity structures, policies relying on the framing mechanism lack explicit institutional pressures for domestic adaptation. This way, we are not able to predict cases of institutional non-adaptation on the basis of an institution-based assumption, stating that domestic change is only possible as long as European adaptation requirements remain within the institutional core patterns. For the same reasons mentioned in the context of road haulage policy, the restricted explanatory value of this condition does not imply its invalidity. Rather we can assume these conditions to be generally fulfilled. Given their voluntaristic, institutionally non-demanding character, policies of framing domestic beliefs and expectations generally refer to changes *within* rather than *of* the (changing) core of national administrative traditions.

This statement can be illustrated by considering the content of railway reforms which took place in the member states in the context of

[5] Council Directive 91/440/EEC of 29 July 1991 on the development of the Community's railways (OJ No. L/237).

corresponding policy initiatives at the European level (Héritier *et al.* 2001). Notwithstanding important differences in the scope and scale of domestic reforms, these developments still remained within the range of options defined by the macro-institutional background of administrative traditions in each country. In Britain, to begin with, we observe not only a radical privatisation programme (including infrastructure), but also the introduction of highly competitive regimes with respect to network operations. In view of the fundamental changes in the British public sector (see chapter 5 in this book), these developments are fully in line with the 'changed' core patterns of British administrative traditions. The radical changes in Britain contrast with the developments in the Netherlands and Germany, where infrastructure is still in public ownership and network operations are privatised and subject to competition to only a limited extent. These differences in the scope and content of national reforms can be traced to the fact that, in these countries, state intervention and public/private co-operation constitute traditional features of the political-administrative system. The emphasis of the state as the provider of public services is even more pronounced in France and Italy, where the structure of the railways as a public sector monopoly is more or less still in place.

Given the limited explanatory relevance of an institution-based perspective, the question of whether and how Europeanisation triggers domestic changes therefore can only be answered from ex *post*, by applying a less abstract agency-based perspective. Unlike European policies whose domestic impact emerges from changes in domestic opportunity structures, policies based on the framing mechanism are basically confined to altering the 'cognitive input' into these opportunity structures rather than directly affecting these structures. Hence, the question is whether European legislation has contributed to altering expectations and beliefs of domestic actors in such a way as to motivate domestic institutional change. Has European legislation sufficiently altered the constellation of domestic preferences and beliefs and hence favoured reforms which would otherwise not have emerged?

As a consequence, the domestic impact of European framing might vary from member state to member state, hence confirming the mixed patterns of administrative transformation already observed in environmental policy and road haulage. Referring to the example of European railways policy, European framing had a considerable impact on national reforms in Germany and Netherlands, while only limited effects can be observed in Britain, France and Italy.

In the British case, this statement seems surprising, given that the 1993 privatisation of British Rail can be classified as the most radical and far-reaching reform of the railways throughout the EU. However, as these reforms basically emerged in the light of endogenous national developments to restructure the public sector, the impact of the European Directive was highly limited (Knill 2001). In France and Italy, the limited influence of European policies becomes apparent in the fact that the existing administrative arrangements in the railways sector remained basically unchanged. Although in France a new organisation was created which is in charge of the infrastructure (*Réseau ferré de France*), the SNCF still manages infrastructure on behalf of this body and still holds the monopoly for all operational services. In Italy, the only changes so far concern the 1992 privatisation of the Italian railways, which, however, remained at a formal and symbolic stage (Knill and Lehmkuhl 2000). Although the concepts embodied in European railways policy were actively used by political and administrative actors in order to promote and legitimise corresponding reforms of the Italian railways, the support provided by European legislation was not sufficient to trigger substantial changes.

In contrast to these countries, European framing played a more decisive role in triggering domestic change in Germany and the Netherlands. Although in both countries there was already a strong political commitment to reform the national railways in view of their increasing financial problems, corresponding policy proposals had failed in the light of the strong political opposition they faced. Solutions only became feasible in the context of European activities. European legislation served not only as a concept to solve domestic problems, but also provided political executives with additional legitimacy to enact their policy ideas. Moreover, the reference to European policy activities significantly altered the expectations of reform opponents and hence affected their strategies. The question was no longer how to block the general developments, which would be inevitable in the long run in the light of Europeanisation, but how to influence the shape of the reform as far as possible. In short, by changing the expectations of domestic actors, European legislation helped to overcome domestic veto points without altering given institutional constraints and opportunities (Lehmkuhl 2001; Teutsch 2001).

10.4   Conclusion

The central objective of this book was to investigate the impact of European policies on national administrative styles and structures. To what extent do we observe domestic administrative change under the impact of European policies and how can we explain the varying patterns of administrative transformation? To address these questions, a modified institutionalist framework has been proposed. This framework is based on the complementary linkage of institution-based and agency-based approaches in order to avoid the problem of determinism inherent in many institutionalist approaches. Moreover, it takes a dynamic perspective on institutional development, explicitly acknowledging that institutional stability is nothing to be taken for granted, but varies with the structural capacity for administrative reform given in a country.

The analytical distinction of different mechanisms of Europeanisation basically confirms the general validity of this modified institutionalist model in order to account for the varying domestic responses to European policies. The absence of direct institutional adaptation pressure, which distinguishes the mechanisms of changing domestic opportunity structures and framing domestic beliefs and expectations from Europeanisation by institutional compliance, however, has certain implications with respect to the explanatory relevance of institution-based and agency-based approaches. To be precise, the assumption that European adaptation only takes place as long as European adaptation requirements remain within the core of national administrative traditions is of limited relevance in cases where European policies imply no explicit institutional pressures for change. This is not to say that the condition is not valid in these cases. Rather it is exactly the institutionally less demanding nature of these policies that implies that this condition can generally be taken for granted.

As a consequence, the application of institution-based explanations (taking institutions as an independent explanatory factor) is of explanatory relevance only with respect to policies relying on the mechanism of Europeanisation by institutional compliance. Given the explicit institutional pressure for adaptation underlying these policies, we are able to hypothesise *ex ante* in the light of the compatibility of these requirements with national administrative traditions. We can identify cases where adaptation will be resisted (challenges of the core) and cases where adaptation is possible within the core of national administrative traditions. Therefore, it is only for explaining the actual occurrence or non-occurrence of changes within the core, that we have to apply a less abstract agency-based perspective, taking account of interests, beliefs, strategies and institutional opportunity structures.

The institution-based explanation is of limited explanatory relevance, however, in order to account for the domestic impact of European policies whose impact is restricted to changing domestic opportunity structures or altering the beliefs and expectations of domestic actors. In the absence of concrete institutional requirements, it is impossible to hypothesise on the compatibility of European policies and national administrative traditions. In these constellations, patterns of domestic change can only be explained *ex post*, by applying an agency-based perspective. In short, the explanatory relevance of institutions in order to explain the domestic impact of European policies varies with the particular mechanism of Europeanisation, i.e., the basic pattern by which European policies exert their influence on national administrative styles and structures. The institution-based concept of adaptation pressure can hardly be applied in order to account for different patterns of administrative change in cases where European policies prescribe no concrete model for institutional compliance. In contrast to the suggestion by Cowles and Risse (2001) who identify European adaptation pressure as the necessary condition for domestic change, the analytical findings presented in this book indicate the need for a more differentiated perspective, taking account of the varying explanatory value of institution-based and agency-based approaches with respect to different mechanisms of Europeanisation.

Taken together, these considerations allow for two general statements on the impact of European policies on national administrations. On the one hand, we know that the scope of domestic adaptation is constrained by the macro-institutional context of national administrative traditions, notwithstanding the fact that Europeanisation may sometimes imply sectoral revolutions at the domestic level. On the other hand, the form, logic and scope of everything that happens within this macro-institutional range varies with European policies, domestic interest constellations, beliefs and expectations as well as institutional opportunity structures in which domestic actors operate.

References

Aberbach, J. D., R. D. Putnam, and B. A. Rockman (1981). *Bureaucrats and Politicians in Western Democracies*. Cambridge, Mass.: Harvard University Press.

Abromeit, Heidrun (1991). 'Staatsentwicklung in der Thatcher-Ära: Weniger Staat – mehr Staat?' In: Roland Sturm (ed.), *Thatcherismus. Eine Bilanz nach zehn Jahren*. Bochum: Universitätsverlag, 295–324.

Alder, John (1993). 'Environmental Impact Assessment – The Inadequacy of English Law'. *Journal of Environmental Law* 5 (2), 203–20.

Allum, Percy (1995). *State and Society in Western Europe*. Cambridge: Polity Press.

Ambrosius, Gerold (1994). 'Privatisierungen in historischer Perspektive: Zum Verhältnis von öffentlicher und privater Produktion'. *Staatswissenschaften und Staatspraxis* 5, 415–38.

Andersen, Sven and Kjell Eliassen (eds.) (1993). *Making Policy in Europe. The Europeification of National Policy-Making*. London: Sage.

Arthur, W. Brian (1988). 'Self-Reinforcing Mechanisms in Economics'. In: Philipp W. Anderson *et al.* (eds.), *The Economy as an Evolving Complex System*, Redwood City: Addison-Wesley Publishing Company, 9–31.

Ashford, Douglas E. (1982). *Policy and Politics in France. Living with Uncertainty*. Philadelphia: Temple University Press.

Aspinwall, Mark and Gerald Schneider (1997). 'Same Menu, Separate Tables. The Institutionalist Turn in Political Science and the Study of European Integration'. Paper presented at the 1997 research session of the European Consortium of Political Research, Bergen, 18–21 September.

Atkinson, Michael M. and William D. Coleman (1989). 'Strong States and Weak States. Sectoral Policy Networks in Advanced Capitalist Economies'. *British Journal of Political Science* 19 (1), 48–67.

Badie, Bertrand and Pierre Birnbaum (1983). *The Sociology of the State*. Chicago: Chicago University Press.

Baggott, Rob (1989). 'Regulatory Reform in Britain: The Changing Face of Self-Regulation'. *Public Administration* 67 (4), 435–454.

Baier, Vicki E., James G. March and Harald Sætren (1990). 'Implementierung und Ungewißheit'. In: James G. March (ed.), *Entwicklung und Organisation. Kritische und konstruktive Beiträge, Entwicklungen und Perspektiven*. Wiesbaden: Gabler, 170–84.

Baldock, D. and G. Bennett (1991). *Agriculture and the Polluter Pays Principle*. London: Institute for European Environmental Policy.

228

Banner, G. (1994). 'Steuerung kommunalen Handelns'. In: R. Roth and H. Wollmann (eds.), *Kommunalpolitik*. Opladen: Leske & Budrich, 350–61.

Barnett, M. (1999). 'Culture, Strategy and Foreign Policy: Israel's Road to Oslo'. *European Journal of International Relations* 1, 5–36.

Bekke, Hans A. G. M., James L. Perry and Theo A. J. Toonen (eds.) (1996). *Civil Service Systems in Comparative Perspective*. Indiana: Indiana University Press.

Benz, Arthur (1990). 'Verhandlungen, Verträge und Absprachen in der öffentlichen Verwaltung'. *Die Verwaltung* 1, 83–98.

——— (1995). 'Verfassungspolitik im Bundesstaat'. In: K. Bentele, R. Schettkat and B. Reissert (eds.), *Die Reformfähigkeit von Industriegesellschaften*. Frankfurt/Main: Campus, 145–63.

Benz, Arthur and Klaus H. Goetz (1996). 'The German Public Sector: National Priorities and the International Reform Agenda'. In: Arthur Benz and Klaus H. Goetz, (eds.), *A New German Public Sector? Reform, Adaptation and Stability*. Aldershot: Dartmouth, 1–26.

Beuermann, Christiane and Reinhard Burdick (1997). 'The Sustainability Transition in Germany: Some Early Stage Experiences'. *Environmental Politics* 6 (1), 83–107.

Beyme, Klaus von (1991). *Das politische System der Bundesrepublik Deutschland nach der Vereinigung*. München: Piper.

BGW (Bundesverband der deutschen Gas- und Wasserwirtschaft) (1995). *Trinkwasser*. Bonn: BGW.

BGW/DVGW (1993). *Erfahrungen mit dem 12–Punkte-Proghramm aus der Sicht der Wasserwirtschaft in Nordrhein-Westfalen*. Bonn: BGW/DVGW.

Böckenförde, E. W. (1991). *Recht, Staat, Freiheit. Studien zur Rechtsphilosophie, Staatstheorie und Verfassungsgeschichte*. Frankfurt/Main: Suhrkamp.

Bodiguel, Maryvonne (ed.) (1996). *La Qualité des Eaux dans l'Union Européenne*. Paris: Edition L'Harmattan.

Boehmer-Christiansen, Sonja and Jim Skea (1991). *Acid Politics. Environmental and Energy Policies in Britain and Germany*. London: Belhaven Press.

Bohne, E. (1981). *Der informale Rechtsstaat*. Berlin: Duncker & Humblot.

Böhret, Carl (1982). 'Reform und Anpassungsflexibilität der öffentlichen Verwaltung'. In: Joaschim Jens Hesse (ed.), *Politikwissenschaft und Verwaltungswissenschaft*, PVS Sonderheft 13, Opladen: Westdeutscher Verlag, 134–50.

Bongaerts, Jan C. (1989). 'Die Entwicklung der europäischen Umweltpolitik'. *WSI-Mitteilungen* 10, 575–584.

Börzel, Tanja A. (1999). 'Towards Convergence in Europe? Institutional Adaptation to Europeanization in Germany and Spain'. *Journal of Common Market Studies* 39 (4), 573–96.

Börzel, Tanja A. and Thomas Risse (2000). 'When Europe Hits Home: Europeanization and Domestic Change'. Paper presented at the Annual Convention of the American Political Science Association, Washington DC, 31 August–3 September 2000.

Bouma, Jan Jaap (2000). 'Environmental Management Systems and Audits as Alternative Environmental Policy Instruments'. In: Christoph Knill and Andrea Lenschow (eds.), *Implementing EU Environmental Policy: New Directions and Old Problems*. Manchester: Manchester University Press, 116–33.

Bowman, John C. (1992). 'Improving the Quality of Our Water: The Role of

Regulation by the National Rivers Authority'. *Public Administration* 70, 565–75.

Boynton, John (1986). 'Judicial Review of Administrative Decisions – A Background Paper'. *Public Administration* 64, 147–61.

BSI (British Standards Institution) (1993). *Guidance to Sector Working Groups in the BS 7750 Pilot Programme on the Production of Sector Application Guides (SAGS) for Use with the New British Standard on Environmental Management Systems*. Milton Keynes: British Standards Institution.

Budge, Ian and David McKay (1988). *The Changing British Political System. Into the 1990s*. Essex: Longman.

Bulmer, Martin (1988). 'Social Science Expertise and Executive-Bureaucratic Politics in Britain'. *Governance* 1 (1), 26–49.

Burch, Martin and Ian Holliday (1996). *The British Cabinet System*. London: Prentice Hall.

Burley, Anne-Marie and Walter Mattli (1993). 'Europe before the Court: A Political Theory of Legal Integration'. *International Organization* 47 (1), 41–77.

Burmeister, Joachim H. (1990). 'Akteneinsicht in Großbritannien'. In: Gerd Winter (ed.), *Öffentlichkeit von Umweltinformationen. Europäische und nordamerikanische Rechte und Erfahrungen*. Baden-Baden: Nomos, 211–48.

Burmeister, Joachim H. and Gerd Winter (1990). 'Akteneinsicht in der Bundesrepublik'. In: Gerd Winter (ed.), *Öffentlichkeit von Umweltinformationen. Europäische und nordamerikanische Rechte und Erfahrungen*. Baden-Baden: Nomos, 87–128.

Busse, Volker (1996). 'Verfahrenswege zu einem "schlankeren Staat"'. *Die öffentliche Verwaltung* 49 (10), 389–96.

Butler, Robin (1993). 'The Evolution of the Civil Service – A Progress Report'. *Public Administration* 71, 395–406.

Campbell, Colin and Graham K. Wilson (1995). *The End of Whitehall. Death of a Paradigm?* Oxford: Blackwell.

Campbell, Colin and Margaret J. Wyszomirski (1991). 'Introduction'. In: Colin Campbell and Margaret J. Wyszomirski (eds.), *Executive Leadership in Anglo-American Systems*. Pittsburgh: Pittsburgh University Press.

Caporaso, James, Maria Cowles and Thomas Risse (eds.) (2001). *Transforming Europe. Europeanization and Domestic Change*. Ithaca, NY: Cornell University Press.

CEC (Commission of the European Communities) (1993). *Report from the Commission of the Implementation of Directive 85/337/EEC on the Assessment of the Effects of Certain Public and Private Projects on the Environment*. Brussels: Commission of the European Communities.

—— (1996). *Thirteenth Annual Report on Monitoring the Application of Community Law (1995)*. Luxembourg: Office for Official Publications of the EC.

Checkel, Jeffrey T. (2001). 'The Europeanization of Citizenship?' In: James A. Caporaso, Maria Green Cowles and Thomas Risse (eds.), *Transforming Europe. Europeanization and Domestic Change*. Ithaca, NY: Cornell University Press, 180–97.

Christoph, James B. (1993). 'The Effects of Britons in Brussels: The European Community and the Culture of Whitehall'. *Governance* 6 (4), 518–37.

Coenen, R. and Jörissen, J. (1988). *Umweltverträglichkeitsprüfung in der Europäischen Gemeinschaft. Derzeitiger Stand der Umsetzung der EG-Richtlinie in zehn Staaten der EG.* Berlin: Erich Schmidt-Verlag.

Collier, David (1991). 'The Comparative Method: Two Decades of Change'. In: Dankwart A. Rustow and Kenneth Paul (eds.), *Comparative Political Dynamics: Global Research Perspectives.* New York: Harper Collins.

Collier, Ute (1995). *Electricity Privatisation and Environmental Policy in the UK. Some Lessons for the Rest of Europe.* EUI Working Paper RSC 95/2. Florence: European University Institute.

Collins, Ken and David Earnshaw (1992). 'The Implementation and Enforcement of European Community Environment Legislation'. *Environmental Politics* 1 (4), 213–49.

Conrad, J. (1990). *Nitrate Pollution and Politics. Great Britain, the Federal Republic of Germany and the Netherlands.* Aldershot: Avebury.

Cowles, Maria Green and Thomas Risse (2001). 'Transforming Europe: Conclusions'. In: James A. Caporaso, Maria Green Cowles and Thomas Risse (eds.), *Transforming Europe. Europeanization and Domestic Change.* Ithaca, NY: Cornell University Press, 217–38.

Crozier, M. (1964). *The Bureaucratic Phenomenon.* Chicago: Chicago University Press.

Cupei, Jürgen (1994). *Vermeidung von Wettbewerbsverzerrungen innerhalb der EG durch UVP? Eine vergleichende Analyse der Umsetzung der UVP-Richtlinie in Frankreich, Großbritannien und den Niederlanden.* Baden-Baden: Nomos.

Czada, Roland (1993). 'Konfliktbewältigung und politische Reform in vernetzten Entscheidungsstrukturen'. In: Roland Czada and Manfred G. Schmidt (eds.), *Verhandlungsdemokratie, Interessenvermittlung, Regierbarkeit.* Opladen: Westdeutscher Verlag, 73–100.

—— (1994). 'Schleichwege in die "Dritte Republik". Politik der Vereinigung und politischer Wandel in Deutschland'. *Politische Vierteljahresschrift* 35, 245–70.

Damaska, Mirian R. (1986). *The Faces of Justice and State Authority. A Comparative Approach to the Legal Process.* New Haven: Yale University Press.

Derlien, Hans-Ulrich (1988). 'Repercussions of Government Change on the Career Civil Service in West Germany: the Cases of 1969 and 1982'. *Governance* 1 (1), 50–78.

—— (1995). 'Public Administration in Germany: Political and Societal Relations'. In: Jon Pierre (ed.), *Bureaucracy in the Modern State. An Introduction to Comparative Public Administration.* Aldershot: Edward Elgar, 64–91.

—— (1996a). 'Germany: The Intelligence of Bureaucracy in a Decentralized Polity'. In: Johan P. Olsen and B. Guy Peters (eds.), *Lessons from Experience. Experimental Learning in Administrative Reforms in Eight Democracies.* Oslo: Scandinavian University Press, 146–79.

—— (1996b). 'Patterns of Postwar Administrative Development in Germany'. In: Arthur Benz and Klaus H. Goetz, (eds.), *A New German Public Sector? Reform, Adaptation and Stability.* Aldershot: Dartmouth, 27–44.

Derlien, Hans-Ulrich et al. (1988). *CES II: Einstellungen der politisch-administrativen Elite des Bundes.* Bamberg: Verwaltungswissenschaftliche Beiträge No. 25.

DiMaggio, Paul J. and Walter W. Powell (1991). 'The Iron Cage Revisited. Institutionalised Isomorphism and Collective Rationality in Organizational Fields'. In: Walter W. Powell and Paul J. DiMaggio (eds.), *The New Institutionalism in Organizational Analysis*. Chicago: Chicago University Press, 63–82.

Dobbin, Frank (1994). *Forging Industrial Policy. The United States, Britain, and France in the Railway Age*. Cambridge: Cambridge University Press.

DoE (Department of the Environment) (1991). *Integrated Pollution Control. A Practical Guide*. London: HMSO.

—— (1996). *Reducing National Emissions of Sulphur Dioxide. A Strategy for the United Kingdom*. London: DoE.

Douillet, Anne-Cécile and Dirk Lehmkuhl (2001). 'Pushing Reform and Opposition Alike: Europe's Differential Impact on the French Transport Sector'. In: Adrienne Héritier, Dieter Kerwer, Christoph Knill, Dirk Lehmkuhl and Michael Teutsch, *Differential Europe. New Opportunities and Constraints for National Policy-Making*. Lanham: Rowman and Littlefield, 99–132.

Dunleavy, Patrick (1991). *Democracy, Bureaucracy and Public Choice*. London: Harvester Wheatsheaf.

—— (1993). 'Introduction: Stability, Crisis or Decline?' In: Patrick Dunleavy, Andrew Gamble, Ian Holliday and Gillian Peele (eds.), *Developments in British Politics*. London: Macmillan, 1–18.

DWI (Drinking Water Inspectorate) (1996). *Drinking Water 1995. A Report by the Chief Inspector of the Drinking Water Inspectorate*. London: HMSO.

Dyson, Kenneth A. (1980). *The State Tradition in Western Europe. A Study of an Idea and Institution*. Oxford: Martin Robertson.

—— (1982). 'West Germany: The Search for a Rationalist Consensus'. In: Jeremy Richardson (ed.), *Policy Styles in Western Europe*. London: Allen and Unwin.

—— (1992). 'Theories of Regulation and the Case of Germany'. In: Kenneth A. Dyson (ed.), *The Politics of German Regulation*. Aldershot: Dartmouth, 1–28.

Eichener, Volker (1996). 'Die Rückwirkungen der europäischen Integration auf nationale Politikmuster'. In: Markus Jachtenfuchs and Beate Kohler-Koch (eds.), *Europäische Integration*. Opladen: Leske & Budrich, 249–80.

Eifert, Martin (1994). 'Umweltinformation als Regelungsinstrument'. *Die öffentliche Verwaltung* 13, 544–52.

Eisen, Andreas (1993). 'Zur Entwicklung der Umweltverwaltung in den neuen Bundesländern – Ein Vergleich der Bundesländer Sachsen und Brandenburg'. *Die öffentliche Verwaltung* 46 (16), 677–88.

Eising, Rainer and Beate Kohler-Koch (1994). 'Inflation und Zerfaserung: Trends der Interessenvermittlung in der Europäischen Gemeinschaft'. In: Wolfgang Streeck (ed.), *Staat und Verbände*. PVS Sonderheft 25/1994, Opladen: Westdeutscher Verlag, 175–206.

Ellwein, Thomas (1985). 'Geschichte der öffentlichen Verwaltung'. In: Klaus König, Hans Joachim von Oertzen and Frido Wagener (eds.), *Öffentliche Verwaltung in der Bundesrepublik Deutschland*. Baden-Baden: Nomos, 37–51.

—— (1989). 'Verwaltungsgeschichte und Verwaltungstheorie'. In: Thomas Ellwein *et al.* (eds.), *Jahrbuch zur Staats- und Verwaltungswissenschaft*. Baden-Baden: Nomos.

(1990). 'Über Verwaltungskunst oder: Grenzen der Verwaltungsführung und der Verwaltungswissenschaft'. *Staatswissenschaften und Staatspraxis* 1, 89–104.

(1993a). *Der Staat als Zufall und Notwendigkeit. Die jüngere Verwaltungsentwicklung in Deutschland am Beispiel Ostwestfalen-Lippe. Band 1*. Opladen: Westdeutscher Verlag.

(1993b). 'Tradition – Anpassung – Reform. Über die Besonderheit der Verwaltungsentwicklung in den neuen Bundesländern'. In: Wolfgang Seibel, Arthur Benz and Heinrich Mäding (eds.), *Verwaltungsreform und Verwaltungspolitik im Prozeß der deutschen Einigung*. Baden-Baden: Nomos, 30–40.

(1994). *Das Dilemma der Verwaltung. Verwaltungsstruktur und Verwaltungsreformen in Deutschland*. Mannheim: B.-I.-Taschenbuchverlag.

(1996). 'Perioden und Probleme der deutschen Verwaltungsgeschichte'. *Verwaltungs-Archiv* 87 (1), 1–18.

Ellwein, Thomas and Joachim Jens Hesse (1989). *Das Regierungssystem der Bundesrepublik Deutschland*. Opladen: Westdeutscher Verlag.

(1994). *Der überforderte Staat*. Baden-Baden: Nomos.

Engel, Rüdiger (1992). 'Der freie Zugang zu Umweltinformationen nach der Informationsrichtlinie der EG und der Schutz von Rechten Dritter'. *NVwZ* (2), 111–14.

Environment Agency (1996). *A Guide to Information Available to the Public*. Bristol: Environment Agency.

Erbguth, Wilfried (1991). 'Das UVP-Gesetz des Bundes: Regelungsgehalt und Rechtsfragen'. *Die Verwaltung* 24 (3), 283–324.

Erdmenger, Jürgen (1997). 'Verkehrspolitik'. In: Werner Weidenfeld and Wolfgang Wessels (eds.), *Jahrbuch der europäischen Integration*. Bonn: Europa-Union Verlag, 167–72.

Erichsen, Hans-Uwe (1992). 'Das Recht auf freien Zugang zu Informationen über die Umwelt'. *NVwZ* (5), 409–19.

Esping-Andersen, Gösta (1990). *The Three Worlds of Welfare Capitalism*. Cambridge: Polity Press.

Feick, Jürgen (1983). 'Internationale Vergleichbarkeit staatlicher Interventionsprogramme – Konzeptionelle und methodische Probleme'. In: Renate Mayntz (ed.), *Implementation politischer Programme II*, Opladen: Westdeutscher Verlag, 197–220.

Finnemore, M. and K. Sikkink (1998). 'International Norm Dynamics and Political Change'. *International Organization* 52 (4), 887–917.

Flynn, Norman (1996). 'The United Kingdom'. In: Norman Flynn and Franz Strehl (eds.), *Public Sector Management in Europe*. London: Prentice Hall, 50–83.

Flynn, Norman and Franz Strehl (eds.) (1996). *Public Sector Management in Europe*. London: Prentice Hall.

FoE (Friends of the Earth) (1996). *Insisting on our Right to Know. Friends of the Earth's Experiences in Using the New Legislation to Access Environmental Information*. London: FoE.

Foster, C. D. (1992). *Privatization, Public Ownership and the Regulation of Natural Monopoly*. Oxford: Blackwell.

Frankel, Maurice (1978). *The Social Audit Pollution Handbook*. London: Social Audit.

Führ, Martin (1990). 'Umweltinformation im Genehmigungsverfahren. Eine Fallstudie'. In: Gerd Winter (ed.), *Öffentlichkeit von Umweltinformationen. Europäische und nordamerikanische Rechte und Erfahrungen*. Baden-Baden: Nomos, 129–58.

Gamble, Andrew (1988). *The Free Economy and the Strong State. The Politics of Thatcherism*. London: Macmillan.

Gehring, Thomas (1996). 'Institutionalizing Environmental Policy-Making: The Case of Packaging Waste'. Paper presented at the conference 'Social Regulation Through European Committees: Empirical Research, Institutional Politics, Theoretical Concepts and Legal Developments'. Florence, European University Institute, 9–10 December.

Grande, Edgar (1996). 'Das Paradox der Schwäche. Forschungspolitik und die Einflußlogik europäischer Politikverflechtung'. In: Markus Jachtenfuchs and Beate Kohler-Koch (eds.), *Europäische Integration*. Opladen: Leske & Budrich, 373–400.

Gray, Andrew and William Jenkins (1985). *Administrative Politics in British Government*. Sussex: Wheatsheaf Books.

Greenwood, John and David Wilson (1989). *Public Administration in Britain Today*. London: Unwin Hyman.

Greenwood, Justin and Laura Cram (1996). 'European Level Business Collective Action: The Study Agenda Ahead'. *Journal of the Common Market Studies* 34 (3), 449–63.

Grimm, Dieter (1991). 'The Modern State: Continental Traditions'. In: Franz-Xavier Kaufmann (ed.) *The Public Sector – Challenge for Coordination and Learning*. Berlin: de Gruyter, 117–40.

Haigh, Nigel (1990). *EEC Environmental Policy and Britain*. Harlow: Longman.

(1996). *The Manual of Environmental Policy: the EC and Britain*. London: Catermill Publishing.

Hall, Peter (1986). *Governing the Economy. The Politics of State Intervention in Britain and France*. Cambridge: Cambridge University Press.

(1992). 'The Movement from Keynesianism to Monetarism: Institutional Analysis and British Economic Policy in the 1970s'. In: Kathleen Thelen, Sven Steinmo, and Frank Longstreth (eds.), *Structuring Politics. Historical Institutionalism in Comparative Analysis*. Cambridge: Cambridge University Press.

(1993). 'Policy Paradigms, Social Learning and the State. The Case of Economic Policymaking in Britain'. *Comparative Politics* 25, 275–96.

Hall, Peter A. and Rosemary C. R. Taylor (1996). *Political Science and the Three New Institutionalisms*. MPIFG Discussion Paper 96/6. Köln: Max-Planck-Instititut für Gesellschaftsforschung.

Hanf, Kenneth and Fritz W. Scharpf (eds.) (1978). *Interorganizational Policy-Making: Limits to Coordination and Central Control*. London: Sage.

Hanf, Kenneth and Paul B. Downing (1982). 'Introduction: A Perspective for the Study of Regulatory Enforcement'. In: Paul Downing and Kenneth

Hanf (eds.), *International Comparisons in Implementing Pollution Law*. Dordrecht: Kluwer-Nijhoff, 1–25.

Harcourt, A. J. (2000). 'European Institutions and the Media Industry. European Regulatory Politics between Pressure and Pluralism'. Ph.D. Dissertation, Department of Government, University of Manchester.

Haverland, Markus (2000). 'National Adaptation to European Integration: The Importance of Veto Points'. *Journal of Public Policy* 20 (1), 83–103.

Hawkins, K. (1984). *Enforcement and Environment*. Oxford: Clarendon Press.

Heady, Ferrel (1979). *Public Administration. A Comparative Perspective*. New York: Marcel Dekker.

Heclo, Hugh and Aaron Wildavsky (1974). *The Private Government of Public Money: Community and Policy Inside British Politics*. London: Macmillan.

Hellstern, Gerd-Michael (1986). 'When Courts Intervene: Judicial Control in a Comparative Institutional Perspective'. In: Franz-Xavier Kaufmann, Giandomenico Majone and Vincent Ostrom (eds.), *Guidance, Control and Evaluation in the Public Sector*. Berlin: de Gruyter, 663–90.

Hennessy, Peter (1989). *Whitehall*. London: Secker & Warburg.

Héritier, Adrienne, Dieter Kerwer, Christoph Knill, Dirk Lehmkuhl and Michael Teutsch (2001). *Differential Europe. New Opportunities and Constraints for National Policy-Making*. Lanham: Rowman and Littlefield.

Héritier, Adrienne and Christoph Knill (2001). 'Differential Responses to European Policies: A Comparison'. In: Adrienne Héritier, Dieter Kerwer, Christoph Knill, Dirk Lehmkuhl and Michael Teutsch, *Differential Europe. New Opportunities and Constraints for National Policy-Making*. Lanham: Rowman and Littlefield, 257–94.

Héritier, Adrienne, Christoph Knill and Susanne Mingers (1996). *Ringing the Changes in Europe. Regulatory Competition and the Transformation of the State*. Berlin: de Gruyter.

Héritier, Adrienne, Susanne Mingers, Christoph Knill and Martina Becka (1994). *Die Veränderung von Staatlichkeit in Europa: Ein regulativer Wettbewerb. Deutschland, Großbritannien, Frankreich*. Opladen: Leske und Budrich.

Hesse, Jens J. and Arthur Benz (1990). *Die Modernisierung der Staatsorganisation*. Baden-Baden: Nomos.

Hey, Christian and Uwe Brendle (1992). *Umweltverbände und EG. Handlungsmöglichkeiten der Umweltverbände für die Verbesserung des Umweltbewußtseins und der Umweltpolitik in der Europäischen Gemeinschaft*. Freiburg: EURES.

Hix, Simon (1994). 'The Study of the European Community: The Challenge to Comparative Politics'. *West European Politics* 17 (1), 1–30.

Holliday, Ian (1993). 'Organised Interest after Thatcher'. In: Patrick Dunleavy, Andrew Gamble, Ian Holliday and Gillian Peele (eds.), *Developments in British Politics*. London: Macmillan, 307–19.

Hood, Christopher (1991). 'A Public Management for all Seasons?' *Public Administration* 69, 3–19.

(1995). '"Deprivileging" the UK Civil Service in the 1980s: Dream or Reality?' In: Jon Pierre (ed.), *Bureaucracy in the Modern State. An Introduction to Comparative Public Administration*. Aldershot: Edward Elgar, 92–117.

(1996). 'United Kingdom: From Second Chance to Near-Miss Learning'. In:

Johan P. Olsen and B. Guy Peters (eds.), *Lessons from Experience. Experimental Learning in Administrative Reforms in Eight Democracies*. Oslo: Scandinavian University Press, 36–70.

House of Lords (1996). *Freedom of Access to Information on the Environment. Select Committee on the European Communities. Session 1996–97, 1st Report*. London: HMSO.

Immergut, Ellen M. (1992). *Health Politics: Interests and Institutions in Western Europe*. Cambridge: Cambridge University Press.

—— (1997). 'The Normative Roots of the New Institutionalism'. In: Arthur Benz and Wolfgang Seibel (eds.), *Beiträge zur Theorieentwicklung in der Politik- und Verwaltungswissenschaft*, Baden-Baden: Nomos, 325–56.

Ingram, Helen and Anne Schneider (1990). 'Improving Implementation Through Framing Smarter Statutes'. *Journal of Public Policy* 10 (1), 67–88.

Ismayr, W. (1992). *Der deutsche Bundestag: Funktionen, Willensbildung, Reformansätze*. Opladen: Leske & Budrich.

Jachtenfuchs, Markus and Beate Kohler-Koch (eds.) (1996). *Europäische Integration*. Opladen: Leske & Budrich.

Jann, Werner (1983). *Staatliche Programme und 'Verwaltungskultur'*. Opladen: Westdeutscher Verlag.

Jansen, Dorothea (1997). 'Mediationsverfahren in der Umweltpolitik'. *Politische Vierteljahresschrift*, 38 (2), 274–97.

Jenkins, B. (1993). 'Reshaping the Managment of Government. The Next Steps Initiative in the United Kingdom'. In: F. L. Seidle (ed.), *Rethinking Government: Reform or Revolution?* Quebec: Institute for Research on Public Policy, 73–103.

Jennings, Ivor (1966). *The British Constitution*. Cambridge: Cambridge University Press.

Jepperson, Ronald L. (1991). 'Institutions, Institutional Effects and Institutionalism'. In: Walter W. Powell and Paul J. DiMaggio (eds.), *The New Institutionalism in Organizational Analysis*. Chicago: Chicago University Press.

Johnson, Nevil (1977). *In Search of the Constitution*. Oxford: Oxford University Press.

—— (1994). 'Der Civil Service in Großbritannien: Tradition und Modernisierung'. *Die öffentliche Verwaltung* 47 (5), 196–200.

Johnson, Stanley P. and Guy Corcelle (1989). *The Environmental Policy of the European Communities*. London: Graham and Trotman.

Jordan, Andrew (1993). 'Integrated Pollution Control and the Evolving Style and Structure of Environmental Regulation in the UK'. *Environmental Politics* 2 (3), 405–28.

—— (1997). 'The Impact on UK Environmental Administration'. In: P. Lowe and S. Ward (eds.), *British Environmental Policy and Europe*. London: Routledge, 173–94.

Jordan, Grant (1981). 'Iron Triangles, Woolly Corporatism or Elastic Nets? Images of the Policy Process'. *Journal of Public Policy* 1, 95–124.

Jordan, Grant and Jeremy Richardson (1982). 'The British Policy Style or the Logic of Negotiation'. In: Jeremy Richardson (ed.), *Policy Styles in Western Europe*. London: Allen and Unwin, 80–109.

Jowell, Jeffrey and Patrick Birkinshaw (1996). 'English Report'. In: Jürgen Schwarze (ed.), *Administrative Law under European Influence*. Baden-Baden: Nomos, 273–333.

Judge, David (1981). 'Specialists and Generalists in British Central Government: A Political Debate'. *Public Administration* 59, 1–14.

Katzenstein, Peter (1987). *Politics and Policy in West Germany: The Growth of a Semi-sovereign State*. Philadelphia: Temple University Press.

Katzenstein, P., R. Keohane and S. Krasner (1998). 'International Organization and the Study of World Politics'. *International Organization* 52 (4), 645–85.

Kay, John, Colin Mayer and David Thompson (eds.) (1989). *Privatisation and Regulation. The UK Experience*. Oxford: Clarendon Press.

Keeler, John (1987). *The Politics of Neocorporatism in France*. New York: Oxford University Press.

Keohane, Robert O. and Stanley Hoffmann (eds.) (1991). *The New European Community*. Boulder: Westview.

Kerwer, Dieter (2001). 'Going Through the Motions. The Modest European Impact on Italian Transport Policy'. In: Adrienne Héritier, Dieter Kerwer, Christoph Knill, Dirk Lehmkuhl and Michael Teutsch, *Differential Europe. New Opportunities and Constraints for National Policy-Making*. Lanham: Rowman and Littlefield, 173–216.

Kerwer, Dieter and Michael Teutsch (2001). 'The Dynamics of the EC's Common Transport Policy'. In: Adrienne Héritier, Dieter Kerwer, Christoph Knill, Dirk Lehmkuhl and Michael Teutsch, *Differential Europe. New Opportunities and Constraints for National Policy-Making*. Lanham: Rowman and Littlefield, 27–56.

Kickert, Walter M. and Richard J. Stillman (1996). 'Introduction'. *Public Administration Review* 56 (1), 65–7.

Kimber, Clíona (2000). 'Implementing European Environmental Policy and the Directive on Access to Environmental Information'. In: Christoph Knill and Andrea Lenschow (eds.), *Implementing EU Environmental Policy: New Directions and Old Problems*. Manchester: Manchester University Press.

King, Desmond (1993). 'Government Beyond Whitehall'. In: Patrick Dunleavy, Andrew Gamble, Ian Holliday and Gillian Peele (eds.), *Developments in British Politics*. London: Macmillan, 194–220.

King, Gary, Robert O. Keohane and Sidney Verba (1994). *Designing Social Inquiry. Scientific Interference in Qualitative Research*. Princeton: Princeton University Press.

Kingdom, J. E. (1989). 'Britain'. In: J. E. Kingdom (ed.), *The Civil Service in Liberal Democracies. An Introductory Survey*. London: Routledge, 11–35.

Klages, Helmut and Elke Löffler (1996). 'Germany. Part I: Public Sector Modernization in Germany – Recent Trends and Emerging Strategies'. In: Norman Flynn and Franz Strehl (eds.), *Public Sector Management in Europe*. London: Prentice Hall, 132–71.

Kloepfer, Michael and Wolfgang Durner (1997), 'Der Umweltgesetzbuch-Entwurf der Sachverständigenkommission'. *Deutsches Verwaltungsblatt* 112 (18), 1081–1107.

Knight, Jack (1992). *Institutions and Social Conflict*. Cambridge: Cambridge University Press.

Knill, Christoph (1995). *Staatlichkeit im Wandel. Großbritannien im Spannungs-feld innenpolitischer Reformen und europäischer Integration*. Opladen: Deutscher Universitätsverlag.

(1997a). 'The Europeanisation of Domestic Policies: The Development of EC Environmental Policy'. *Environmental Policy and Law* 27 (1), 48–56.

(1997b). 'The Implementation of EU Environmental Policy in the UK'. In: Christoph Knill (ed.), *The Impact of National Administrative Traditions on the Implementation of EU Environmental Policy*. Florence: European University Institute.

(1998). 'European Policies: The Impact of National Administrative Traditions'. *Journal of Public Policy* 18 (1), 1–28.

(1999). 'Explaining Cross-National Variance in Administrative Reform: Autonomous versus Instrumental Bureaucracies'. *Journal of Public Policy* 19 (2), 113–39.

(2001). 'Reforming Transport Policy in the United Kingdom: Concurrence with Europe but Separate Developments'. In: Adrienne Héritier, Dieter Kerwer, Christoph Knill, Dirk Lehmkuhl and Michael Teutsch, *Differential Europe. New Opportunities and Constraints for National Policy-Making*. Lanham: Rowman and Littlefield, 57–98.

Knill, Christoph and Adrienne Héritier (1996). 'Neue Instrumente in der europäischen Umweltpolitik: Strategien für eine effektivere Implementation'. In: Gertrude Lübbe-Wolff (ed.), *Der Vollzug des europäischen Umweltrechts*. Berlin: Erich Schmidt Verlag, 209–34.

Knill, Christoph and Dirk Lehmkuhl (1998). Integration by Globalisation: The European Interest Representation of the Consumer Electronics Industry. *Current Politics and Economics of Europe* 8 (2), 131–153.

(1999). 'How European Matters: Different Mechanisms of Europeanization'. *European Integration online Papers (EIoP)* 3 (7), http://eiop.or.at/eiop/texte/1999-007a.htm.

(2000). 'European Integration by Support-Building: The Implementation of the Community's Railways Policy'. *West European Politics* 23 (1), 65–88.

Knill, Christoph and Andrea Lenschow (1998). 'Coping with Europe: The Implementation of EU Environmental Policy and Administrative Traditions in Britain and Germany'. *Journal of European Public Policy* 5(4), 595–614.

(2000a). 'On Deficient Implementation and Deficient Theories. The Need for an Institutional Perspective in Implementation Research'. In: Christoph Knill and Andrea Lenschow (eds.), *Implementing EU Environmental Policy: New Directions and Old Problems*. Manchester: Manchester University Press, 9–38.

(2000b). 'Do New Brooms Really Sweep Cleaner? Implementation of New Instruments in EU Environmental Policy'. In: Christoph Knill and Andrea Lenschow (eds.), *Implementing EU Environmental Policy: New Directions and Old Problems*. Manchester: Manchester University Press, 251–86.

(2001a). 'Adjusting to EU Environmental Policy: Change and Persistence of Domestic Administrations'. In: James A. Caporaso, Maria Green Cowles and Thomas Risse (eds.), *Transforming Europe. Europeanization and Domestic Change*. Ithaca, NY: Cornell University Press, 116–36.

(2001b). '"Seek and Ye Shall Find": Linking Different Perspectives on Institutional Change'. *Comparative Political Studies* 34 (2), 187–215.

Knill, Christoph and Andrea Lenschow (eds.) (2000). *Implementing EU Environmental Policy: New Directions and Old Problems*. Manchester: Manchester University Press.

Kohler-Koch, Beate (1994). 'Changing Paterns of Interest Intermediation in the European Union'. *Government and Opposition* 29, 166–80.

—— (1996). 'The Strength of Weakness. The Transformation of Governance in the EU'. In: S. Gustavsson and L. Lewin (eds.), *Essays on Cultural Pluralism and Political Integration*. Stockholm: Nerenius & Santerus, 169–210.

—— (1999). 'The Evolution and Transformation of European Governance'. In: Beate Kohler-Koch and Rainer Eising (eds.), *The Transformation of Governance in the European Union*. London: Routledge, 14–36.

Kohler-Koch, Beate (ed.) (1998). *Interaktive Politik in Europa. Regionen im Netzwerk der Integration*. Opladen: Leske & Budrich.

Kohler-Koch, Beate and Rainer Eising (eds.) (1999). *The Transformation of Governance in the European Union*. London: Routledge.

König, Klaus (1996). 'Unternehmerisches oder exekutives Management – die Perspektive der klassischen öffentlichen Verwaltung'. *Verwaltungs-Archiv* 87 (1), 19–37.

—— (1997). 'Drei Welten der Verwaltungsmodernisierung'. In: Klaus Lüder (ed.), *Staat und Verwaltung. Fünfzig Jahre Hochschule für Verwaltungswissenschaften Speyer*. Berlin: Duncker & Humblot, 399–424.

Kooiman, Jan (ed.) (1993). *Modern Governance. New Government–Society Interactions*. London: Sage.

Kraemer, Andreas R. and A. Warnke (1992). *Zukunftsperspektiven der Trinkwasserversorgung*. Bonn: Büro für Technikfolgenabschätzung des Deutschen Bundestages.

Krasner, Stephen D. (1988). 'Sovereignty: An Institutional Perspective'. *Comparative Political Studies* 21 (1), 66–94.

Kromarek, P. (1986). *Die Trinkwasserrichtlinie der EG und die Nitratwerte*. Berlin: Wissenschaftszentrum für Sozialforschung.

Kunzlik, Peter (1995). 'Environmental Impact Assessment: The British Cases'. *European Environmental Law Review* (December), 336–44.

Ladeur, Karl-Heinz (1990). 'Selbstorgnaisation sozialer Systeme und Prozeduralisierung des Rechts. Von der Schrankenziehung zur Steuerung von Beziehungsnetzen'. In: Dieter Grimm (ed.), *Wachsende Staatsaufgaben – sinkende Steuerungsfähigkeit des Rechts*. Baden-Baden: Nomos, 187–216.

Lambrechts, Claude (1996). 'Environmental Impact Assessments'. In: Gerd Winter (ed.) *European Environmental Law. A Comparative Perspective*. Aldershot: Dartmouth, 63–79.

Lane, Jan-Erik (1995). *The Public Sector. Concepts, Models and Approaches*. London: Sage.

Lavenex, Sandra (1999). 'The Europeanization of Refugee Policy: Between Human Rights and Internal Security'. Ph.D. Thesis, European University Institute, Florence.

Lee, Norman (1995). 'Environmental Assessment in the European Union: A Tenth Anniversary'. *Project Appraisal* (June), 77–90.

Lehmbruch, Gerhard (1976). *Parteienwettbewerb im Bundesstaat.* Stuttgart: Kohlhammer.

(1987). 'Administrative Interessenvermittlung'. In: Adrienne Windhoff-Héritier (ed.), *Verwaltung und ihre Umwelt.* Opladen: Westdeutscher Verlag, 11–43.

(1990). 'Die improvisierte Vereinigung: Die dritte deutsche Republik'. *Leviathan* 18, 462–86.

(1997). 'From State of Authority to Network State: The German State in a Comparative Perspective'. In: Michio Muramatsu and Frieder Naschold (eds.), *State and Administration in Japan and Germany: A Comparative Perspective on Continuity and Change.* Berlin: de Gruyter, 39–62.

Lehmbruch, Gerhard *et al.* (1988). 'Institutionalle Bedingungen ordnungs-politischen Strategiewechsels im internationalen Vergleich'. In: Manfred G. Schmidt (ed.), *Staatstätigkeit*, PVS Sonderheft 19, Opladen: Westdeutscher Verlag, 251–83.

Lehmkuhl, Dirk (1996). 'Privatizing to Keep it Public? The Reorganization of the German Railways'. In: Arthur Benz and Klaus H. Goetz, (eds.), *A New German Public Sector? Reform, Adaptation and Stability.* Aldershot: Dartmouth, 71–92.

(1999). *The Importance of Small Differences. The Impact of European Integration on Road Haulage Associations in Germany and the Netherlands.* The Hague: Thela Thesis.

(2001) 'From Regulation to Stimulation: The Reform of Dutch Transport Policy'. In: Adrienne Héritier, Dieter Kerwer, Christoph Knill, Dirk Lehmkuhl and Michael Teutsch, *Differential Europe. New Opportunities and Constraints for National Policy-Making.* Lanham: Rowman and Littlefield, 217–56.

Lenschow, Andrea (1997). 'The Implementation of EU Environmental Policy in Germany'. In: Christoph Knill (ed.), *The Impact of National Administrative Traditions on the Implementation of EU Environmental Policy.* Florence: European University Institute.

(1999). 'Transformation in European Environmental Governance'. In: Beate Kohler-Koch and Rainer Eising (eds.), *The Transformation of Governance in the European Union.* London: Routledge, 39–60.

Lijphart, Arend (1971). 'Comparative Politics and Comparative Method'. *American Political Science Review* 65, 682–93.

Lindenberg, Siegwart (1991). 'Die Methode der abnehmenden Abstraktion: Theoriegesteuerte Analyse und empririscher Gehalt'. In: Hartmut Esser and Klaus G. Troitsch (eds.), *Modellierung sozialer Prozesse.* Bonn: Informationszentrum Sozialwissenschaften, 29–78.

Linder, Stephen and B. Guy Peters (1989). 'Instruments of Government: Perceptions and Contexts'. *Journal of Public Policy* 9 (1), 35–58.

Lipsky, M. (1980). *Street-Level Bureaucracy.* New York: Russell Sage.

Lowndes, Vivien (1996). 'Varieties of New Institutionalism. A Critical Appraisal'. *Public Administration* 74 (2), 181–197.

Lübbe-Wolff, Gertrude (1994). 'Die EG-Verordnung zum Umwelt-Audit'. *Deutsches Verwaltungsblatt* 109 (7), 361–74.

(1996). 'Stand und Instrumente der Implementation des Umweltrechts in

Deutschland'. In: Gertrude Lübbe-Wolff (ed.), *Der Vollzug des europäischen Umweltrechts*. Berlin: Erich Schmidt Verlag, 77–106.

Lüder, Klaus (1996). '"Triumph des Marktes im öffentlichen Sektor?" Einige Anmerkungen zur Verwaltungsreformdiskussion.' *Die öffentliche Verwaltung* 49 (3), 93–100.

Luhmann, Niklas (1972). *Soziologische Aufklärung. Aufsätze zur Theorie sozialer Systeme. Band 3.* Opladen: Westdeutscher Verlag.

Majone, Giandomenico (1989). 'Regulating Europe: Problems and Prospects'. In: Thomas Ellwein *et al.* (eds.), *Jahrbuch zur Staats- und Verwaltungswissenschaft*. Baden-Baden: Nomos, 159–77.

Majone, Giandomenico (ed.) (1996). *Regulating Europe*. London: Routledge.

Maloney, William A. and Jeremy Richardson (1994). 'Water Policy-Making in England and Wales: Policy Communities under Pressure?' *Environmental Politics* (3), 110–37.

—— (1995). *Managing Policy Change in Britain: The Politics of Water*. Edinburgh: Edinburgh University Press.

March, James G. and Johan P. Olsen (1984). 'The New Institutionalism: Organizational Factors in Political Life'. *American Political Science Review* 78 (3), 734–49.

—— (1989). *Rediscovering Institutions*. New York: Free Press.

—— (1996). 'Institutional Perspectives on Political Institutions'. *Governance* 9 (3), 247–64.

Marks, Gary, Lisbet Hooghe and Kermit Blank (1996). 'European Integration from the 1980s: State-centric v. Multi-level Governance'. *Journal of Common Market Studies* 34 (3), 341–78.

Massey, Andrew (1992). 'Managing Change: Politicians and Experts in the Age of Privatization'. *Government and Opposition* 27, 486–501.

—— (1995). *After Next Steps: An Examination of the Implications for Policy Making of the Developments in Executive Agencies*. A Report to the Office of Public Service and Science. London: OPSS.

Matthews, Duncan and John Pickering (1997). 'Corporate Responses to European Environmental Law: The Case of the Water Industry and the Drinking Water Directive'. *International Journal of Biosciences and the Law* 1, 265–99.

Mayntz, Renate (1978). *Soziologie der öffentlichen Verwaltung*. Heidelberg: Decker & Müller.

—— (1983). 'Implementation von regulativer Politik'. In: Renate Mayntz, (ed.), *Implementation politischer Programme II*. Opladen: Westdeutscher Verlag, 50–74.

—— (1990). 'Entscheidungsprozesse bei der Entwicklung von Umweltstandards'. *Die Verwaltung* (2), 137–51.

Mayntz, Renate and Hans-Ulrich Derlien (1989). 'Party Patronage and the Politicization of the West German Administrative Elite, 1970–1987: Towards Hybridization?' *Governance* 2, 384–404.

Mayntz, Renate and Jochen Hucke (1978). 'Gesetzesvollzug im Umweltschutz, Wirksamkeit und Probleme'. *Zeitschrift für Umweltpolitik* (2), 217–44.

Mayntz, Renate and Fritz W. Scharpf (1975). *Policy-Making in the German Federal Bureaucracy*. Amsterdam: Elsevier.

(1995). 'Der Ansatz des akteurzentrierten Institutionalismus'. In: Renate Mayntz and Fritz W. Scharpf (eds.), *Gesellschaftliche Selbstregelung und politische Steuerung*. Frankfurt/Main: Campus, 39–72.

Mayntz, Renate *et al.* (1978). *Vollzugsprobleme der Umweltpolitik: Empirische Untersuchung der Implementation von Gesetzen im Bereich der Luftreinhaltung und des Gewässerschutzes*. Stuttgart: Kohlhammer.

McGillivray, Donald (1997). 'Policy Networks and EC Environmental Policy: A Case Study of the Implementation of the Drinking Water Directive in the UK'. Paper presented at the European Communities Studies Association Conference, Seattle, 29 May–1 June.

McLoughlin, J. (1982). *The Law and Practice Relating to Pollution Control in the United Kingdom*. London: Graham and Trotman.

Mény, Yves (1993). *Government and Politics in Western Europe. Britain, France, Italy, West Germany*. Oxford: Oxford University Press.

Mény, Yves, Pierre Muller and Jean-Louis Quermonne (eds.) (1996). *Adjusting to Europe. The Impact of the European Union on National Institutions and Policies*. London: Routledge.

Metcalfe, Les und Sue Richards (1987). *Improving Public Management*. London: Sage.

Moe, Terry M. (1990). 'Political Institutions: The Neglected Side of the Story. Journal of Law'. *Economics and Organization* 6 (Special Issue), 213–53.

Moravcsik, Andrew (1991). 'Negotiating the Single European Act: National Interests and Conventional Statecraft in the European Community'. *International Organization* 45 (1), 19–56.

(1994). 'Why the European Community Strengthens the State: Domestic Politics and International Cooperation'. Paper presented at the Annual Convention of the American Political Science Association, 1–4 September, New York.

Müller, Edda (1986). *Innenwelt der Umweltpolitik: Sozial-liberale Umweltpolitik – (Ohn)macht durch Organisation?* Opladen: Westdeutscher Verlag.

Nettl, J. P. (1968). 'The State as a Conceptual Variable'. *World Politics* 7, 559–92.

Nørgaard, Asbjørn (1996). 'Rediscovering Reasonable Rationality in Institutional Analysis'. *European Journal of Political Research* 29 (1), 31–57.

North, Douglass C. (1990). *Institutions, Institutional Change and Economic Performance*. Cambridge: Cambridge University Press.

Olsen, Johan P. (1995). *Europeanization and Nation State Dynamics*. Working Paper 9/95. Oslo: ARENA.

Olsen Johan P. and B. Guy Peters (1996). 'Learning from Experience?' In: Johan P. Olsen and B. Guy Peters (eds.), *Lessons from Experience. Experimental Learning in Administrative Reforms in Eight Democracies*. Oslo: Scandinavian University Press, 1–16.

Olsen, Johan P. and B. Guy Peters (eds.) (1996). *Lessons from Experience. Experimental Learning in Administrative Reforms in Eight Democracies*. Oslo: Scandinavian University Press.

Olson, Mancur (1982). *The Rise and Decline of Nations. Economic Growth, Stagflation and Social Rigidities*. New Haven: Yale University Press.

O'Riordan, Timothy (1979). 'The Role of Environmental Quality Objectives in the Politics of Pollution Control'. In: Timothy O'Riordan and Ralph D'Arge (eds.), *Progress in Resource Management and Environmental Planning Vol. 1*. Chichester: John Wiley, 221–58.

Page, Edward C. (1992). *Political Authority and Bureaucratic Power. A Comparative Analysis*. New York: Harvester Wheatsheaf.

Page, Edward C. and Linda Wouters (1995). 'The Europeanization of National Bureaucracies?' In: Jon Pierre (ed.), *Bureaucracy in the Modern State. An Introduction to Comparative Public Administration*. Aldershot: Edward Elgar, 185–204.

Peele, Gillian (1993). 'The Constitution'. In: Patrick Dunleavy, Andrew Gamble, Ian Holliday and Gillian Peele (eds.), *Developments in British Politics*. London: Macmillan, 19–39.

Peters, B. Guy (1988). *Comparing Public Bureaucracies: Problems of Theory and Method*. Tuscaloosa: University of Alabama Press.

(1992). 'Bureaucratic Politics and the Institutions of the European Community'. In: Alberta M. Sbragia (ed.), *Europolitics. Institutions and Policy-Making in the 'New' European Community*. Washington: The Brookings Institution, 75–122.

(1993). 'Alternative Modelle des Policy-Prozesses: Die Sicht "von unten" und die Sicht "von oben"'. In: Adrienne Héritier (ed.), *Policy-Analyse. Kritik und Neurorientierung*, PVS Sonderheft 24/1993, 289–306.

(1995). *The Politics of Bureaucracy*. New York: Longman.

(1996). 'Theory and Methodology'. In: Hans A. G. M. Bekke, James L. Perry and Theo A. J. Toonen (eds.), *Civil Service Systems in Comparative Perspective*. Indiana: Indiana University Press, 13–41.

Pierre, Jon (ed.) (1995). *Bureaucracy in the Modern State. An Introduction to Comparative Public Administration*. Aldershot: Edward Elgar.

Pierson, Paul (1996). 'The Path to European Integration. A Historical Institutionalist Analysis'. *Comparative Political Studies* 29 (2), 123–63.

Pollitt, Christopher (1993). *Managerialism and the Public Service*. Oxford: Blackwell.

(1996). 'Antistatist Reforms and New Administrative Directions: Public Administration in the United Kingdom'. *Public Administration Review* 56 (1), 81–94.

Powell, Walter W. (1991). 'Expanding the Scope of Institutionalism in Organizational Analysis'. In: Walter W. Powell and Paul J. DiMaggio (eds.), *The New Institutionalism in Organizational Analysis*. Chicago: Chicago University Press, 183–203.

Powell, Walter W. and Paul J. DiMaggio (eds.) (1991). *The New Institutionalism in Organizational Analysis*. Chicago: Chicago University Press.

Pressman, J. and A. Wildavsky (1973). *Implementation*. Berkeley: University of California Press.

Przeworski, Adam and Henry Teune (1970). *The Logic of Comparative Social Inquiry*. New York: John Wiley.

Raadschelders, Jos C. N. and Mark A. Rutgers (1996). 'The Evolution of Civil Service Systems'. In: Hans A. G. M. Bekke, James L. Perry and Theo A. J. Toonen (eds.), *Civil Service Systems in Comparative Perspective*. Indiana: Indiana University Press, 67–99.

Radaelli, Claudio (2000). 'Whither Europeanization? Concept Stretching and Substantive Change'. *European Integration online papers (EIoP)* 4 (8), http://eiop.or.at/eiop/texte/2000–008a.htm.

Ragin, Charles (1989). 'New Directions in Comparative Research'. In: Melvin L. Kohn (ed.), *Cross-National Research in Sociology.* Newbury Park: Sage.

RCEP (Royal Commission on Environmental Pollution) (1976). *5th Report. Air Pollution Control. An Integrated Approach.* London: HMSO.

(1984). *10th Report. Tackling Pollution – Experience and Prospects.* London: HMSO.

Rehbinder, E. and R. Stewart (1985). *Environmental Protection Policy. Integration Through Law.* Berlin: de Gruyter.

Reichard, Christoph (1994). *Umdenken im Rathaus. Neue Strategiemodelle in der deutschen Kommunalverwaltung.* Berlin: Sigma.

Reinhardt, Michael (1997). 'Das Umweltinformationsgesetz vom 8. Juli 1994 als Beispiel konzeptionsdefizitärer Transformationsgesetzgebung'. *Die Verwaltung* 30 (2), 161–84.

Rhodes, R. A. W. (1991). 'Now Nobody Understands the System'. In: Philip Norton (ed.), *New Directions in British Politics. Essays on the Evolving Constitution.* Aldershot: Edward Elgar, 83–112.

(1996). 'The New European Agencies. Agencies in British Government: Revolution or Evolution?' EUI Working Papers RSC No. 96/51, Florence: European University Institute.

Richardson, Geneva (1983). 'The Enforcement of Water Pollution Controls in the United Kingdom'. In: Paul Dowding and Kenneth Hanf (eds.), *International Comparisons in Implementing Pollution Law.* Dordrecht: Kluwer-Nijhoff, 281–98.

Richardson, Jeremy (1994a). 'EU Water Policy: Uncertain Agendas, Shifting Networks and Complex Coalitions'. *Environmental Politics* 3 (4), 139–67.

(1994b). 'Doing Less by Doing More: British Government 1979–1993'. In: Wolfgang C. Müller and Vincent Wright (eds.), *The State in Western Europe. Retreat or Redefinition?* Ilford: Frank Cass, 179–97.

Richardson, Jeremy J., William A. Maloney and Wolfgang Rüdig (1992). 'The Dynamics of Policy Change: Lobbying and Water Privatisation'. *Public Administration* 70, 157–75.

Ridley, F. F. (1995). 'Die Wiedererfindung des Staates – Reinventing British Government. Das Modell einer Skelettverwaltung'. *Die öffentliche Verwaltung* 48 (14), 569–78.

Ridley, F. F. (ed.) (1979). *Government and Administration in Western Europe.* Oxford: Oxford University Press.

Ritter, Ernst-Hasso (1990). 'Das Recht als Steuerungsmedium im kooperativen Staat'. In: Dieter Grimm (ed.), *Wachsende Staatsaufgaben – sinkende Steuerungsfähigkeit des Rechts.* Baden-Baden: Nomos, 69–112.

Rose, Richard (1987). 'Steering the Ship of State. One Tiller but Two Pairs of Hands'. *British Journal of Political Science* 17, 409–53.

(1989). *Politics in England. Change and Persistence.* London: Macmillan.

(1991). 'Comparing Forms of Comparative Analysis'. *Political Studies* 39, 446–62.

Rowan-Robinson, Jeremy, Andrea Ross, William Walton and Julie Rothnie (1996). 'Public Access to Environmental Information. A Means to What End?' *Journal of Environmental Law* 8 (1), 19–42.

Rüdig, Wolfgang and R. Andreas Kraemer (1994). 'Networks of Cooperation: Water Policy in Germany'. *Environmental Politics* 3 (4), 52–79.

Sabatier, Paul A. (1993). 'Advocacy-Koalitionen, Policy-Wandel und Policy-Lernen: Eine Alternative zur Phasenheuristik'. In: Adrienne Héritier (ed.), *Policy-Analyse. Kritik und Neurorientierung*, PVS Sonderheft 24/1993, 116–48.

Sandholtz, Wane (1996). 'Membership Matters: Limits of the Functional Approach to European Institutions'. *Journal of Common Market Studies* 34 (3), 403–29.

Sartori, Giovanni (ed.) (1984). *Social Science Concepts. A Systematic Analysis.* Beverly Hills: Sage.

Scharpf, Fritz W. (1970). *Die politischen Kosten des Rechtsstaats. Eine vergleichende Studie der deutschen und amerikanischen Verwaltungskontrolle.* Tübingen: Mohr.

(1973). *Planung als politischer Prozeß. Aufsätze zur Theorie der planenden Demokratie.* Frankfurt: Suhrkamp.

(1994). *Mehrebenenpolitik im vollendeten Binnenmarkt.* MPIFG Discussion Paper 94/4. Köln: Max-Planck-Institut für Gesellschaftsforschung.

Scharpf, Fritz W., Bernd Reissert and Fritz Schnabel (1976). *Politikverflechtung: Theorie und Empirie des kooperativen Föderalismus in der Bundesrepublik.* Kronberg: Scriptor.

Scherzberg, Arno (1994). 'Freedom of Information – deutsch gewendet: Das neue Umweltinformationsgesetz'. *Deutsches Verwaltungsblatt* 109, 733–45.

Schmid, Josef (1993). 'Parteien und Verbände. Konstitution, Kontingenz und Koevolution im System der Interessenvermittlung'. In: Roland Czada and Manfred G. Schmidt (eds.), *Verhandlungsdemokratie, Interessenvermittlung, Regierbarkeit.* Opladen: Westdeutscher Verlag, 171–91.

Schmidt, Susanne K. (1996). 'Privatizing the Federal Postal and Telecommunication Services'. In: Arthur Benz and Klaus H. Goetz (eds.), *A New German Public Sector? Reform, Adaptation and Stability.* Aldershot: Dartmouth, 45–70.

(1997a). 'Sterile Debates and Dubious Generalisations: An Empirical Critique of European Integration Theory Based on the Integration Processes in Telecommunications and Electricity'. *Journal of Public Policy* 17 (3), 233–71.

(1997b). *Behind the Council Agenda: The Commission's Impact on Decisions.* MPIFG Discussion Paper 97/4. Köln: Max-Planck-Institut für Gesellschaftsforschung.

Schmidt, Vivien A. (1996). *From State to Market? The Transformation of French Business and Government.* Cambridge: Cambridge University Press.

Schmitter, Philippe and Gerhard Lehmbruch (eds.) (1979). *Trends Toward Corporatist Intermediation.* London: Sage.

Schneider, Jens-Peter (1995). 'Öko-Audit als Scharnier einer ganzheitlichen Regulierungsstrategie'. *Die Verwaltung* 28 (3), 361–87.

Schneider, Volker (2001). 'Institutional Reform in Telecommunications: The

European Union in Transnational Policy Diffusion'. In: James A. Caporaso, Maria Green Cowles and Thomas Risse (eds.), *Transforming Europe. Europeanization and Domestic Change*. Ithaca, NY: Cornell University Press, 60–78.

Schoppa, L. (1999). 'The Social Context in Coercive International Bargaining'. *International Organization* 53 (2), 307–42.

Schumann, Wolfgang (1991). 'EG-Forschung und Policy-Analyse. Zur Notwendigkeit, den ganzen Elefanten zu erfassen'. *Politische Vierteljahresschrift* 2, 232–57.

Schwanenflügel, Matthias von (1993). 'Die Richtlinie über den freien Zugang zu Umweltinformationen als Chance für den Umweltschutz'. *Die öffentliche Verwaltung* 3, 95–102.

Schwarze, Jürgen (1996). 'Deutscher Landesbericht'. In: Jürgen Schwarze (ed.), *Administrative Law under European Influence*. Baden-Baden: Nomos, 123–227.

Schwarze, Jürgen, Ulrich Becker and Christiana Pollak (1994). *The Implementation of Community Law*. Baden-Baden: Nomos.

Scott, Richard W. (1995). *Institutions and Organizations. Foundations for Organizational Science*. London: Sage.

Seibel, Wolfgang (1986). 'Entbürokratisierung in der Bundesrepublik Deutschland'. *Die Verwaltung* 2, 137–61.

Seibel, Wolfgang (1996). 'Administrative Science as Reform: German Public Administration'. *Public Administration Review* 56 (1), 74–81.

Sellner, Dieter and Jörn Schnutenhaus (1993). 'Umweltmanagement und Umweltbetriebsprüfung ("Umwelt-Audit") – ein wirksames, nicht ordnungsrechtliches System des betrieblichen Umweltschutzes'. *NVwZ* 12 (10), 928–34.

Shepsle, Kenneth A. (1989). 'Studying Institutions. Some Lessons from the Rational-Choice Approach'. *Journal of Theoretical Politics* 1 (2), 131–47.

Shepsle, Kenneth A. and Barry R. Weingast (1987). 'The Institutional Foundations of Committee Power'. *American Political Science Review* 81, 85–104.

Siedentopf, H. and J. Ziller (eds.) (1988). *Making European Policies Work. L'Europe des Administrations? Vol. 2, National Reports, Rapports Nationaux*. London: Sage.

Skowronek, Stephen (1982). *Building a New American State. The Expansion of National Administrative Capacities 1877–1920*. Cambridge: Cambridge University Press.

Spindler, Edmund A. (1992). 'Neues Denken beim Umweltmanagement. Die Umweltverträglichkeitsprüfung für Industriebetriebe'. *Entsorgungs-Technik. Zeitschrift für Abfallwirtschaft, Umweltschutz, Recycling* (5), 50–6.

Spoerr, Wolfgang (1991). 'Verwaltungsrechtschutz in Großbritannien – Entwicklung und Reform'. *Verwaltungs-Archiv* 82, 12–53.

SRU (Sachverständigenrat für Umweltfragen) (1987). *Stellungnahme zur Umsetzung der EG-Richtlinie über die Umweltverträglichkeitsprüfung in das nationale Recht*. Stuttgart: Metzler-Poeschel.

—— (1996). *Umweltgutachten 1996*. Stuttgart: Verlag Metzler-Poeschel.

Steinmo, Sven (1993). *Taxation and Democracy: Swedish, British and American*

Approaches to Financing the Modern State. New Haven: Yale University Press.

Sterett, Susan (1994). 'Judicial Review in Britain'. *Comparative Political Studies* 26 (4), 421–42.

Stewart, John and Kieron Walsh (1992). 'Change in the Management of Public Services'. *Public Administration* 70 (4), 499–518.

Stone, Diane (1996). 'From the Margins of Politics: The Influence of Think-Tanks in Britain'. *West European Politics* 19 (4), 675–92.

Sturm, Roland (1995). 'Das Vereinigte Königreich von Großbritannien und Nordirland. Historische Grundlagen und zeitgeschichtlicher Problemaufriß'. In: Hans Kastendiek, Karl Rohe and Angelika Volle (eds.), *Groß-britannien. Geschichte, Politik, Wirtschaft, Gesellschaft.* Frankfurt: Campus, 68–84.

Suleiman, Ezra (ed.) (1984). *Bureaucrats in Policymaking.* New York: Holmes and Meier.

Tant, A. P. (1990). 'The Campaign for Freedom of Information: A Participatory Challenge to Elitist British Government'. *Public Administration* 68, 477–91.

Taylor, Paul (1983). *The Limits of European Integration.* London: Croom Helm.

Teutsch, Michael (2001). 'Regulatory Reform in the German Transport Sector: How to Overcome Multiple Veto Points'. In: Adrienne Héritier, Dieter Kerwer, Christoph Knill, Dirk Lehmkuhl and Michael Teutsch, *Differential Europe. New Opportunities and Constraints for National Policy-Making.* Lanham: Rowman and Littlefield, 133–72.

Thelen, Kathleen and Sven Steinmo (1992). 'Historical Institutionalism in Comparative Politics'. In: Kathleen Thelen, Sven Steinmo and Frank Longstreth (eds.), *Structuring Politics. Historical Institutionalism in Comparative Analysis.* Cambridge: Cambridge University Press, 1–32.

Thomas, Rosamund M. (1978). *The British Philosophy of Administration.* London: Longman.

Toonen, Theo A. J. (1992). 'Europe of the Administrations. The Challenges of 1992 (and Beyond)'. *Public Administration Review* 52 (2), 108–15.

Troja, Markus (1997). 'Zulassungsverfahren, Beschleunigung und Mediation. Ansätze zur Verbesserung konfliktträchtiger Verwaltungsentscheidungen im Umweltbereich'. *Zeitschrift für Umweltpolitik* (3), 317–41.

Tromans, Stephen (1996). 'EMAS and ISO 14001: Vive La Différence!' *Business and the Environment's ISO 14000 Update,* September 1996, 1–7.

Turnbull, Robert (1988). 'Environmental Impact Assessment in the United Kingdom'. In: Michael Clark and John Herrington (eds.), *The Role of Environmental Impact Assessment in the Planning Process.* London: Mansell Publishing, 17–29.

Vogel, David (1983). 'Cooperative Regulation. Environmental Protection in Great Britain'. *The Public Interest* 72, 88–106.

(1986). *National Styles of Regulation. Environmental Policy in Great Britain and the United States.* Ithaca: Cornell University Press.

Vogel, Stephen K. (1997). 'International Games with National Rules: How Regulation Shapes Competition in "Global" Markets'. *Journal of Public Policy* 17 (2), 169–93.

Waarden, Frans van (1995). 'National Regulatory Styles. A Conceptual Scheme and the Institutional Foundations of Styles'. In: Brigitte Unger and Frans van Waarden (eds.), *Convergence or Diversity? Internationalization and Economic Policy Response*. Aldershot: Avebury, 45–97.

Ward, N., H. Buller and P. Lowe (1995). *Implementing European Environmental Policy at the Local Level: The British Experience with Water Quality Directives*. Newcastle: University of Newcastle upon Tyne.

Weale, Albert (1992). *The New Politics of Pollution*. Manchester: Manchester University Press.

Weale, Albert (1996a). 'Environmental Regulation and Administrative Reform in Britain'. In: Giandomenico Majone (ed.), *Regulating Europe*. London: Routledge, 106–30.

(1996b). 'Environmental Rules and Rule-making in the European Union'. *Journal of European Public Policy* 3 (4), 594–611.

Weale, Albert, Timothy O'Riordan and L. Kramme (1992). *Controlling Pollution in the Round*. Manchester: Manchester University Press.

Weber, Max (1972). *Wirtschaft und Gesellschaft*. Tübingen: Mohr.

Wegener, Bernd (1993). 'Die unmittelbare Geltung der EG-Richtlinie über den freien Zugang zu Umweltinformationen'. *Zeitschrift für Umweltrecht* 1, 17–21.

Weidner, Helmut (1996). *Umweltkooperation und alternative Konfliktregelungsverfahren in Deutschland*. Schriften zu Mediationsverfahren im Umweltschutz No. 16. Berlin: Wissenschaftszentrum für Sozialforschung.

Weidner, Helmut (ed.) (1997). *Performance and Characteristics of German Environmental Policy. Overview and Expert Commentaries from 14 Countries*. Berlin: Wissenschaftszentrum für Sozialforschung.

Wessels, Wolfgang and Dietrich Rometsch (1996). 'German Administrative Interaction and the European Union: the Fusion of Public Policies'. In: Yves Mény, Pierre Muller and Jean-Louis Quermonne (eds.), *Adjusting to Europe. The Impact of the European Union on National Institutions and Policies*. London: Routledge, 73–109.

Williamson, Oliver E. (1985). *Markets and Hierarchies. Analysis and Antitrust Implications*. New York: Free Press.

(1985). *The Economic Institutions of Capitalism*. New York: Free Press.

Wilson, James Q. (1989). *Bureaucracy. What Government Agencies Do and Why They Do It*. New York: Basic Books.

Windhoff-Héritier, Adrienne (1987). *Policy-Analyse. Eine Einführung*. Frankfurt: Campus.

Winter, Gerd (1996). 'Freedom of Environmental Information'. In: Gerd Winter, (ed.), *European Environmental Law. A Comparative Perspective*. Aldershot: Dartmouth, 81–94.

Wolf, Rainer (1990). 'Normvertretende Absprachen und normvorbereitende Diskurse: Konfliktmanagement im 'hoheitsreduzierten Staat' – Aufgabenfelder für Konfliktvermittler?' In: Wolfgang Hoffmann-Riem and Eberhard Schmidt-Aßmann (eds.), *Konfliktbewältigung durch Verhandlungen Band II*. Baden-Baden: Nomos, 129–53.

Wright, Vincent (1994). 'Reshaping the State. The Implications for Public Administration'. *West European Politics* 17 (2), 102–37.

WSA (Water Services Association) (1996). *Water Facts '96*. London: WSA.

Zito, Anthony R. and Michelle Egan (1997). *Environmental Management Standards, Corporate Strategies and Policy Networks*. Manuscript. Florence: European University Institute.

Index

abstraction levels, 5, 24, 25, 26, 27, 28, 30, 31, 39, 48, 52, 54, 55, 65, 137, 205
access, 40, 69, 139, 142–3, 149, 179, 181, 185
    equal, 134
Access to Environmental Information Directive (1990), 2, 54, 126, 129, 132, 134
    Britain, 3, 165, 180–1, 186–7, 188ff., 195–6, 206, 207
    and divergence, 208, 211
    Germany, 4, 129, 135, 141–3ff., 203, 204, 206
accountability, 79, 143, 187, 189, 191, 193
accreditation, 159, 161, 166, 167
actors, 3, 4, 5, 11, 13–14, 18, 22, 23, 24, 26, 28, 44, 46, 85, 86, 93, 202, 221ff., 226
    domestic, 31, 135, 148, 156, 157, 190, 192, 207, 214, 215, 217, 219–20
    societal, 39, 40, 64, 68, 69, 160, 161, 162, 179
    see also agency-based approaches; domestic support
adaptation pressure, 5, 13, 14, 22, 41–56
    and administrative change, 46–50
    comparative view, 201–7
    concept, 41–3, 53
    dynamic aspect, 42, 45–6, 47, 53, 164
    high, 5, 46, 48, 54, 140, 164, 206
    institutional dimension, 43–5, 47, 53
    levels, 4, 5, 21, 46–9, 162, 205
    low, 45, 47, 136
    moderate, 46–7, 48, 135, 150, 157, 161, 168, 174, 192, 205, 215
    and national changes, 45
    reduction of, 190–2
    sectoral dimension, 42, 43, 47, 53
adjustments, 3, 4, 5, 122, 124, 133, 201, 204–5, 211
administration bound to law, 65–6, 155

administrative change, 2, 5, 9, 42, 49, 50, 161
    comparative view, 201–7
    degrees of, 4
    explanatory models, 10–14, 17, 135–6
    inconsistencies in, 3–4
    institutional approach, 20, 21ff., 135
    see also institutional change; reforms
administrative interest intermediation, 3, 39–40, 41, 55, 61, 72, 73, 113, 114, 134, 137, 174, 177, 180, 181, 182, 185, 186, 209
    see also intervention; mediation
administrative law, 45, 69, 79, 91
administrative policies, 35–6
administrative reform capacity, 5, 34, 42, 45, 46, 85, 86, 90, 202
administrative structures, 2–3, 4, 5, 15, 26, 40–1, 42, 43, 44, 53, 69–73, 90–2
    Britain, 77, 80, 83, 84, 104–6, 166, 169ff., 178, 183–4, 189, 191, 194
    convergence, 12
    Germany, 104–6, 139–40, 149, 151, 158–9
    and institutional change, 21, 22, 23
administrative styles, 2, 3, 4, 39–40, 42, 43, 44, 53, 84
    Britain, 165, 169, 177–8, 180, 181–3, 185, 189
    convergence, 12
    environmental policies, 132, 134, 137–9
    Germany, 137–9, 141, 152, 153, 158
    see also intervention; mediation
agency-based approaches, 5, 14, 21, 23–5, 136, 150, 157, 160, 162, 165, 173–4, 188, 202, 213, 224
    and adaptation pressures, 42, 48, 205
    and institutional approaches, 25–30ff., 215, 219, 226, 227
    see also actors; domestic support
agriculture, 156–7

air pollution, 54, 71, 121, 122, 123,
    127–8, 137–8, 168, 176–8, 180, 192,
    210
    see also Large Combustion Plants (LCP)
    Directive (1988)
allocation of competencies, 40–1, 45,
    69–71, 80–1, 83, 110
ambiguity, 26, 146, 186–7, 222, 223
analytical factors, 4, 5, 27, 28, 35, 38–9,
    119, 122, 213, 215
Andersen and Eliassen (1993), 12
auditing, 159, 165, 166, 185, 208
authorisation, 177, 178, 183
autonomy, 11, 62, 86–7, 90, 93, 95–7, 99,
    106, 107, 110

Baden-Württemberg, 139n., 157, 161
Badie and Birnbaum (1983), 44, 65, 74,
    75, 76, 77
bargaining, 40, 63, 68, 88, 90, 96, 103,
    113, 114, 138, 183, 209
BATNEEC, 126, 177, 182
Bavaria, 139n., 157, 161
behaviour, 26, 27
beliefs, 13, 14, 26, 33, 42, 44, 161, 214,
    221–5, 226
benefits, 24
Benz and Goetz (1996), 63, 64, 86, 92, 97,
    98, 99, 149, 160
Best Available Technology (BAT), 137–8
    see also BATNEEC
Best Practicable Environmental Option
    (BPEO), 182
best practicable means (bpm), 176, 177
Britain, 2, 16n., 44, 45, 52–4, 56, 93, 202,
    211, 224, 225–6
    active role of, 165, 169
    administrative reforms, 75, 100, 106,
        109, 110, 111–15, 164–5, 181, 184,
        189–91, 193, 196
    administrative structure, 77, 80, 83, 84,
        104–6, 166, 169, 170–1, 178, 183–4,
        189, 191, 194
    administrative style, 165, 169, 177–8,
        180, 181–3, 185, 189
    civil service, 78–80ff., 94, 104ff., 112
    Drinking Water Directive, 3, 178–80,
        184–6, 188ff., 203, 206, 209–10
    EIA Directive, 3, 168–74, 203, 205, 209
    EMAS Regulation, 3, 165–8, 203, 208
    energy sector, 194–5
    executive leadership, 100–4, 106
    implementation, 110, 114, 189–90, 196
    Information Directive, 3, 129, 164,
        180–1, 186–7, 188ff., 195–6, 203,
        206, 208

lack of rules, 104, 105
LCP Directive, 3, 122, 123, 127–8,
    175–8, 181–4, 188ff., 203, 206, 209
legal system, 76–8, 104, 105, 110
local government, 80, 81–3, 84, 101,
    106, 111, 112, 113
national plan, 182, 193, 209
neglected adaptation, 171–3, 174
organisational structure, 105
planning law, 169–73
political role of bureaucracy, 106–9, 189
privatisation, 28, 29, 31
road haulage liberalisation, 217, 218,
    219
state structure, 80–4, 101
state tradition, 73–6, 83
BS 7750, 165–6, 167, 168
bureaucracy, 15, 16–17, 29, 46, 55, 63,
    86–7, 90, 92–7, 99
    influence on policy-making, 85, 86, 94,
        189
    and politics, 92–7, 106–9

cabotage, 216–17
Central Electricity Generating Board
    (CEGB), 190, 194
central government, 80, 82, 106, 110, 111,
    115, 191
centralisation, 3, 40, 41, 63, 70, 80, 86,
    100, 101, 143, 191
    legal, 139, 140
centre-local relations, 69–70ff., 80, 82–3,
    84, 105, 106, 174, 178, 183–4, 191
charges, 146, 192
circulars, administrative, 65, 66, 140, 171,
    184
civil service, 43, 46, 61, 67–9, 78–80ff.,
    91, 94–5, 98, 104, 105ff., 112
    see also bureaucracy
civil society, 74, 76, 78
coalitions, 48, 89, 135, 220, 221
cognition, 26, 27, 221, 224
Collier (1991), 52, 53, 54
'command and control' regulation, 38, 39,
    131, 137
Common Law, 64, 76, 77
Common Market, 37, 120, 215
comparative approach, 2, 10, 14, 38, 43,
    51–5, 84, 201
    convergence and divergence, 207–12
    public administration, 14–17
    sectoral compatibility, 202–4
compatibility, 3, 4, 13, 42, 43, 53, 135,
    136, 139, 153, 154, 166, 169, 202–4,
    217, 226
compensation, 123, 127, 156, 157

competition, 9, 88, 102, 124–5, 216, 217, 219
competitive reregulation, 30
competitive tendering, 98, 112, 113
compliance, 17, 18, 48–9, 51, 123–4, 181, 196, 213, 214–15
    limits to, 31, 154–7
    without change, 136–41, 167–8
comprehensiveness, 119–22, 124, 125
confidentiality, 187
consensualism, 40, 61, 68, 83, 91, 138, 174, 188, 195
conservatism, 4, 5, 22, 24, 30, 32–3, 91, 201
Conservative Party, 76, 79, 83, 100, 103, 108, 111, 191
constitutional law, 65, 101
consultation, 40, 90, 103
consumer organisations, 179, 185, 186, 192
continuity, 5, 21, 28, 32, 97, 99, 104, 209
    see also persistence
contracting-out, 98, 112, 113, 114, 115
control, 40, 41, 45, 69, 81, 132, 143, 159, 161, 182
control technologies, 121
convergence, 2, 3, 12, 16, 17n., 29, 41–50, 51, 207–12
co-operation, 11, 89, 177, 195
co-ordination, 40, 41, 45, 69, 81, 88, 89, 95, 143, 147, 170, 173, 190, 196
    'negative', 72
core, see institutional core
corporatism, 61ff., 68, 72, 89, 103, 157, 160, 161, 205, 208, 219, 220
costs, 9, 24, 124, 150, 155, 156, 176, 192
courts, 65, 76, 77, 148, 172, 173
Cowles and Risse (2001), 13, 227
cross-country approaches, 12, 15, 28, 49–50, 51–4, 55, 201, 203
cross-media approaches, 121, 147
cross-policy comparison, 51, 55, 201

data, administrative 53, 56, 183, 185, 186
    see also information
decentralisation, 3, 40, 41, 46, 63, 70, 87, 98, 152n.
decision-making, supranational, 122–6, 136
'decreasing levels of abstraction', 5, 26
deductive approaches, 39, 40, 65, 134, 137
delayed change, 3, 135, 150, 154, 156, 157, 184, 206
Department of the Environment (DoE), 166, 167, 168, 172, 178, 182, 195
dependent variables, 9, 10, 11, 41, 55

deregulation, 29, 31, 98, 161, 216
Derlien (1995, 1996), 15, 16n., 67, 68, 87, 91, 94, 95, 98, 99
determinism, 4, 22, 23, 24, 25, 26–7, 30, 54, 165, 188, 201, 204, 226
DiMaggio and Powell (1991), 17n., 22n.
discretion, 3, 66, 68, 71, 77, 78, 79, 81, 103, 132, 169, 171, 176, 177, 179, 180, 194, 195
distribution, 24, 26, 28, 32
divergence, 3, 12, 41, 49, 50, 51, 53, 125, 207–12
domestic change, see administrative change; institutional change
domestic policies, 122–6, 129, 131
    initiatives, 124–5
    see also Europeanisation
domestic structures, 11, 12, 205
domestic support, 148–9, 157, 160–1, 167, 168, 192, 193, 204, 205, 206, 207, 222ff.
Drinking Water Directive (1980), 54, 123, 126, 128–9, 132, 134, 209–11
    Britain, 3, 178–80, 184–6, 188ff., 203, 206, 207
    Germany, 3, 135, 150–7, 203, 205, 206
Drinking Water Inspectorate (DWI), 184, 185–6, 191, 195, 196
Dunleavy, Patrick (1991,1993), 101, 102, 115
dynamic view, 5, 13, 32–3, 42, 45–6, 47, 53, 110, 111, 113, 115, 165, 202, 207

economics, 24, 67, 176
efficiency, 24
Eising and Kohler-Koch (1994), 11
electoral systems, 32, 88, 102
Ellwein (1969, 1985, 1993), 62, 69, 71, 86, 90, 92, 96, 97
embedded administrative patterns, 4, 43, 44–5, 47, 140–1, 150, 201, 204
emissions, 138, 176, 177, 186, 193
    'bubbles', 121, 127, 132, 139, 182, 182, 193, 194, 209
    standards, 38, 121, 136, 179, 182
empirical factors, 2, 3, 5, 12, 14, 18, 21n., 24, 26, 27, 28, 52, 205, 213, 214
endogenous pressures, 22, 162, 164, 225
Environment Agency, 167, 168, 170, 172, 173, 182, 183, 184–5, 187, 192, 194, 196, 209, 210
environmental action programmes, 38, 120, 121
Environmental Impact Assessment (EIA) Directive (1985), 2, 54, 126, 129–31, 132, 133, 134

Britain, 3, 165, 168–74, 203, 205, 209
Germany, 4, 123–4, 143–5, 147–8,
   149–50, 203, 204, 206, 208
and persistence, 208–9, 211
environmental legislation, 38–9, 69, 121,
   122, 126–33
Environmental Management and Auditing
   Systems (EMAS) Regulation (1993),
   2, 54, 126, 131, 132, 133, 134, 211
Britain, 3, 165–8, 203, 208
and convergence, 208
Germany, 3, 131, 157–61, 162, 203,
   205, 208
environmental organisations, 52, 148, 156,
   159, 161, 172, 174, 179, 180, 183,
   185, 192, 193, 204, 205, 207
environmental policy (EU), 9, 12, 36, 37
   administrative implications, 132–4
   analytical advantages, 2, 38–9, 119,
      122
   domestic impact, 122–6, 129, 131,
      132–4ff.
   general view, 119–26
   methodology, 52–4
Environmental Protection Act (1990), 181,
   182, 186, 187
equilibrium solution, 214, 218, 219
EU legislation, 37, 44, 47, 54, 126–31
European Commission, 37n., 38, 56, 120,
   123, 124–5, 184, 191, 195, 222
European Court of Justice (ECJ), 39, 140,
   184
European Parliament, 38
European policies, 9, 18, 19, 31, 51
   administrative impact, 1–2, 35, 36,
      122ff.
   differential impact, 12
   see also EU legislation; Europeanisation
Europeanisation, 1, 38
   and domestic change, 10–14
   and domestic opportunity structures,
      215–21, 226
   by framing domestic beliefs, 221–5, 226
   institutional approach, 20
   institutional compliance, 213, 214–15
   mechanisms of, 14, 213ff., 226–7
   traditional theories, 10–12
executive leadership, 33, 46, 85, 86,
   100–4, 106
   limits of, 87–90, 97, 99
executive power, 79, 81
exemptions, 123, 129, 145, 146, 169, 187,
   196
exogenous pressures, 4, 22, 47
expectations, 13, 26, 42, 124, 171, 201,
   211, 221–5, 226

explanation, 14, 21, 22, 26–7, 31, 32, 52,
   53, 214, 217, 218, 226

federal structures, 61, 62, 63, 68, 69ff.,
   87–8, 92, 146
flexibility, 3, 39, 40, 66, 68, 69, 71, 80, 96,
   106, 132, 134, 169, 172, 174, 176,
   177, 179, 180, 188, 193, 194, 196,
   197, 209, 210
Flynn and Strehl (1996), 1, 15
formality, 3, 26, 40, 46, 68, 86, 113, 132,
   134, 138, 149, 152, 177, 181, 182,
   183, 185, 209
fragmentation, 72, 87, 88, 92, 114, 144,
   147, 149–50, 151, 186, 192, 196
Framework Directive (1984), 126, 177,
   178, 181, 183, 188, 191
   see also Large Combustion Plants (LCP)
   Directive (1988)
France, 12, 28, 44, 62, 63, 71, 82, 127,
   217, 218–19, 221, 224, 225
functional division of labour, 69, 70, 80

generalism, 78, 79, 81, 83, 109, 114, 137
Germany, 2, 16n., 28, 52–4, 56, 61–73,
   103, 211, 224, 225
   administrative reform, 86, 87, 90, 91,
      95, 96–7, 98, 106, 140–1
   administrative structure, 104–6,
      139–40, 141, 149, 151, 158–9
   administrative style, 137–9, 141, 152,
      153, 158
   Basic Law, 68, 70, 91, 93
   bureaucracy, 63, 86–7, 90, 92–7, 99,
      106, 107
   civil service, 67–9, 91, 94–5, 98, 104,
      149
   corporatism, 61, 62, 63, 64, 68, 72, 89,
      157, 160, 161, 205, 208, 220
   Drinking Water Directive, 3, 135,
      150–7, 203, 205, 206
   EIA Directive, 4, 123–4, 143–5, 147–8,
      149–50, 203, 204, 206, 208
   electoral system, 88, 148
   EMAS Regulation, 3, 131, 157–61, 162,
      203, 205, 208
   environmental law, 143–4
   government organisation, 87, 89
   Information Directive, 4, 129, 135,
      141–3, 145–6, 148–9, 203, 204, 206,
      208
   LCP Directive, 3, 135, 136–40, 203
   legal system, 64–7, 91, 155
   limits of executive leadership, 87–90, 97,
      99
   party competition, 87–8

Germany (*cont.*)
  political system, 90, 92, 93ff.
  Rechtsstaat, 62, 63, 64ff., 88–9, 91, 94,
    149, 155
  regional governments, 61, 69, 70–2, 98,
    99, 143, 144, 149, 151, 157
  re-unification, 98, 99
  road haulage liberalisation, 218, 220–1
  rule of law, 62, 63, 67, 146
  state structure, 69–73, 92, 96
  state tradition, 61–4, 65ff., 73, 149, 155,
    160
global reforms, 16, 28, 29, 98

Hall (1986, 1993), 23, 44
Hall and Taylor (1996), 20, 23
health and safety at work, 9, 71, 176, 214
health sector, 27, 151, 152, 155, 160
Her Majesty's Inspectorate of Pollution
  (HMIP), 183
Héritier *et al.* (1994, 2001), 9, 10, 12, 14,
  125
Héritier and Knill (2001), 13, 218
Héritier, Knill and Mingers (1996), 2, 9,
  10, 12, 13, 52, 53, 122, 124, 125, 129,
  131, 136, 137, 146, 158, 159
hierarchical structures, 3, 39, 61, 65, 70–1,
  72, 73, 81, 92, 150, 151, 178, 188
hierarchical styles, 132, 133, 134, 137,
  141, 181
historical institutionalism, 4, 5, 20, 21, 23,
  25–6, 28, 29, 31, 34, 44
Hood (1996), 16
horizontal structures, 3, 40, 41, 81, 89, 92,
  133, 151
  segmentation, 72, 73, 144

ideal types, 55, 61, 92, 93, 132–3, 137
  see also administrative interest
    intermediation
Immergut (1997), 20, 23, 24n., 27, 46
implementation, 2, 9, 68, 70, 71, 92, 95,
  110, 114, 145–6, 147, 159, 189–90,
  196
  deficiencies, 38–9
  effectiveness, 17, 18, 19, 161, 162
  minimalist, 171
  process, 18
  research, 17–19, 20, 69, 71–2, 203–4
incremental change, 21, 28, 32, 86, 87,
  97–100, 111, 153, 202
independent agencies, 113, 114, 115, 160,
  189, 196
independent variables, 22–3, 25, 26, 27,
  32, 41, 47, 53, 201
indeterminate approaches, 30

individual rights, 67, 69, 143, 149
inductive approaches, 39, 40, 76, 83
Industrial Air Pollution Inspectorate
  (IAPI), 176, 177, 178, 183
industrial companies, 121, 131, 159, 168
industrial plants, 126, 127, 137, 138, 141,
  147, 168, 175, 176, 178, 182, 193–4,
  209
  see also Large Combustion Plants (LCP)
    Directive (1988)
informality, 3, 26, 40, 69, 83, 96, 113,
  114, 132, 138, 174, 177, 180, 188,
  209
information, 170, 172, 173, 177
  see also Access to Environmental
    Information Directive (1990)
innovations *see* reforms
  see also administrative change;
    institutional change
institutional change, 21–5
  agency-based approaches, 21, 23–5
  dynamic view of, 32–3
  institution-based approaches, 21–3, 25,
    214–15
  levels of abstraction, 27–31
  modification of, 204–7
  routine, 22, 29
  see also administrative change;
    institutional core
institutional core, 4, 5, 44, 72, 80
  challenges to, 4, 43, 46, 47–8, 50, 51,
    141, 148, 206
  changes of, 42, 47, 110, 113, 164,
    175ff., 188, 192, 202, 204, 206
  changes within, 42, 47, 48, 87, 97, 111,
    135, 150–61, 168–9, 174, 175ff.,
    190, 192, 202, 204, 205, 206, 214,
    215, 218, 223, 226
  confirmation of, 48–9, 50, 136–41,
    165–8, 206, 211
  contradiction of, 4, 47, 48, 49, 54,
    141–50, 158, 188, 202
  moving, 189
  stability, 87
  see also dynamic view; static core
institutional entrenchment, 85, 86, 90, 91,
  97, 104, 115
  see also embedded administrative
    patterns
institution-based approaches, 4–5, 14,
  20–3, 135, 136, 150, 154, 164, 174
  adaptation pressure, 42, 43–5, 54
  and agency-based model, 25–30ff., 226
  comparative view, 201, 202–7
  Europeanisation mechanisms, 213,
    214–15

limits of, 5, 22, 25, 55, 214–15, 218, 219, 223–4, 226
institutions, 20, 26
  as explanatory factor, 4, 21
  as independent variables, 22–3, 25, 201
  structuring impact, 21, 22, 23
  see also institutional change; institution-based approaches
instrumentality, 86, 95, 106, 110, 115
Integrated Pollution Control (IPC), 182, 183
integration, 95
  negative, 122, 215–16, 222
  positive, 214, 221
  research, 11, 12
interests, 4, 5, 11, 13, 23, 24, 26, 27, 64
  see also administrative interest intermediation; societal interests
intergovernmentalism, 10–11
interpretation, 186–7
intervening variables, 23, 24, 26, 27, 28, 52, 55, 202
intervention, 3, 132, 133
  British model, 83, 110, 177, 181, 185, 188
  German model, 61, 68, 72, 137, 138, 141, 152, 153, 155, 160, 163, 218, 219
  styles of, 39, 40, 41, 61, 114, 134
ISO 14001, 167–8
Italy, 217, 218, 219, 220, 224, 225

Japan, 28, 29
judicial review, 45, 65, 66, 77, 88, 101, 170

Keohane and Hoffmann (1991), 11
Knill (1997, 1998, 1999), 13, 38, 46, 75, 83, 85, 101, 103, 113, 114, 120, 122, 123, 125, 128, 155, 160, 177, 184, 192, 193, 196, 225
Knill and Héritier (1996), 38, 120
Knill and Lehmkuhl (1998), 11, 14, 37, 213, 222, 223, 225
Knill and Lenschow (1998, 2000, 2001a), 12, 13, 17, 27, 30, 38, 39, 121, 128, 148, 152, 192
Kohler-Koch (1994, 1999), 11, 14
Kohler-Koch and Eising (1999), 11
Kohler Koch and others (1998), 12
Krasner (1988), 22

Labour Party, British, 75, 83, 103
Large Combustion Plants (LCP) Directive (1988), 2, 54, 126–8, 132, 134, 209–11
  Britain, 3, 165, 175–8, 181–4, 188ff., 203, 206, 207

Germany, 3, 135, 136–40, 203
  see also Framework Directive (1984)
law, 83, 155
  see also Common Law; legal systems; Roman Law
legal systems, 2, 4, 43, 44, 45, 53, 64–7, 76–8, 91, 104, 105, 110
legalism, 3, 40, 46, 61, 68, 72, 73, 86, 91, 113, 132, 134, 138, 139, 141, 149, 152, 155, 163, 209
legislature, 63, 66
Lehmkuhl (1999), 13
Lenschow (1999), 11, 160, 161
liberalisation policies, 216–21, 222–5
licensing, 178
Lindenberg (1991), 5, 26
linkages, 44, 48, 53, 92, 105, 150, 214, 226
local authorities, 56, 101, 106, 112, 113, 170ff., 178, 179, 183, '84
local government, 62, 70–1, 80, 82–3, 84, 101, 106, 111, 112, 113, 188, 189, 191
lock-in effects, 23, 26, 32

Maastricht Treaty (1992), 120
macro-institutional context, 4, 15, 27, 28, 29, 30, 31, 32, 33, 34, 42, 44, 45, 46, 85, 201, 227
  Britain, 84, 110
  Germany, 73, 84, 148
Majone (1996), 13, 36, 37n.
majority-voting, 120, 125
management reforms, 98–9, 112, 114, 189
markets, 28, 29, 37, 64, 75, 136, 214, 215–16, 217, 219
Mayntz (1978, 1983, 1990), 18, 66, 67, 70, 71, 72, 96, 158
Mayntz and Derlien (1989), 95
Mayntz and Scharpf (1995), 21, 22, 26, 98
measurement, 154, 155, 156, 183
mediation, 3, 40, 55, 61, 73, 83, 84, 132, 133, 174, 188, 208
Member States, 1, 9, 37, 51, 122–6, 129, 130, 131, 216, 222
  misunderstanding by, 123–4
  regulatory contest among, 124–5
  see also domestic policies
Mény, Muller and Quermonne (1996), 12
methodology and procedure, 5, 51–5, 56
modernisation, 71, 90, 98, 104, 111
Moe (1990), 25, 28
monitoring, 153, 155, 176, 186
Moravcsik (1991, 1994), 11

national administrative traditions, 2, 4, 42,
    43–6, 55, 61, 136, 141, 162, 164,
    189, 190, 204, 205
  see also institutional core
national governments *see* Member States;
    see also domestic policies
national implementation, 9–10
National Rivers Authority (NRA), 183,
    185, 191
nationalised industries, 28–9, 75, 82, 189
neglected adaptation, 49
neofunctionalism, 10–12
Netherlands, 224, 225
new institutionalism, 20–1, 24
new regulatory policies, 36, 37, 38, 122
Next Steps initiative, 113, 189
non-adaptation, 50, 148, 156, 201, 206
non-hierarchical structures, 40, 81–2, 83,
    84
norms, 20, 26, 140, 145
North (1990), 23, 24, 26
North-Rhine Westphalia, 139n., 157
NPM concepts, 15, 16, 113

Office of Water Services (OFWAT), 185,
    186, 190, 192, 196
Olsen, Johan P. (1995), 13, 22
Olsen and Peters (1996), 1, 15, 16
Olson, Mancur (1982), 115
ontology, 20, 21, 22, 27, 33
openness, 24, 26, 27, 30, 32, 39, 48, 113,
    132, 142, 165, 170, 183, 186, 187,
    188
opportunity structures, 13, 14, 24, 27, 154,
    161, 190, 207, 214
  changes of, 215–21, 226

Page (1992), 15, 67, 68, 77, 80, 82, 83,
    105
Page and Wouters (1995), 16, 17
Parliament, 62, 63, 65, 66, 74, 75, 77, 79,
    81, 100, 101, 102, 104
parsimonious model, 22, 24, 26, 53, 54
participation, public, 38, 46, 121, 132,
    134, 139, 170, 183, 186
path-dependency, 21–2, 23, 29, 31, 32
performance, 113, 114, 189, 190
peripheral changes, 44, 45
persistence, 3, 4, 5, 22n., 24, 28, 49–50,
    51, 190, 193, 195, 197, 208, 211,
    212
pesticides, 153, 154, 156
Peters (1988, 1993, 1996), 15, 18, 19, 55,
    65, 68, 78, 79, 80, 81, 82, 89, 155
Pierre (1995), 1, 15, 16n.
policy instruments, 38, 39

policy-making, 46, 65, 68, 70
  bureaucracy and, 85, 86, 93, 94, 106–9,
    189
political-administrative system, 2, 4, 32,
    43, 44, 53, 61
political outcomes, 4, 21, 23, 24, 26, 27
political parties, 46, 87, 88, 94–5, 102,
    103
politics, 12, 15, 22, 27, 28, 32, 33, 45, 46,
    86, 148, 188
  and bureaucracy, 92–7
  and environmental policy, 122–3, 161
pollution, 151, 152, 156, 157, 168, 170,
    178, 179, 80, 181, 182, 191, 192
Powell (1991), 22
power distribution, 24, 26, 28
practice, 15, 18, 24
pragmatism, 3, 26, 31, 40, 69, 78, 83, 114,
    176, 177, 180, 188, 193, 194, 209
precautionary principle, 132
prediction, 31, 33, 42, 85, 201, 205
preferences, 14, 18, 23, 24, 33, 42, 110,
    221
prescription, 213, 214–15, 216
private law, 65
private sector, 16, 64, 75, 81, 98, 112, 159,
    189
privatisation, 28–9, 76, 91, 98, 112, 113,
    114, 115, 189, 190–1, 192, 194, 195,
    196, 224
procedural regulation, 38, 40, 66, 83, 121,
    133, 134, 174, 176, 188
product standards, 121, 137, 138
proportionality principle, 66, 78
Prussia, 44, 63, 67, 71
public administration, 1, 10, 20, 45, 65,
    80–1
  comparative, 14–17, 55
public law, 65, 77, 78, 91
public-private interactions, 39, 40, 64, 77,
    179, 180, 182, 224
public registers, 183, 185, 186, 187, 192
public sector, 16, 81, 91, 98, 99, 111,
    112–13, 114, 189, 224, 225

quality standards, 121, 128, 137, 138, 176,
    180, 185, 195, 209, 210

railways, 213, 222–5
rational choice theories, 23, 24–5, 27, 28,
    29, 30
redistribution of power, 11–12
reforms, 5, 13, 14, 16, 33, 34, 45, 46, 124
  Britain, 75, 100, 106, 109, 110, 111–15,
    189–90
  Germany, 86, 87, 90, 91, 95, 96–7, 161

internally-driven, 97–100
  see also administrative reform capacity
registration, 177, 178
  see also public registers
regulations, 3, 44, 65, 66, 68, 131, 138,
  140, 147, 159, 160, 171–2
  variety of, 38, 119, 121–2, 124, 125
regulatory policies, 36–7
regulatory processes, 3, 113–14, 121
resistance, 3, 4, 39, 42, 47–8, 49, 50, 202,
  203, 205, 206, 222
  Britain, 173, 184, 192, 193, 196
  Germany, 131, 141, 145–8, 149, 150,
    153–7, 207, 208
road transport, 37, 52, 213, 216–21
Roman Law, 64–5, 76
Rose (1991), 52, 55
Royal Commission for Environmental
    Pollution (RCEP), 180, 192, 193
rules, 40, 45, 65, 68, 91, 92, 137, 139,
  180
  lack of, 104, 105

Schmidt, Susanne K., 11n.
Schmidt, Vivien, 12
Schneider (2001), 13
science, 66, 78, 123, 129
secrecy, 114, 180, 183, 188, 193, 195
sectoral levels, 27, 29, 30, 32, 33, 39, 141,
  169, 217
  adaptation pressure, 42, 43, 47, 53
  'fit', 4, 43, 47, 201, 202–4
  'misfit', 47, 141, 143, 175, 187, 201,
    202–4
sectoral reform capacity, 13
segmentation, 72, 73, 89, 144, 156
self-adaptation, 86–7, 97, 99, 111
self-regulation, 3, 38, 39, 75, 121, 131,
  132, 134, 158, 159, 160, 162, 165,
  167, 168, 174, 180, 186, 188, 205,
  208
separation of powers, 107–9, 110, 151
Shepsle (1989), 24
Shepsle and Weingast (1987), 24
similarity, 50, 51, 52, 53
Single European Act (1986), 120
single media instruments, 121, 147
societal interests, 11, 18, 39, 40, 102–3,
  179
society, 29, 44, 45, 61, 62, 63, 68, 69, 73,
  74
sociological institutionalism, 20, 23, 25, 26
Spain, 127, 128
special agencies, 71, 92
specialisation, 79, 93, 94
stability, 21, 24, 32, 34, 45, 48, 87, 90–2,

93, 99, 104, 105, 136, 141, 149, 150,
  202, 204, 226
standards, 121, 128, 132, 136, 137, 138,
  153, 165–6, 179, 180, 184, 187, 194,
  195
state, 28
  and society, 29, 44, 45, 61, 65, 73–4
  structure, 45, 53, 61, 69–73, 80–4, 92,
    96, 101
state tradition, 2, 4, 43, 44, 53, 61–4,
  65ff., 73–6, 83
static core, 5, 42, 136, 162, 163, 202
statutory law, 65, 66, 77
strategic interactions, 14, 22, 25, 27, 28,
  161, 207
structures, *see* administrative structures
subnational actors, 11, 12
substantive outcomes, 39, 65, 66, 132,
  134, 135, 137, 149, 153, 189, 209
supranational policies, 5, 9, 10, 11, 17, 18,
  36, 37, 38, 42, 56, 119, 120
symbolism, 26, 48, 222

technical guidance notes, 65
technocratic reforms, 97, 98
technological standards, 121, 123
telecommunications sector, 28–9, 30–1,
  112
Thatcher, Margaret, 76, 79, 102, 103, 108,
  111, 189
Thelen and Steinmo (1992), 22, 23, 26, 32
theory, 5, 16
  limits of, 12–14, 15, 17, 18–19, 20
  'think tanks', 94, 108, 109n.
third-parties, 40, 76, 129, 139, 142, 172,
  173, 183, 186
Toonen (1992), 16–17
Town and Country Planning Act , 169,
  170, 171
transparency, 40, 114, 121, 132, 134, 142,
  170, 177, 181, 182, 183, 185, 186,
  188, 189, 191, 192–3
transposition, 140, 145, 153–4, 169, 171,
  184
Treaty of Rome (1957), 119, 120, 125, 184
tribunals, administrative, 77

uniform standards, 138, 153, 179, 180,
  181
United States, 73, 78, 94

variables, 4, 9, 13, 17, 22, 41, 52, 53, 55
  see also dependent variables; independent
    variables; intervening variables
verification, 131, 159, 161, 165, 167, 208
vertical structures, 40, 41, 72

veto points, 24, 28, 32, 33, 46, 85, 86, 87, 90, 100, 149, 207, 219, 220, 225
Vogel (1986, 1997), 29, 30, 43, 79, 176
voluntary agreements, 38, 39, 121, 132, 162, 165, 176

Waarden, Frans van (1995), 40, 68, 78, 79, 94
waste disposal, 183
water authorities, 152, 156, 178, 179, 185, 190, 191, 195, 210

water policy, 71, 121, 128–9, 142, 150–7, 168, 181, 184–6, 190–1, 192, 195, 210
    see also Drinking Water Directive (1980)
Weale (1996), 38
Weber, 15, 78, 92, 93, 94
welfare state, 74, 75
Wessels and Rometsch (1996), 16, 35
within-case comparisons, 54–5
Wright (1994), 1, 15, 16, 98